Endorsements

Svend Brinkmann
Professor of Psychology, Aalborg University, Denmark

This is a helpful and well-written book on strain psychology by a highly experienced practitioner and scholar in the field—a book I can warmly recommend.

Wilmar B. Schaufeli
Professor emeritus of Work and Organizational Psychology, Utrecht University, The Netherlands

As a psychologist and researcher, I highly recommend this book: it is an accessible, comprehensive, and practical resource for professionals at risk of psychotrauma, combining multiple perspectives with robust scientific insight.

Miranda Olff
Professor of Clinical Psychology, Amsterdam UMC, University of Amsterdam, The Netherlands

This book is an accessible and practice-oriented guide to understanding psychological strain in high-risk professions. A valuable resource for professionals facing traumatic or morally injurious events and high emotional demands, combining clinical experience, research, and systemic perspectives.

Jette Albinus
Major General and Commander, Multinational Division North (NATO)

From military operations to civilian frontline work, this book offers essential tools for navigating strain and safeguarding psychological health. An important contribution for anyone working under high mental demands.

Klas Backholm
Senior University Lecturer (Docent) in Journalism and Trauma Studies, Åbo Akademi University, Finland

This book is a very welcome addition to the literature on how individuals and organizations in high-risk professions can understand and address psychological trauma. It combines theoretical and practical perspectives in an accessible and engaging way.

Fundamentals of Strain Psychology

Fundamentals of Strain Psychology

Preventing Burnout, Primary and Secondary Traumatisation in Psychologically Demanding Work

Rikke Høgsted

With contributions by Agnes Ringer

Registered Office(s)

John Wiley & Sons, Inc., 111 River Street, Hoboken, NJ 07030, USA

John Wiley & Sons Ltd, New Era House, 8 Oldlands Way, Bognor Regis, West Sussex, PO22 9NQ, UK

For details of our global editorial offices, customer services, and more information about Wiley products visit us at www.wiley.com.

The manufacturer's authorized representative according to the EU General Product Safety Regulation is Wiley-VCH GmbH, Boschstr. 12, 69469 Weinheim, Germany, e-mail: Product_Safety@wiley.com.

Library of Congress Cataloging-in-Publication Data has been applied for:

Paperback: 9781394402328
ePDF: 9781394402342
ePub: 9781394402335
oBook: 9781394402359

Cover Design and Image: Alette Bertelsen

Set in 9.5pt and STIXTwoText by Lumina Datamatics

Dedicated to those who were left without support when it mattered most. May we build systems that catch them next time.

Contents

Foreword

During my 23 years in the UK Armed Forces, I encountered my fair share of trauma, and intense stress. This was both direct exposure, seeing an enemy rocket explode metres from where I was taking cover is seared in my mind, and vicariously through the multitude of service personnel I spoke with informally and the patients I saw as a military psychiatrist.

I have also spent a lot of my life researching the possible impacts of trauma upon individuals who work in organisations that predictably place their staff in harm's way. If you reflect on who this group of trauma-exposed workers are, it is probably larger than you imagine. It is not just the military and emergency responders but also media professionals, legal professionals, healthcare and transportation workers; the list goes on and on.

Even if someone's job is unlikely to expose them to trauma, sustained high emotional demands are commonplace. Such intense demands can also have a detrimental impact on both mental health, including causing burnout and moral injury, as well as performance. It is thus imperative that all managers should have an excellent understanding how to protect their staff's mental health. Understanding this topic well, will increase the likelihood that their organisation is successful and will help avoid the risk of a disgruntled, underperforming, workforce who may leave or bring legal claims.

As readers will undoubtably be aware, uncertainty across the globe is the new normal. Uncertainty often generates anxiety whether the threat is from climate change, war or financial crises. It is thus more important now than ever, that every employer has a good understanding of the possible impacts of stress and trauma on their workforce and the consequential impact on their business. It is age old wisdom that 'failing to prepare is preparing to fail'. Whilst those who run higher-risk organisations, such as a police force or a newsgathering company, are likely to have legal duties to take reduce the impact of unavoidable highly stressful events, even those who run coffee shops, libraries, or supermarkets would be well advised to have a good understanding of what to do if the unthinkable happens.

This book provides the necessary knowledge, and practical advice, that employers need about the possible impacts of trauma and highly stressful situations. It also speaks directly to the professionals who undertake highly stressful work. Importantly, it does not merely describe the impact of these sorts of events, often referred to as 'admiring the problem', it also tells readers what to do about them. Whilst there is no magic way of stopping the potential negative impacts of trauma, and intense stress, if an organisation handles it right then not only will a workforce weather the post-trauma psychological storm well but there is also a fighting chance that they will come out on top. Woven throughout this useful tome, is the formula for fostering what is known as post-traumatic growth. This concept was at the heart of what the well-known philosopher Nietzsche was thinking when he wrote '*Out of life's school of war—what doesn't kill me, makes me stronger*'.

I hope you enjoy reading this book as much as I did. More importantly, I hope that you use the wisdom contained in these pages to better support your workforce and, in doing so, success where others who are less knowledgeable unfortunately fail.

Neil Greenberg
Professor of Defence Mental Health, King's College London;
President of the Society of Occupational Medicine

Other Books by the Author

Psykologisk førstehjælp og medmenneskelig støtte
[Psychological First Aid and Human Support] (1997)—with Lise Knudsen and Peter Berliner

Assertiv kommunikation i teori og praksis [Assertive Communication in Theory and Practice] (1998)—with Anne Sofie Møller Petersen

FN-polititjeneste i det tidligere Jugoslavien, Rigspolitiet *[UN Police Service in the Former Yugoslavia, Danish National Police]* (1999)—with Lea Sand, Peter Berliner and Anne Sofie Møller Petersen

Når sjælen rystes
[When the Soul is Shaken] (1999)—with Anne Sofie Møller Petersen

Til minde om ... —en mindebog til børn og unge, der har mistet en nærtstående [In Memory Of ... —A Memorial Book for Children and Young People Who Have Lost a Loved One] (2005)

Sorgbogen, Mindebogen og Med kærlig hilsen—en trilogi
[The Book of Mourning, The Book of Remembrance and With Love—A trilogy] (2008)

Baglandet—beretninger fra pårørende til soldater [The Hinterland—Stories from Relatives of Soldiers] (2008)

Kom på benene igen—sådan klarer du en fyring [Get Back on Your Feet—How To Cope With a Layoff] (2009)

Missionen går til—en selvhjælpsbog til børnefamilier i forbindelse med internationale operationer [The mission goes to—a self help book to families related to international operations] (2009), translated also into Swedish and Norwegian

De unge i baglandet—til soldater, der fik set for meget [The Young People in the Hinterland—For Soldiers Who Have Seen Too Much] (2015)

De voksne i baglandet—til soldater, der fik set for meget [The Adults in the Hinterland—For Soldiers Who Have Seen Too Much] (2015)

Børnene i baglandet—til soldater, der fik set for meget [The Children in the Hinterland—For Soldiers Who Have Seen Too Much] (2015)

Kort og godt om kriser og traumer [Short on crises and trauma] (2023)—with Anne Sofie Møller Sparre og Anne Sophie Byder

Håndbog i Psykologisk Tryghed—Tør vi? Tør vi lade være? Psykologisk tryghed fra et belastningspsykologisk ståsted [Handbook of Psychological Safety—Do We Dare? Can We Afford Not To? Grounded in Strain Psychology] (2024)

Grundbog i psykisk førstehjælp og krisehåndtering ved akkumuleret og akut belastning [Fundamentals of Psychological First Aid and Crisis Management—In Response to Accumulated and Acute Strain] (2025)

Acknowledgements

This book is a revised and expanded version of the original Danish edition, and I remain deeply grateful to all those who contributed to its early development—through insight, critique, stories, or presence.

Special thanks to Annette Carlsen, whose beautiful illustrations helped shape the book's visual identity, and to Alette Bertelsen, for her thoughtful and dedicated graphic design of the Danish edition.

This international edition would not have happened without the many voices who insisted—persistently and generously—that it should. Thank you to all who believed that these ideas deserved wider reach.

Special thanks to Simon Grund Sørensen for stepping in with energy and clarity at the very beginning of the process, and to Jake Opie and Nathanael Mcgavin at Wiley, whose early support made it clear that this book had found the right home.

I'm also deeply grateful to Agnes Ringer for taking on the dual role of co-editor and co-author, and for helping refine and strengthen the manuscript.

I'm grateful to my colleagues at the Institute for Strain Psychology, whose expertise, commitment, and shared reflections have shaped the thinking behind this book—and strengthened it in countless ways.

Thank you to Neil Greenberg for contributing such a thoughtful and beautifully written foreword. I am honoured by the generous endorsements from Svend Brinkmann, Wilmar B. Schaufeli, and Miranda Olff—your recognition means more than I can say.

Finally, my deepest thanks to Thomas Middelboe—psychiatrist, medical consultant at the Institute for Strain Psychology, and my husband. His clarity, insight, and grounded presence carried me through the writing process. He is, in every way, my strongest foundation. As are our four daughters, whose perspective and presence shape more than they know.

Rikke Høgsted
Copenhagen, September 2025

About the Institute for Strain Psychology

The Institute for Strain Psychology develops research-informed, practice-based approaches to strengthening occupational psychological health in psychologically demanding professions. Across sectors such as healthcare, education, emergency response, social services, and law enforcement, the Institute supports organisations in building sustainable psychosocial work environments.

Founded by psychologist Rikke Høgsted, the Institute works at the intersection of theory, organisational culture, and professional responsibility. Its approach is grounded in the recognition that psychological strain is embedded in organisational structures, professional culture, and in the inherent demands of core professional tasks, and must therefore be addressed through collective awareness and systematic action.

This volume forms part of a broader implementation framework designed to translate psychological knowledge into sustainable professional practice. It is accompanied by two structured, digital, group-based Foundation Programmes developed for collective learning and organisational anchoring. Both programmes combine structured group reflection, short instructional films, guided exercises, and practical implementation tools designed for integration into everyday professional contexts. The programmes are delivered through the Institute's digital implementation platform, *MentiMove*.

The Foundation Programme in Strain Psychology provides a structured and systemic framework for understanding and managing the psychological demands embedded in everyday professional practice. Participants develop a shared professional language and strengthen collegial and managerial responsibility for the ordinary yet demanding conditions of daily work.

The Foundation Programme in Psychological First Aid and Crisis Management provides a structured and systemic framework for collegial and organisational support when work-related strain escalates or when critical situations occur. It equips professionals and leaders with clear procedures for early support, stabilisation, coordinated response, and responsible follow-up, including practical action cards designed to support confident intervention when it is most needed.

Together, the two programmes form a coherent framework addressing both the ongoing psychological demands of professional life and the structured support required when strain intensifies.

Further information is available at: www.strainpsychology.com

Note on the Structure and Key Concepts of the Book

It is my ambition to make the book's content easy for the reader to understand and use. The book is divided into three parts:

1. **The Impacts:** What causes mental strain?
2. **The Reactions:** How do we react to mental strain?
3. **The Strategies:** How do we prevent mental strain from escalating into mental injury?

This book draws on empirical research on crisis psychology. While the causes of primary trauma and post-traumatic stress disorder (PTSD) are well-documented in research, the study of secondary trauma is still in its early stages, though there have been significant advancements in recent years. For this reason, some of the topics in the book are based on clinical experience, rather than research.

The book begins with a prologue, inspired by the theatre's tradition of delivering a brief speech as a prelude to the main performance. There are several thoughts I wish to share with you before you dive into the book, which are included here. I have titled the prologue 'The Myth of the Invulnerable Helper, the Omnipotent Leader, and The Big Why'.

Part I—The Impacts—explores the people who are in harm's way—directly and indirectly during critical events. Here I introduce the core concepts of *protective factors* and *risk factors*, and the *Strain model* on page 108. I provide a comprehensive overview of the key considerations required to make a *risk analysis*—and, from that foundation, an effective *prevention plan* for mental injury.

Part II—The Reactions—examines the different ways in which individuals and groups react to mental strain—reactions important to recognise and act upon before strain progresses to injury. If the warning signs are ignored, mental strain may develop into *stress* or *trauma-related mental disorders*, all of which are described and defined in this part of the book.

This part of the book also includes a chapter on the challenges of detecting such warning signs, as well as a key chapter on maintaining constructive contact: the art of balancing between under- and over-involvement, when faced with frightening, provocative, sad, or otherwise challenging situations.

Part III—The Strategies—begins with the *strain square*: a model that illustrates objective strains and subjective vulnerabilities. We highlight key elements that a preventive staff policy should include. This is followed by suggestions for sustainable strategies at all levels of the organisation, along with practical advice on what you can do—as an organisation, a leader, a team, or an individual—to build and maintain a psychologically healthy workplace culture.

Strain Psychology

Strain psychology refers to a distinct field within applied psychology concerned with the causes and consequences of sustained psychological strain—particularly in professions marked by emotional exposure, moral complexity, and significant responsibility. It encompasses:

- the **contexts and conditions** that create lasting emotional and mental pressure—including both direct and indirect exposure to trauma, suffering, and human crisis, and
- the psychological, relational, **reactions and systemic responses** that arise when such strain becomes a core part of one's professional role.

While the primary focus of this book is on strain in occupational settings, many of the mechanisms described—including the cumulative effect of exposure, the weight of responsibility, and the struggle to remain engaged without becoming overwhelmed—may also apply to personal life contexts such as caregiving, grief, or existential crisis.

Strain Psychology recognises that these responses are not signs of individual weakness. Rather, they reflect the profound human impact of being persistently exposed to pain one cannot prevent, fix, or turn away from. Framing these experiences within a professional and systemic perspective allows us to address them not as private shortcomings, but as shared, ethical, and organisational challenges.

Strain Psychology therefore also draws on insights from psychotraumatology, as well as from organisational psychology and occupational health—disciplines that examine responses to trauma, workplace structure, leadership, culture, and employee well-being.

Strain Psychology and Psychological Safety

In recent years, the concept of *psychological safety* has become widely used in different kinds of workplaces. It describes the shared belief that it is safe to speak up, ask for help, or show uncertainty—without fear of being judged or ignored (Edmondson, 2019).

Psychological safety matters because it influences how people deal with emotional strain, especially in jobs where the stakes are high and the work affects others deeply.

In strain psychology, the idea of psychological safety appears in different ways. It connects to central themes such as support, communication, teamwork, leadership, and the ability to talk about what affects us—both as professionals and as people.

In some chapters in the book, psychological safety is discussed directly. In others, it is part of broader reflections about care, belonging, and trust. In this sense, psychological safety is not an add-on to strain psychology. It is part of the relational foundation that helps people face demanding work—and stay engaged over time.

Key Concepts

There are several key concepts in the book, which I will briefly define here.

A mentally high-risk job is a job that involves regular confrontations with accidents, threats, trauma, abuse, death, or violent events—either directly or indirectly—via encounters with people in crisis or trauma. Such jobs place high emotional demands on an employee to empathise with others and handle painful emotions.

Mental tilting is a term used in strain psychology to describe a state of emotional imbalance. Professionals may find themselves becoming either emotionally detached (*under-involved*) or overly engaged (*over-involved*). It is a warning sign that their capacity to cope with psychological strain is being stretched.

Warning signs are used here as another word for symptoms. A symptom is a physical or psychological reaction that can either be sensed by the person themselves or observed by others.

A sustainable organisation of work is one that strikes a balance between utilising and protecting resources. These resources should be understood broadly, as including time, finances, and—most importantly—the professional and human competencies of individuals or teams.

As an author, I have made several stylistic choices to enhance both accessibility and readability. One consideration was whether to use a single, consistent term for key concepts and roles—such as 'a violent incident' or 'the professional'—for the sake of clarity. However, I found that strict consistency made the text feel repetitive and mechanical. Instead, I have chosen to vary the terminology, using the words that best fit each specific context while remaining true to the meaning.

Throughout the book, I thus use different adjectives to describe what **triggers reactions**, including: stressful, mentally or emotionally demanding, violent, critical, traumatic, or trauma-inducing incidents or events.

I use terms such as 'employee', 'professional', 'carer', 'helping professional', and 'helper' throughout the book to describe individuals **working in roles that place them at risk of mental strain**. I am aware that many volunteers generously take on essential responsibilities without financial compensation, and I hope they will forgive me for not consistently using the term 'volunteer'. My hope is that you will still recognise yourself in the word 'helper'—and perhaps in 'professional' as well.

Finally, different fields have their own traditions for referring to the **individuals professionals interact with**:

- In healthcare, the individual is called a **patient.**
- In social services, the individual is often referred to as a **service user.**
- Amongst psychologists and lawyers, the term **client** is used.
- In prisons and correctional settings, the person is referred to as an **inmate.**

To create as broad a resonance with my readers as possible, I use the terms interchangeably, and often together, as **patient, client, or service user.**

Some readers may recognise many of the strategies for preventing mental strain from their own workplaces—especially if their organisation is already working actively to protect staff from fatigue and mental tilting. Others may realise that their workplace still has a long way to go before reaching a reasonable level of prevention. My hope is that all readers, wherever they begin, will find inspiration for their journey towards a more psychologically sustainable work environment. The concepts and models in this book are intended to offer a shared language—one that can make it easier to talk about strain, and to find solutions that suit the unique conditions of your workplace.

This book is deeply grounded in first-hand empirical experience. It is fundamentally built on the belief that creating resilience and preventing mental tilting should be approached as a *team effort*—requiring collaboration at all levels of an organisation.

The book ends with a short epilogue about some of the people who have inspired me.

Prologue

The Myth of the Invulnerable Helper, the Omnipotent Leader, and The Big WHY

> No human being is capable of handling everything. We all have a breaking point—a moment when we can no longer endure.

This is not new knowledge. It has been recognised since at least the Second World War. Until then, there was a widespread belief in the existence of a special kind of soldier—one who, with the right training, could become immune to the psychological toll of war. But military psychological studies gradually revealed a different truth: any soldier could break under pressure (Heaton et al., 1966). The likelihood of breakdown increased with the intensity and duration of combat. It became clear that psychological trauma was not a sign of weakness or failure—it could affect anyone.

Both early and current large-scale studies of military and emergency personnel show that no amount of training, personal coping skill, or innate resilience makes anyone bulletproof; what truly helps is having organised peer support when things get tough (Greenberg, Langston and Jones, 2008). Even those we see as rock-solid—the quiet professional, the decorated hero—remain human; no one is immune. And yet, the myth persists.

In many workplaces today—across countless professions—there remains an unspoken ideal: the 'true' professional is the one who never falters, no matter how great the pressure. This notion of the invulnerable helper continues to cast its shadow over what it means to be a 'real' doctor, nurse, lawyer, police officer, prison guard, aid worker, war reporter, psychologist, social worker, or healthcare assistant.

There is also the enduring myth of the omnipotent leader—the one who shoulders immense responsibility without ever faltering, who leads with such strength and grace that everyone in the organisation feels seen, heard, and understood.

Both myths claim that—despite years of witnessing death, suffering, trauma, threats, and tragedies—some employees remain mentally and emotionally immune. Deep down, we all recognise these as myths, but, in practice, we may mistake them for truths. The myths of the invulnerable helper and omnipotent leader revolve around themes of power, responsibility, and guilt.

Power, Responsibility, Guilt, Shame, and Powerlessness

Power, responsibility, and guilt are closely linked. If you have power, you have responsibility; if you fail in an area of your responsibility, you inevitably feel guilty. As a professional, you will occasionally—or perhaps even often—find yourself in situations where you are powerless, in the sense that you cannot solve the 'problem'. The *problem* may be terminal illness, death, or chronic trauma from war experiences or neglect. For a manager, the unsolvable *problem* may be the inevitable tolls of cost-cutting practices or mergers that can have a major impact on the group.

The feeling of powerlessness is harsh and frightening—a stark reminder that we have no real control over our lives. It is a fundamental reality, one we must accept as something that will not simply disappear.

Yet many helpers and managers instinctively take on responsibility and blame, convinced that outcomes might have been different—if only they had been more skilled, more experienced, or simply better at their jobs. In their minds, they often conjure an idealised version of a colleague: someone endlessly competent, calm, and composed, no matter the situation. Compared to this imaginary figure, they inevitably fall short. Confronting the pain of powerlessness can be so emotionally overwhelming that blaming oneself may feel strangely easier. It seems less painful to carry the weight of guilt—to believe you were not good enough—than to accept the unsettling truth that sometimes, nothing could have changed the outcome.

Guilt, however, rarely comes alone. It is often accompanied by an even more harsh emotion: shame. While guilt arises from falling short of your own values or expectations, shame strikes at the core of your identity—it says not just *you did wrong*, but *you are wrong*. Shame often takes root early in life, in moments of rejection or when one's needs were unmet. It's a deeply painful emotion, bound up with feelings of humiliation, alienation, and the sense of being fundamentally flawed or unworthy.

The opposite of shame is pride—the feeling that arises when you live up to your own or others' expectations and demands. Shame often underlies the relentless efforts (and occasional anger) of the thin-skinned helper or leader, just as it may fuel the trivialisation or apparent indifference of their thick-skinned counterpart. These behaviours can be seen as different ways employees attempt to cope with—or defend against—feelings of shame. While sharing professional pride can bring joy and serve as a powerful source of renewal during difficult times, many professionals find it so excruciatingly embarrassing to talk about their professional shame that they avoid it altogether.

The only good thing about shame is that its opposite is worse: shamelessness. At least the feeling of shame shows that we still have some proud professional values.

When we, as employees, feel powerless but are unable to admit it, feelings of guilt and shame often erode our ability to mentalise and maintain genuine connection with the person we aim to help. The individual we are helping will quickly sense the weakened connection and feel abandoned. This dynamic can easily turn into a negative self-fulfilling prophecy: to prevent a patient or client from feeling powerless and alone, the helper assumes responsibility—and with it, blame—for something beyond their control. The shame of lacking influence over the situation can become so overwhelming that, on a psychological level, the helper withdraws from the interaction—depriving the other person of a meaningful, human connection.

Throughout my years of working as a crisis psychologist, I have engaged in conversations with numerous employees from all of this book's target groups. These conversations revolved around stressful work events that quite naturally—and thankfully—made a particular impression on the employees. I emphasise 'thankfully' because only inanimate objects, like robots, remain unaffected by violent or tragic events. We humans are affected, and we *must* be so—for it is essential to our psychological vitality and our ability to do our jobs well. There is absolutely no shame in being emotionally affected when you routinely witness violent or tragic situations. The far more concerning alternative is becoming emotionally frozen, retreating into an armoured version of oneself, disconnected from one's own emotions and those of others.

Good Luck and Bad Luck

Fortunately, working in a high-risk job does not automatically mean you are personally at risk of psychological strain. Often, it comes down to a matter of luck or misfortune as to who gets affected the most. Those impacted are usually individuals who happened to be in the wrong place at the wrong time—the person driving over a roadside bomb, the one on duty during a major accident, or the individual who became the unintended victim of a psychotic inpatient. The recent graduate who, in the absence of an experienced colleague meant to assist, was assigned a case involving severe neglect. Or the woman who spent years working alone on assignments because no one at the main office recognised that solo work is one of the greatest risk factors for mental strain.

As is often evident, good luck and bad luck play a significant role in determining who bears the brunt. Luck refers to circumstances beyond your control that lead to a positive outcome; bad luck is when those uncontrollable factors result in a negative one. At the heart of this is the concept of power—and, more specifically, the lack of it. While much lies outside a person's control, there are still areas where influence can be exercised. Acknowledging this is about more than just seeing who is lucky and who is not; it is about recognising where your power lies and learning how to harness it.

Responsibility for the Psychological Work Environment

The ultimate responsibility for the physical and psychological work environment—both legally and morally—always rests with the organisation. Just as any organisation handling physically harmful substances must have knowledge of those substances, along with policies and procedures for managing them, an organisation dealing with psychologically harmful conditions must also have the necessary expertise, policies, and procedures in place to safeguard its employees. While work that involves death, suffering, trauma, violence, and threats inevitably poses risks to employees' mental well-being—and can therefore never be made entirely safe—these risks can be minimised as much as possible.

Organisations operating in mentally high-risk environments—such as healthcare, social services, media, or emergency response—need a strong HR policy framework. Such a policy helps managers lead with clarity, distribute responsibilities wisely, and ensure that teams and individuals have the tools and support required to manage the psychological demands of their work.

The Risk—or Opportunity—of Development

Taking good care of—and safeguarding—employees is not only the legal and moral responsibility of the organisation; it is also in the organisation's best interest. Mental wear and tear, as well as workplace injuries, lead to sick leave (Anagnostopoulos and Niakas, 2010) and increased staff turnover (Scanlan and Still, 2019), both of which incur financial costs and deplete the organisation of the vital expertise and experience needed to serve the target population effectively.

The risks of this type of work do not just concern employees' wear and tear, or work-related injuries, but also the risk—or opportunity—of innovation, creativity, and growth. When employees trust that their leaders will provide unwavering support when required, they gain the professional courage to take bold steps and embrace calculated risks—fostering progress and achievement. Courage flourishes in organisations that establish a solid safety net for both employees and managers, supported by their corporate culture and staff policies. This foundation empowers individuals to maximise their potential when circumstances demand it. Likewise, mental health thrives in environments where employees feel secure and assured that addressing their own or their colleagues' well-being is both recognised and valued.

Respect for the Affected

Being at the receiving end of any violent incident inevitably involves an element of bad luck—and it is our responsibility to acknowledge that to those who have been affected.

Although the myth of the invulnerable helper and the omnipotent leader—with its clear divide between the 'weak' and the 'strong'—is compelling, we must remember that in mentally high-risk workplaces, luck—whether good or bad—plays a significant role.

Employees who have already suffered mental harm in a high-risk job and those who are at risk of future harm must be shown due respect. Most likely, they just happened to be in the wrong place at the wrong time. Confusing luck with individual competencies sends an implicit message to professionals that being injured on the job is their own fault.

The Big WHY

Nietzsche's famous words, 'He who has *why* to live can bear almost any *how*', can in this context be paraphrased as 'The one who knows *why* he or she works can tolerate almost any *how*'.

For many employees in a mentally high-risk job, the answer to the question WHY revolves around the experience of having a meaningful job. This may involve helping other people, defending democracy, creating safety and security, taking care of the planet, or perhaps documenting the history of the oppressed.

As you will read in the WHY section in Part III, employees with high compassion satisfaction—i.e., the pleasure derived from helping others—have a lower risk of developing work-related mental injuries than those who have less satisfaction—even when performing the same difficult or tragic tasks under similar conditions. There may be many explanations for this phenomenon, but reminding yourself and each other WHY you chose your profession is an effective way to reconnect with the overall joy, gratitude, and pride in your work.

If you can find good answers to WHY you have chosen your profession or your role, this book offers valuable insights and good advice on HOW you can handle it.

References

Anagnostopoulos, F. and Niakas, D. (2010) "Job burnout, health-related quality of life, and sickness absence in Greek health professionals," *European Psychologist, 15*(2), pp. 132–141. Available at: https://doi.org/10.1027/1016-9040/a000013.

Edmondson, A.C. (2019) *The Fearless Organization: Creating Psychological Safety in the Workplace for Learning, Innovation, and Growth.* Hoboken, NJ: Wiley.

Greenberg, N., Langston, V. and Jones, N. (2008) "Trauma risk management (TRiM) in the UK Armed Forces," *Journal of the Royal Army Medical Corps, 154*(2), pp. 124–127. Available at: https://doi.org/10.1136/jramc-154-02-11.

Heaton, L.D. et al. (1966) *Military Surgical Practices of the United States Army in Viet Nam.* Year Book Medical Publishers, Inc. (Current Problems in Surgery), pp. 1–59.

Scanlan, J.N. and Still, M. (2019) "Relationships between burnout, turnover intention, job satisfaction, job demands and job resources for mental health personnel in an Australian mental health service," *BMC Health Services Research, 19*(1), p. 62. Available at: https://doi.org/10.1186/s12913-018-3841-z.

Introduction

This book is for people who work in mentally high-risk jobs—jobs that involve facing illness, accidents, threats, trauma, abuse, death, or violence. These are jobs that require deep empathy and the ability to navigate painful emotions.

A mentally high-risk job puts you at risk of emotional strain through direct (primary) or indirect (secondary) exposure to trauma and crisis. Your role requires maintaining professionalism, enduring whatever challenges arise—for yourself and those around you. But no matter how strong, competent, and experienced you are, it is impossible to go through such a work life unaffected. At times, you may find yourself listing to one side—becoming emotionally detached and thick-skinned; at other times, you may tip the other way, feeling thin-skinned and overly involved. Like a boat that leans with the weight it carries, your emotional balance shifts depending on what you're navigating.

As a crisis and military psychologist, I have met people like you and witnessed the profound pain and despair of countless professionals—whether from experiencing suffering directly or through the stories of those they care for. I recognise the emotional and physical fatigue that these painful encounters bring, from my own work with people in crisis and trauma.

In this book, I have compiled everything I have learnt about working in mentally high-risk jobs and what you can do to prevent work-related psychological strain from progressing to temporary or lasting illness. Importantly, my years of experience have taught me *one* thing. Long-term resilience in the workplace is only possible when everyone—employees, management, and colleagues—works together and collaborates effectively. Share this book with your team and embark on the journey to build a sustainable workplace that thrives—not in spite of trauma and challenges—but because of them. Together, we can foster an environment rich in life, meaning, and joy. Ultimately, safeguarding mental health is a collective effort—it requires the entire organisation to prevent individual trauma.

I love my job, but I often wonder if I can continue working. I hope I can, because I can't imagine a job that would be more meaningful to me, or imagine having better colleagues. I'm looking forward to reading your book, so I know how I can persevere.

Working with threats, violence, life-threatening illnesses, and death deeply affects one's sense of existence. Eventually, all employees in these roles must confront the reality that we, too, can lose our loved ones or face mortality ourselves. As my former boss used to say: 'In this business, we all have our ass on the line!'

I have worked at the 'sharp end'—in the desert of Afghanistan, on burning oil rigs, and in treatment rooms alongside grieving parents and dying young people. At times, I got over-involved and thin-skinned, crying the moment clients left the room. Other times, I was under-involved, detached, and thick-skinned, catching myself thinking the older cancer patient in front of me should simply pull himself together now we knew his disease had not spread. I know how shameful such thoughts can be—but I also know how incredibly human and normal they are.

Who Are You?

Maybe you are a police officer working with sexual offences against children, or a doctor who must tell patients their disease is terminal. You could also be a nurse or priest, supporting parents who must identify their dead child after a road accident. Perhaps you are a paramedic, soldier, humanitarian aid worker, or a war photographer, who is regularly confronted with death, mutilation, or famine? Or maybe a psychologist like me—but someone working with survivors of torture, rather than writing books and teaching professionals?

You might be a prison officer, teacher, or social worker who has experienced verbal or physical abuse—or even threats to your life—on multiple occasions. You could also be a lawyer or social worker tasked with removing neglected children from their homes. Perhaps you are an interpreter, court clerk, or medical secretary who, by interpreting or documenting, gains insight into deeply tragic cases you are powerless to change.

You might be working in climate change and have begun to feel the mental toll of your work. Or perhaps you serve as a health and safety representative, union consultant, occupational health and safety advisor, stress counsellor, or coach. You could also be a leader or manager overseeing an entire organisation, responsible for supporting your colleagues—whether in the field, at an accident scene, in a hospital, in prison, or in a newsroom—by ensuring they have optimal conditions to carry out their roles.

Finally, you might be a student preparing for one of these professions, eager to learn how best to prepare yourself for the challenges ahead. Whatever your role, this book will provide insights into what it means to work in a mentally high-risk job and offer strategies to help reduce the risks of mental and emotional exhaustion.

In this book, I will share all I have learnt about mental strain—a topic that has captivated me since my student years. What makes humans capable of enduring the most harrowing challenges? And what is at stake when we do not dare to share our insecurities and fears with others? What makes some organisations resilient to mental strain, while others struggle with sick leaves and injuries? In this book, you will discover answers to these questions—and a whole lot more.

But remember: Regardless of how carefully you read this book—or how mentally strong, competent, and experienced you are—a mentally high-risk career will always involve mental strain. At times, you will find yourself thick-skinned, and, at other times, thin-skinned—it is simply part of being human. The key is to continually assess your state and strive to return to a healthy balance.

Heartfelt thanks to each of you—whether you are still in training or already working. We are all deeply grateful for everything you do for others.

Wishing you an inspiring and insightful read.

Rikke Høgsted

Part I

The Impacts

1

Who Is Affected?

A mentally high-risk job is one where employees must routinely confront disease, accidents, threats, trauma, abuse, death, or other violent events. These roles often involve engaging with individuals in crisis or trauma, and they place significant emotional demands on employees to empathise and navigate deeply painful emotions.

Employees can be broadly classified into first-line and second-line responders.

First-line Responders

First-line responders are individuals *directly* exposed to trauma, as their work involves being at the scene of an accident or crime, in a war zone or in a relief area. During accidents, first-line responders include the police, firefighters, and paramedics. At war or in humanitarian aid zones, such helpers may include soldiers, doctors, nurses, psychologists, and rescue workers. Staff in emergency dispatch centres and other emergency call centres, those responsible for coordinating or overseeing emergency work, as well as journalists and photographers working on the front line, also belong to this category.

First-line responders are present at the scene and experience incidents firsthand through all their senses. This immersive exposure can leave a profound impact, particularly in terms of sounds, smells, and sights; see section 'Sensory Impressions' on page 17.

First-line responders typically work with acute short-term strain or with long-term and sustained strain; see section 'Duration of the Traumatic Event' on page 13.

Second-line Responders

Second-line responders are helpers who are *indirectly* exposed to trauma through their interaction with the traumatised person. They are not at the scene of the accident or crime—rather, they are the helpers to whom first-line responders 'hand over' their cases. Second-line responders include hospital staff, other healthcare professionals or social services. For journalists and photographers, the second line consists of employees at the editing room, who receive reports from the field. The category also includes therapists who work with trauma endured many years ago, as may be the case in childhood sexual abuse treatment.

Second-line helpers can be divided into those who work face-to-face and interact with the traumatised person, and those who work with the incident through documenting or reporting it as administrative staff.

Scale of Impact and Trauma Exposure

Everyone involved is affected in their own unique way—and everyone faces the risk of mental imbalance, or tilting, if the impact goes unacknowledged. The 'Ripples in the Water' model on page 5 illustrates how critical incidents affect different groups of people.

The people in the **first circle** in the 'Ripples in the Water' model are:

- **Victims** of a traumatic event.
- **Witnesses**—those present with the affected person at the time of the incident or those who happened to be bystanders who saw events unfold.
- **Professionals** who are on-site to assist.

All these individuals are directly exposed to the incident, which means that they may experience various major or minor after-effects in the days that follow. For most, these reactions subside within a few days. For some, however, these reactions may persist over a longer period. In such cases, these individuals are considered to be traumatised.

Model 1: The Ripples in the Water Model

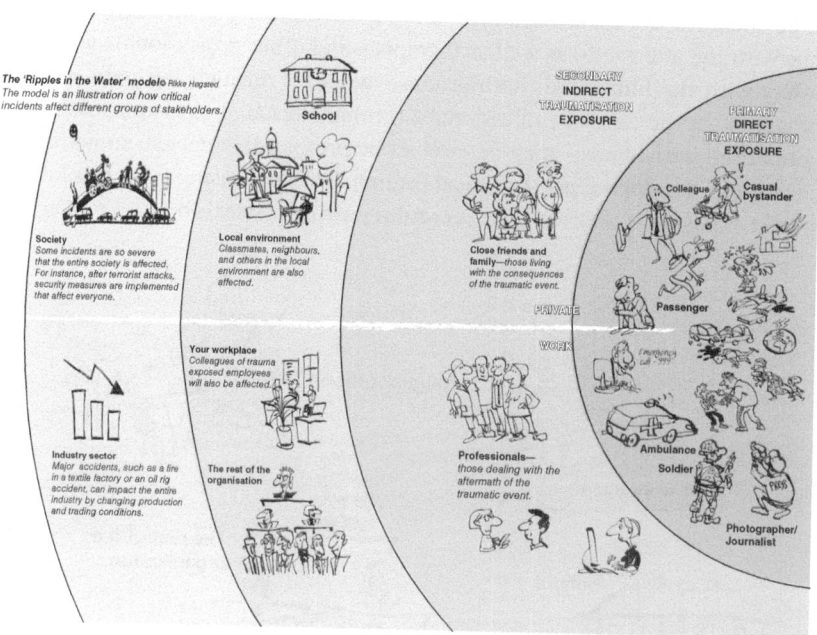

The 'Ripples in the Water' model *Rikke Høgsted.*
The model is an illustration of how critical incidents affect different groups of stakeholders.

School

SECONDARY INDIRECT TRAUMATISATION EXPOSURE

PRIMARY DIRECT TRAUMATISATION EXPOSURE

Colleague **Casual bystander**

Society
Some incidents are so severe that the entire society is affected. For instance, after terrorist attacks, security measures are implemented that affect everyone.

Local environment
Classmates, neighbours, and others in the local environment are also affected.

Close friends and family—those living with the consequences of the traumatic event.

Passenger

PRIVATE

Your workplace
Colleagues of trauma exposed employees will also be affected.

WORK

Industry sector
Major accidents, such as a fire in a textile factory or an oil rig accident, can impact the entire industry by changing production and trading conditions.

The rest of the organisation

Professionals—those dealing with the aftermath of the traumatic event.

Ambulance **Soldier**

Photographer/ Journalist

Psychological trauma caused by exposure to a traumatic event of an exceptionally threatening or catastrophic nature can develop into post-traumatic stress disorder (PTSD). If an individual has been directly exposed to a traumatic event, this is referred to as **primary traumatisation**.

Events or situations that are exceptionally threatening or catastrophic in nature—such as torture, rape, violence, threats of death, natural disasters, or serious transport accidents—are likely to have a profound psychological impact on nearly anyone.

Friends and family—those living with the consequences

Professionals— those working with the consequences

Individuals in the **second** circle of the *Ripples in the Water* model are not directly endangered by the traumatic event but are indirectly affected. This group includes the traumatised person's closest family and friends, who must cope with the aftermath, as well as therapists and other professionals who work closely with the individual. Both groups—whether through intimate, ongoing contact or, in the case of professionals, through repeated exposure to multiple traumatised individuals—may themselves be profoundly affected, sometimes to the point of developing psychological trauma. Trauma arising from this kind of indirect exposure is referred to as **secondary traumatisation**.

Individuals in the **third circle of** the *Ripples in the Water* model include all others who are affected by the incident to varying degrees. These may include the traumatised person's classmates, colleagues, neighbours, and members of the local community, as well as the professional's colleagues. In some cases, the impact may extend to an entire organisation.

Finally, the **outer circle** of the *Ripples in the Water* model represents society at large. Certain events—such as acts of terrorism, natural disasters, or major accidents that disrupt production or trade across entire industries—can be so intense or far-reaching that they have a widespread impact on the broader population.

Proximity to the Traumatic Event

There is generally a strong correlation between the scale of a trauma-inducing event and the scale of the symptoms experienced by a person involved in the event. This implies that individuals in the first circle, or first-line responders, who are at the centre of the violent event, will, in general, experience more after-effects than those in the second and third circles.

High Emotional Demands

When patients, clients, or service users self-harm, behave aggressively, or act offensively, they place significant emotional demands on the professionals who support them. Similarly, prolonged silences, excessive complaining, or helpless behaviour can be equally taxing for those in helping roles. The same holds true in situations where employees are expected to meet unrealistically high demands.

A distinct form of emotional strain emerges when the person being supported displays highly unpredictable behaviour. In such situations, the caregiver must

High emotional demands can look very different.

continually interpret behavioural cues and anticipate actions in order to stay ahead—ensuring the safety of both the individual and those around them.

Even when you understand that this behaviour stems from the individual's helpless or tragic circumstances, or is the result of illness, it can still provoke strong emotional reactions. As a professional, it is essential to acknowledge and manage these emotions in order to maintain a high standard of care and professionalism.

Finally, considerable emotional demands arise when you carry the responsibility of making decisions that profoundly affect another person's life.

2

Factors Affecting the Traumatic Impact

There are several factors to consider when you wish to reduce the risk of traumatisation in the workplace and create the best possible work environment.

The simple answer to what causes stress for professionals in mentally high-risk jobs is clear: violent incidents. This aligns with the well-documented dose-response or exposure-response phenomenon, where the likelihood of stress increases in direct proportion to the number of violent incidents an employee encounters (Gerber et al., 2018). The severity of the impact is also determined by the intensity and magnitude of the violent incident (Masten and Narayan, 2012).

A violent incident, however, never occurs in a social vacuum. It takes place at a particular moment, within a specific organisation, and is handled by individual employees. Typically, employees respond in ways that align with the norms and culture of their workplace, shaped by its unique conditions. As a result, the same type of violent incident can lead to very different outcomes across organisations— depending on their level of preparedness, the employees' experience, and their ability to manage stress and challenges effectively.

The risk of mental tilting amongst employees depends on a wide range of factors. Some of these factors are related to the incident itself (Chapter 3), while others concern how the incident is handled (Chapter 4).

The model shows how various warning signs (Chapter 8) can evolve into either a stress condition (Chapter 10) or an actual trauma-related mental disorder (Chapter 11).

Protective and Risk Factors

The various factors that influence the risk of how severely an employee is affected by a violent incident can be divided into protective factors and risk factors. A *risk factor* is a factor related to either the incident, the task, or the person, which increases the likelihood of a negative outcome for the employee. A *protective factor*, by contrast, is one that either prevents a worsening of outcomes, or increases the likelihood of a positive outcome.

Protective factors cannot eliminate the risk of a negative or traumatic impact, but they can moderate the strain or—figuratively—take the edge off it. There is no one-size-fits-all formula for the relationship between risk and protective factors. Instead, to foster optimal conditions for employees, each workplace must independently evaluate how best to structure and organise work according to its unique context.

Risk and protective factors are grounded in evidence from research and statistics. The value of statistical knowledge lies in its ability to reflect patterns across large groups, offering insight into how many employees are likely to respond in specific ways under certain conditions. However, statistics cannot predict how individual employees will react in any given situation, nor can they explain why something is stressful. Every organisation is different, every employee is unique, and each work task is performed within a particular context—all of which shape the potential impact of a given event.

While knowledge of risk and protective factors can increase awareness and help organisations focus on prevention, it cannot precisely predict or explain how a particular incident will affect an individual. That said, statistical insights remain valuable for strategic planning and for determining what should be examined and addressed in the event of trauma.

The **strain model** provides a comprehensive framework for identifying relevant factors when developing a risk analysis and prevention strategy. Organisations are encouraged to assess not only elements directly related to the traumatic event but also broader contributing conditions. The way such events are managed plays a critical role. The model underscores how these factors influence an organisation's response to stressors and helps identify key warning signs to monitor. Ultimately, it illustrates how these warning signs can escalate into states of strain or, in some cases, develop into mental health disorders.

Model 2: The Strain Model

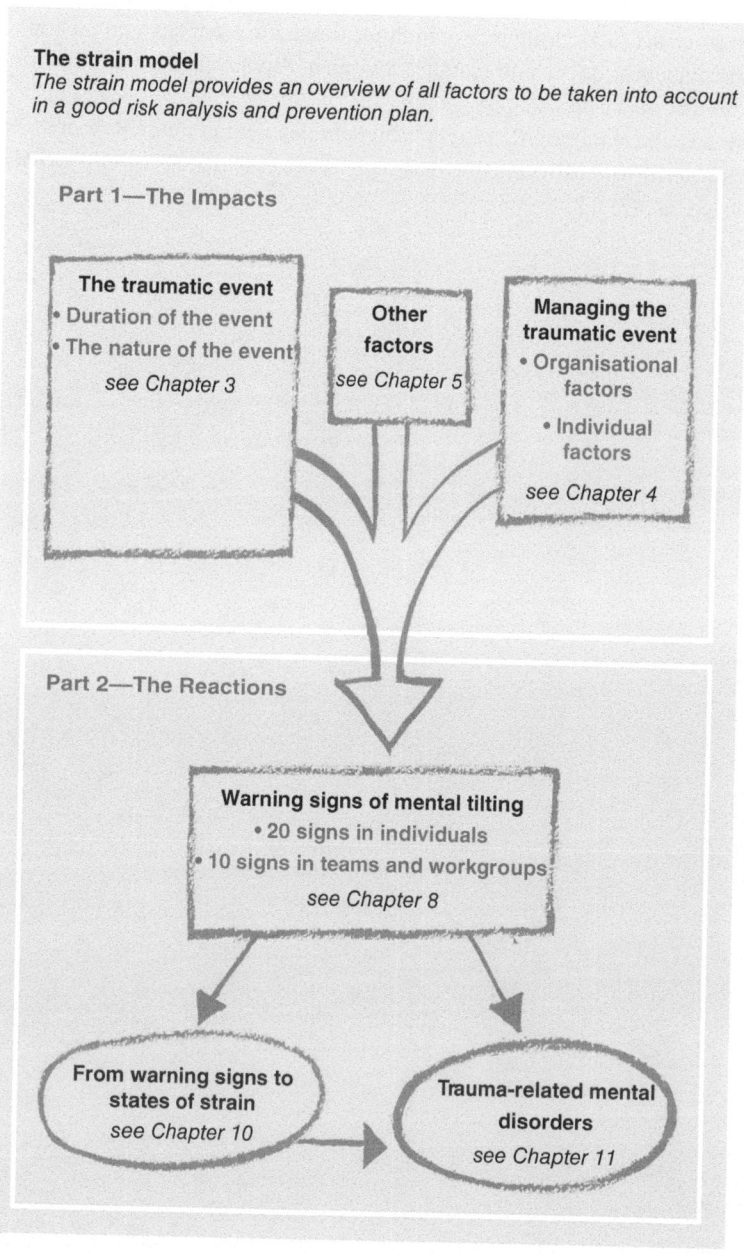

The strain model

The strain model provides an overview of all factors to be taken into account in a good risk analysis and prevention plan.

Part 1—The Impacts

The traumatic event
• Duration of the event
• The nature of the event
see Chapter 3

Other factors
see Chapter 5

Managing the traumatic event
• Organisational factors
• Individual factors
see Chapter 4

Part 2—The Reactions

Warning signs of mental tilting
• 20 signs in individuals
• 10 signs in teams and workgroups
see Chapter 8

From warning signs to states of strain
see Chapter 10

Trauma-related mental disorders
see Chapter 11

References

Gerber, M. et al. (2018) "Influence of multiple traumatic event types on mental health outcomes: does count matter?" *Journal of Psychopathology and Behavioral Assessment*, 40(4), pp. 645–654.

Masten, A.S. and Narayan, A.J. (2012) "Child development in the context of disaster, war and terrorism: pathways of risk and resilience," *Annual Review of Psychology*, 63(1), pp. 227–257.

3

The Traumatic Event

There are several factors that both practice and research have identified as central to how traumatic events affect those involved across time and place.

A thorough understanding of these conditions is crucial for fostering the organisation's resilience and minimising the risk of adverse effects on employees. Identifying these factors also serves as a foundation for accurately assessing the severity of a stressful incident, which in turn determines the appropriate level of support to provide. Two key aspects to consider are the duration and nature of the incident.

Duration of the Traumatic Event

As shown in the Ripples in the Water model, a violent event can affect a wide range of people. The impact may be either short-term or long-term. The longer the duration of an incident, the greater the strain on those involved. While some individuals can endure extended periods of high stress without showing symptoms, others may develop delayed or long-term effects (see Chapter 10 for further discussion).

An Acute Short-term Strain

A single traumatic incident may involve a car accident, fire, robbery, rape, or a similar event. As previously mentioned, such sudden incidents are typically managed by emergency responders and medical professionals.

Journalists and photographers may also be present during individual traumatic incidents. Being on the scene of a crime or accident, interacting with people in crisis, or witnessing severe injuries can have a deeply distressing impact. Because these events occur without warning, individuals may be unprepared and lack the readiness to cope with the situation. In such cases, the psychological impact is often particularly intense, as it involves a sudden loss of control and direction. Stress levels tend to be extremely high, as the events usually unfold rapidly within a short period.

A Series of Stressful Events – Accumulated Strain

In professions where employees are routinely exposed to traumatic events—for instance, social workers at a refugee centre, nurses in a cancer ward, or employees in a prison—strain can accumulate (Gerber et al., 2018). Unlike professionals who deal with sudden and violent incidents, those exposed to long-term stressors have the opportunity to mobilise their psychological counterforces, as they are, to some extent, prepared for the demands. However, such professionals risk a gradual buildup of unnoticed stress, which may eventually reach a critical saturation point and trigger a reaction. This is known as a **cumulative reaction**, or a **drop-by-drop impact**—in the end, all it takes is a single drop to make the glass overflow.

> *Over the years as a manager, I've learnt to watch for those who just bleed quietly without much drama. You have to keep an eye out for those too.*

Long-term, Continuous Strain

The last category concerns continuous strains that unfold over longer periods, in which the employee must endure stress as part of their job. Such professional groups include deployed soldiers or employees in humanitarian aid organisations who work in unsafe conditions. While some individuals manage stressors effectively, others may reach a breaking point, with the psychological toll becoming apparent to those around them. Additionally, employees who initially cope well with immediate stressors may, over time, develop psychological reactions or experience delayed effects—even years later (Utzon-Frank et al., 2014).

Risk of Reoccurrence

When the likelihood of a stressful event recurring is low, it is generally easier to cope with than situations where the risk of reoccurrence is high. Incidents that are likely to happen again—perhaps even in a more violent form—increase the risk of employees experiencing feelings of powerlessness and helplessness.

Is the Traumatic Event Over—Or Still Ongoing?

Closely related to the risk of reoccurrence is the question of whether the traumatic event is over or could potentially be brought to an end. If an incident can be clearly delineated in time, with a distinct beginning and end, it is easier for those involved to develop a shared understanding and common narrative of what occurred. This makes it possible to talk about the event with others and, potentially, to gain new professional insights and learning together—an important protective factor.

Conversely, incidents involving unresolved elements or ongoing suffering can place professionals under prolonged psychological pressure. Examples include cases where people go missing in a plane crash and the aircraft is never found, unsolved crimes where the perpetrator remains at large, or long-term treatment scenarios in which a chronically ill patient is in severe physical or mental distress.

The Nature of the Traumatic Event

Trauma-inducing or violent incidents are generally events or situations where individuals:

- Face a direct threat to their life or risk serious harm, or
- Witness the death of others, or observe others being, or having been, in danger of death or serious harm.

Threats

Whereas the psychological impact of threats was previously downplayed with arguments such as 'nothing happened, it was just a threat', research has shown that threats are a serious psychological stressor (Lapid Pickman, Greene and Gelkopf, 2017). In general, the more severe the perceived threat, the greater the psychological impact—and therefore the higher the risk of mental tilting (Pinto et al., 2015). Threats such as workplace violence and bullying have been shown to significantly increase the risk of suicide amongst employees (Magnusson Hanson et al., 2023).

Loss and Death

Experiencing a loss—the loss of the job itself, the loss of a good colleague or the loss of part of one's ability to work—can also increase employees' risks of developing a mental disorder. Furthermore, an assault or accident can result in the loss of some, or all, of an employee's sight or hearing, in the loss of a body part, or in impaired memory and concentration. Whether the injury is physical or psychological, the loss implies being unable to maintain normal work, which many professionals will perceive as a great loss, triggering a psychological crisis.

Human-made or Natural Events

Stressful events can be divided into two groups: *human-made events*, such as threats, violence, and accidents, and *natural events*, such as forest fires, landslides, hurricanes, or other types of natural disasters. Human-made events can be further subdivided into two categories: *intentional incidents*, such as deliberate threats, violence, and acts of terrorism, and *accidental incidents*, such as car accidents, plane crashes, or drowning accidents.

Human-made Events

Human-made incidents are psychologically more stressful to cope with than natural ones (Alisic et al., 2014; Peled-Avram, 2017). Intentional incidents that involve a deliberate act, such as sexual abuse, torture, violence, or gross neglect, will have a profound adverse effect on employees, often leading them to grapple with the concept of evil and question how one human being could inflict such harm on another. Human-made incidents can also prompt reflections on whether the situation could have been avoided or detected earlier, or raise questions about culpability, legal liability, and financial compensation.

Natural Events and Natural Disasters

Natural events and disasters may be typical of certain geographical regions and, as such, may be part of the lived experience of several generations within a family. These events are therefore often understood and accepted as inevitable occurrences that happen from time to time. Those affected typically view such events as a matter of bad luck and rarely take them personally.

Climate-related Natural Disasters

Climate-related natural disasters, such as floods or droughts, are often regarded as purely natural events, despite their potential connection to human activity. This subtle link can make them more difficult to comprehend, amplifying feelings of powerlessness rather than fostering a sense of agency to prevent similar occurrences in the future. Feelings of powerlessness significantly contribute to the risk of psychological trauma in the workplace (see Chapter 6 for further detail on mental strain and other global crises).

Witnessing the Suffering of Acquaintances or Children

Witnessing an event involving trauma, death, injury, or threat is generally psychologically stressful. However, the burden is heavier if you have a personal relationship, whether familial or through work, with the victim (Broberg, Dyregrov and Lilled, 2005). Children who suffer often make a profound impression on employees and are therefore a risk factor in themselves (Sprang, Craig and Clark, 2011).

> *As a young journalist, I was faced with six children dying within a month, and at the same time, I had young children of my own. It was just too much, and I felt awful. When I called my editor to tell him, he just said, 'That's a good story. Write it!' Fortunately, that was a long time ago.*

Number of People Involved

The number of victims or injured individuals significantly influences the psychological strain placed on professionals. For instance, a road accident involving a single vehicle with one or two casualties may impose relatively less strain compared to a major collision involving a bus with up to 50 casualties, or a disaster scene with hundreds or even thousands of injured or deceased. A higher number of casualties can greatly affect employees' ability to maintain a sense of control, gain a clear overview of the situation, and ensure adequate support reaches everyone.

Sensory Impressions

The more sensory impressions an employee is exposed to during a traumatic situation, the more profound the psychological strain. For instance, the sight of dead or severely injured individuals—such as torn body parts or significant blood loss—the feel of diseased or damaged tissue, the screams of those in pain or distress, deafening noise, the smell of burnt flesh, and the extreme temperatures or smoke from a fire can all have a profoundly traumatising impact. The intensity and number of these sensory stimuli increase the likelihood of strain.

Where Did the Incident Occur—And Was It Anticipated?

Incidents that are anticipated—such as those occurring in high-risk areas or involving clients, patients, or service users known for disruptive behaviour—tend to be less psychologically stressful than sudden or unpredictable events in an otherwise safe and tranquil environment (Gleser et al., 2013). Prior warning allows you to keep your psychological defences up and be prepared to act quickly and appropriately. Responding effectively in a predictable and expected situation also tends to leave employees more satisfied with their performance afterwards. By contrast, a sudden, unexpected incident leaves a person psychologically unprepared and unprotected.

> *I got really angry. Damn it! I had worked in war zones all over the world, and I was settling in for some peace and quiet in peaceful Norway. I had deliberately removed myself from high-explosive areas to gain some control.*
> *And now I was standing there in Oslo with broken windows in my office.*

Near Misses

Incidents that narrowly avoid catastrophe can still impose a significant psychological burden in certain industries.

References

Alisic, E. et al. (2014) "Rates of post-traumatic stress disorder in trauma-exposed children and adolescents: meta-analysis," *British Journal of Psychiatry*, 204(5), pp. 335–340. Available at: https://doi.org/10.1192/bjp.bp.113.131227.

Broberg, A.G., Dyregrov, A. and Lilled, L. (2005) "The Göteborg discotheque fire: posttraumatic stress, and school adjustment as reported by the primary victims 18 months later," *Journal of Child Psychology and Psychiatry, and Allied Disciplines*, 46(12), pp. 1279–1286. Available at: https://doi.org/10.1111/j.1469-7610.2005.01439.x.

Gerber, M.M. et al. (2018) "Influence of multiple traumatic event types on mental health outcomes: does count matter?" *Journal of Psychopathology and Behavioral Assessment*, 40(4), pp. 645–654. Available at: https://doi.org/10.1007/s10862-018-9682-6.

Gleser, G.C. et al. (2013) *Prolonged Psychosocial Effects of Disaster: A Study of Buffalo Creek*. Burlington: Elsevier Science.

Lapid Pickman, L., Greene, T. and Gelkopf, M. (2017) "Sense of threat as a mediator of peritraumatic stress symptom development during wartime: an experience sampling study," *Journal of Traumatic Stress*, 30(4), pp. 372–380. Available at: https://doi.org/10.1002/jts.22207.

Magnusson Hanson, L.L. et al. (2023) "Association of workplace violence and bullying with later suicide risk: a multicohort study and meta-analysis of published data," *The Lancet Public Health*, 8(7), pp. e494–e503. Available at: https://doi.org/10.1016/S2468-2667(23)00096-8.

Peled-Avram, M. (2017) "The role of relational-oriented supervision and personal and work-related factors in the development of vicarious traumatization," *Clinical Social Work Journal*, 45(1), pp. 22–32. Available at: https://doi.org/10.1007/s10615-015-0573-y.

Pinto, R.J. et al. (2015) "The strongest correlates of PTSD for firefighters: number, recency, frequency, or perceived threat of traumatic events?" *Journal of Traumatic Stress*, 28(5), pp. 434–440. Available at: https://doi.org/10.1002/jts.22035.

Sprang, G., Craig, C. and Clark, J. (2011) "Secondary traumatic stress and burnout in child welfare workers: a comparative analysis of occupational distress across professional groups," *Child Welfare*, 90(6), pp. 149–168.

Utzon-Frank, N. et al. (2014) "Occurrence of delayed-onset post-traumatic stress disorder: a systematic review and meta-analysis of prospective studies," *Scandinavian Journal of Work, Environment & Health*, 40(3), pp. 215–229. Available at: https://doi.org/10.5271/sjweh.3420.

4

Managing the Traumatic Event

One factor is the nature of the traumatic event itself; another is how the organisation responds to it. The same event occurring in two different organisations can have vastly different impacts on employees, depending on how each organisation manages and supports its staff through the experience.

Put simply, employees in a well-prepared organisation that proactively addresses the risk of mental harm—by fostering resilience and implementing preventive strategies—can carry out their duties professionally, with minimal risk to their mental health. Conversely, in an organisation lacking such awareness and strategies, employees are at greater risk of performing poorly, which poses a threat both to patient or client safety and to their own psychological well-being (Kanno and Giddings, 2017; Ashley-Binge and Cousins, 2020).

> *There was once a crisis psychologist who said, 'It's not the traumatic incident that defines the crisis; it's the crisis that defines the traumatic incident,' and I think that makes a lot of sense.*

This chapter focuses on managing the traumatic event and is divided into two sections. The first examines the role of the organisation; the second focuses on employees in helping professions. In practice, these two areas influence one another and are often difficult to separate. For instance, a poorly defined task performed within an unclear framework increases the risk that an employee feels dissatisfied with their performance—which, in turn, increases the likelihood of being negatively affected by the work. Yet separating the two is important to identify the specific sub-elements that contribute to employees' risk of harm. Fortunately, substantial research has been conducted on this topic, making it possible to highlight at least some of the relevant factors. A thorough understanding of these factors forms the foundation for building the resilience and prevention strategies outlined in Part III of this book.

Organisational Factors

Trauma Education

If you are a professional working with traumatised people, it is important to receive appropriate training on psychological trauma. Identifying what causes trauma, how trauma manifests itself, and how it can affect both the traumatised person and his or her surroundings can reduce the risk of strain (Kanno and Giddings, 2017). Hands-on trauma training that prepares a helping professional for the specific work has a good protective effect.

Supervision

Supervision is a professional learning and development method frequently used by psychologists, psychotherapists, and other professions working with people, such as social workers, teachers, nurses, and doctors. Regular supervision is a protective factor (McFadden, Campbell and Taylor, 2015; Sprang et al., 2019). Supervision can take the form of individual support or occur in a group. Supervision allows a helping professional to explore the problem and reflect on the way they have approached it. An important part of this exploration concerns the relationship between the client and the practitioner. Supervision may explore topics such as the practitioner's emotions in working with the client and whether the practitioner and client are in good contact—or conversely, if the practitioner is either over- or under-involved. This process will frequently result in new and alternative interpretations of the task and lead to new possibilities of action.

Supervision can help create a better understanding of the expectations a practitioner has towards himself or herself and make visible the realistic possibilities inherent in the job as well as the practitioner's own abilities.

Through group supervision, colleagues can witness and share each other's experiences, which can reduce the feeling of loneliness that is typical for many practitioners working on their own.

Social Support

Social support, which grants professionals in helping professions a sense of belonging, is a key protective factor (Hensel et al., 2015). Social support can be provided in several ways. It can include *emotional support* from colleagues, which prioritises empathy, care, and presence. Another form of social support is *feedback-oriented support*, where colleagues engage in conversations to help their colleague or each other reach a better understanding of what happened and what role they each played in the process. *Counselling or advisory support* is an additional form of collegial support, which entails co-workers engaging in mutual sharing of information and advice. Finally, professionals can also engage in *practical support*, where colleagues help each other in carrying out their tasks.

Clarity of Task and Role

Another important protective factor is having a clear understanding of the task at hand, your professional role, and the expectations and demands placed on your performance (Peled-Avram, 2017). When roles and responsibilities are clearly defined—along with decision-making authority and the framework for action—it becomes much easier to create a realistic and effective plan. This allows practitioners to form clear and realistic expectations of themselves. Sharing these expectations with both managers and colleagues increases the likelihood of later satisfaction with one's own performance—another key protective factor.

When tasks are clearly defined, it is especially important to establish clear roles and frameworks in interdisciplinary teams to avoid uncertainty about the specific responsibilities and mandates of different professional groups.

The Organisation of Work—Alone or as Part of a Workgroup?

Being part of a well-functioning, supportive workgroup is one of the most powerful protective factors when managing psychologically demanding tasks (Ashley-Binge and Cousins, 2020). A cohesive team can handle many provocative, frightening, distressing, or challenging events without compromising the quality of their work or causing psychological harm to any of its members. By contrast, working alone—being the sole person responsible for a task—makes an employee significantly more vulnerable and is considered a risk factor (Gleser et al., 2013).

> There are always two paramedics in an ambulance, and there are always two officers in a police car. They have a partner. As a doctor, you're often on your own.

When Are Tasks Carried Out?

As you will discover in Part III, the specific way in which a workday or workweek is organised can serve as a risk factor or a protective factor. An abrupt transition from being a private person to a professional role and back again can make the professional more vulnerable to violent incidents at work. This vulnerability is amplified if the working day, either planned or accidentally, begins or ends with particularly hard, challenging, or otherwise demanding tasks.

Caseload

As mentioned earlier, there is a direct correlation between how often a person is exposed to traumatic incidents and how affected they are by them. Needless to say, the number of traumatised patients, clients, or service users you encounter and must assist has a direct impact on the level of strain—and thus the risk of mental tilting (Hensel et al., 2015; Denkinger et al., 2018).

Leadership Well-being and Responsibility Fatigue

The well-being of managers and leaders is vital to the overall well-being of employees. Consequently, a leader's unhappiness or stress should be regarded as a risk factor (Skakon et al., 2010). Leaders who are responsible for both the quality of the work and the mental health and safety of their employees face immense psychological pressure. Additionally, for leaders operating in high-risk geographic areas, the burden is even greater, as they must ensure not only the safety and performance of the group but also their own personal security.

> *It was only as I headed home and handed over the phone that I realised I was no longer the one on call, no longer the person responsible for everyone else's families.*

A leader's well-being and professional judgement, both in routine operations and during periods of peak pressure, play a crucial role in shaping the team's ability to perform their duties effectively and safely, and to experience a sense of accomplishment. As outlined in the next section, employees' own satisfaction—or dissatisfaction—with their performance is a key factor in their resilience.

Individual Factors

Individual factors concern who was on duty, so to speak, when the violent incident occurred. How an incident is handled often depends on the specific employee assigned to the task. Some individual factors—such as the employee's gender and length of work experience—are objective. Other factors relate to the nature of the task and the overall job satisfaction within the team, while still others pertain to how the individual employee typically copes with stress.

Personal Factors

Gender

Many high-risk jobs are 'gendered'; there is a tradition of a predominance of one gender over the other amongst a particular group of helping professionals. For example, while positions in the health and social care sector are often held by women, most positions in the emergency response sector are typically held by men. Some studies indicate that men are generally more likely to be exposed to traumatic events (Vogt and Mangan, n.d.), which in itself is associated with a risk of developing post-traumatic stress disorder (PTSD). Other studies report that women may have a higher overall risk of developing PTSD than men (Olff, 2017). Several studies could not find any gender differences. The skewed gender distribution makes it difficult to say anything specific about the impact of gender on the development of secondary traumatisation.

Current Life Situation

The helping professional's current life situation has an impact on their vulnerability. If a professional's circumstances are already strained because of financial problems, illness, loss, or if they are in the midst of a conflict-ridden divorce, the professional's ability to cope with violent events is naturally weakened. Consequently, it is important to communicate any personal circumstances to your manager, so that they can take them into account in planning and assigning tasks.

If an employee facing difficult life circumstances is unfortunate to experience a violent incident, despite the management's special care, it is crucial to communicate this clearly so that additional support measures can be implemented to prevent long-term negative reactions.

What Stage of Working Life Are You in?

Employees in high-risk roles can be particularly vulnerable both at the beginning and towards the end of their careers. Increased vulnerability early in working life often stems from a combination of factors: younger employees may have less confidence in their abilities and, due to limited experience, are more likely to face situations where they feel uncertain about what they should or can do (Sinclair et al., 2017). If this uncertainty develops into feelings of helplessness, there is a risk that the individual becomes dissatisfied with their own performance. It is crucial to ensure that this group is well-informed about the critical tasks they may face and reassured that they will receive consistent support throughout.

Helping professionals may also become more vulnerable towards the end of their careers, due to their cumulative exposure to traumatic events over time (Rossi et al., 2012). This is often described as the proverbial straw that breaks the camel's back. Individuals who experience this frequently report being caught off guard, as the final, triggering incident was not more severe than earlier critical events—it was the final drop in an already full cup. It is equally important to pay attention to senior members of staff and maintain an open dialogue about whether special considerations or a senior scheme might be appropriate.

At one point I just couldn't drive with one more terminal patient. This was after a trip where I had to drive a young man and his parents home from the hospital so he could die at home.

Personal Trauma History

Another personal risk factor is a history of childhood trauma (La Mott and Martin, 2019). If a person grew up in an abusive household, or if they were emotionally or physically abused or neglected as a child, this will make a person particularly vulnerable to traumatisation (Hensel et al., 2015; La Mott and Martin, 2019).

Past trauma, such as growing up in an abusive home, does not have to be a vulnerability. If a traumatic experience has been dealt with successfully, it may even become a strength—for example, a personal history of trauma may help the professional develop a deeper understanding and compassion for current clients living with abuse.

Role in the Incident—Active or Passive?

The experience of being active and in control—or having the opportunity to influence a critical situation in the right direction—is an important protective factor. Conversely, the experience of forced passivity or chaos is a significant risk factor (Rohde et al., 2006; Gleser et al., 2013). Professionals who are not required or able to take action but must instead passively observe a situation unfold may be more affected afterwards than colleagues who had the opportunity to act. For example, a soldier without the mandate to intervene in attacks on civilians, or a firefighter unable to save more people from a burning building because the fire has already spread, may experience the psychological strain of being forced into passivity.

Many readers may recall a time as a student or intern when they were emotionally affected while observing an experienced professional at work, feeling like a passive 'fly on the wall'. Witnessing others' suffering without the ability to intervene can be particularly mentally exhausting.

Journalists and photographers working in war zones or in other situations where civilians are in urgent need of assistance sometimes report a similar experience of passivity. This can be psychologically stressful both during the event and afterwards. Unlike relief workers, who can and should help victims directly and actively, journalists' indirect role—reporting on the crisis—can be perceived as passive. Some reporters have also described facing a moral dilemma during such incidents, forced to choose between remaining in their professional role as journalists or stepping in to help the victims directly (Backholm and Idås, 2015; Williamson, Stevelink and Greenberg, 2018).

How You Assess Your Own Performance

Just as it is a protective factor when an employee's manager is satisfied with their work and takes the time to express it explicitly, the employee's own satisfaction with their performance is another important protective factor (Yates and Samuel, 2019). Self-criticism and persistent rumination—about whether one performed well enough, what might have happened if one had acted differently, and so on—constitute a separate risk factor for the development of depression and other mental disorders (Yates and Samuel, 2019).

Perfectionist professionals who set very high standards for themselves are particularly at risk of being dissatisfied with their own performance (Sherman, 2004). This can happen even when colleagues or managers acknowledge their efforts and praise them for performing impeccably or even exceeding expectations. Although recognition from colleagues and leaders is important (Sprang et al., 2019), if a helping professional is not personally satisfied with their performance, they may be left alone with self-criticism and doubt. In some cases, the employee may even begin to believe that others are not applying high enough standards to the task at hand.

It is therefore important to ask for the employee's own assessment of their performance. If they express dissatisfaction, a professional conversation should be arranged to reflect on and discuss the process.

Coping

In speaking about coping, we often refer to coping *ability*—that is, the capacity to manage life's demands, including strains encountered at work. It can be difficult to define which coping strategies are universally good or bad, as their effectiveness depends on the specific situation. As a helping professional, you will likely draw on a range of strategies depending on the context and the people involved (Turgoose and Maddox, 2017). However, research has identified several coping strategies associated with an increased risk of secondary traumatisation (Dunkley and Whelan, 2006; Adams and Riggs, 2008; Furlonger and Taylor, 2013; Gil and Weinberg, 2015; Scanlan and Still, 2019):

- **Emotion-focused coping strategies**, where the emphasis is placed on the emotions that arise from a stressful situation rather than on adopting a solution-oriented approach.
- **Self-sacrificing coping strategies**, where you strive to maintain an image—both to yourself and others—of being kind, helpful, and never angry.

- **Negative coping strategies**, characterised by behaviours such as excessive worry, self-blame, aggressive outbursts, and social isolation.
- **Avoidant coping strategies**, where you attempt to ignore or avoid the problems or keep them entirely to yourself.

Need to Clarify the Causes

Like some victims, helping professionals may become preoccupied with the causes of a traumatic event. Why was the storm surge not forecast in advance? How did the road accident happen? Why was the neglect not identified earlier? These kinds of questions often arise. Placing blame and identifying responsibility can offer a sense of justice and accountability. For both professionals and victims, this process may help bring peace of mind and offer a way to mentally process and move beyond the incident.

Another reason for a strong focus on the causes of a traumatic event is the need to find learning or meaning in an otherwise senseless and tragic situation. If a helping professional is concerned with understanding the causes, a thorough and impartial accident or root cause analysis can serve as a protective factor.

Compassion Satisfaction

Compassion satisfaction refers to a sense of fulfilment at work—the feeling of performing well and being successful (Turgoose and Maddox, 2017). This satisfaction may stem from positive emotions about one's colleagues, or from the sense that one's efforts have a meaningful impact on others, and perhaps even on society as a whole. Compassion satisfaction is closely tied to the 'Big WHY'—the belief that your work carries deeper meaning and purpose.

Employees with high levels of compassion satisfaction tend to experience fewer symptoms of secondary traumatisation (Stamm, 2010). While the exact reasons for this link are not fully understood, the connection is clear and well established. See Chapter 16, The Big WHY, for further discussion.

References

Adams, S.A. and Riggs, S.A. (2008) "An exploratory study of vicarious trauma among therapist trainees," *Training and Education in Professional Psychology*, 2(1), pp. 26–34. Available at: https://doi.org/10.1037/1931-3918.2.1.26.

Ashley-Binge, S. and Cousins, C. (2020) "Individual and organisational practices addressing social workers' experiences of vicarious trauma," *Practice*, 32(3), pp. 191–207. Available at: https://doi.org/10.1080/09503153.2019.1620201.

Backholm, K. and Idås, T. (2015) "Ethical dilemmas, work-related guilt, and posttraumatic stress reactions of news journalists covering the terror attack in Norway in 2011," *Journal of Traumatic Stress*, 28(2), pp. 142–148. Available at: https://doi.org/10.1002/jts.22001.

Denkinger, J.K. et al. (2018) "Secondary traumatization in caregivers working with women and children who suffered extreme violence by the 'Islamic state,'" *Frontiers in Psychiatry*, 9, p. 234. Available at: https://doi.org/10.3389/fpsyt.2018.00234.

Dunkley, J. and Whelan, T.A. (2006) "Vicarious traumatisation in telephone counsellors: internal and external influences," *British Journal of Guidance & Counselling*, 34(4), pp. 451–469. Available at: https://doi.org/10.1080/03069880600942574.

Furlonger, B. and Taylor, W. (2013) "Supervision and the management of vicarious traumatisation among Australian telephone and online counsellors," *Australian Journal of Guidance and Counselling*, 23(1), pp. 82–94. Available at: https://doi.org/10.1017/jgc.2013.3.

Gil, S. and Weinberg, M. (2015) "Secondary trauma among social workers treating trauma clients: the role of coping strategies and internal resources," *International Social Work*, 58(4), pp. 551–561. Available at: https://doi.org/10.1177/0020872814564705.

Gleser, G.C. et al. (2013) *Prolonged Psychosocial Effects of Disaster: A Study of Buffalo Creek*. Burlington: Elsevier Science.

Hensel, J.M. et al. (2015) "Meta-analysis of risk factors for secondary traumatic stress in therapeutic work with trauma victims," *Journal of Traumatic Stress*, 28(2), pp. 83–91. Available at: https://doi.org/10.1002/jts.21998.

Kanno, H. and Giddings, M.M. (2017) "Hidden trauma victims: understanding and preventing traumatic stress in mental health professionals," *Social Work in Mental Health*, 15(3), pp. 331–353. Available at: https://doi.org/10.1080/15332985.2016.1220442.

La Mott, J. and Martin, L.A. (2019) "Adverse childhood experiences, self-care, and compassion outcomes in mental health providers working with trauma," *Journal of Clinical Psychology*, 75(6), pp. 1066–1083. Available at: https://doi.org/10.1002/jclp.22752.

McFadden, P., Campbell, A. and Taylor, B. (2015) "Resilience and burnout in child protection social work: individual and organisational themes from a systematic literature review," *British Journal of Social Work*, 45(5), pp. 1546–1563. Available at: https://doi.org/10.1093/bjsw/bct210.

Olff, M. (2017) "Sex and gender differences in post-traumatic stress disorder: an update," *European Journal of Psychotraumatology*, 8(sup4), p. 1351204. Available at: https://doi.org/10.1080/20008198.2017.1351204.

Peled-Avram, M. (2017) "The role of relational-oriented supervision and personal and work-related factors in the development of vicarious traumatization," *Clinical*

Social Work Journal, 45(1), pp. 22–32. Available at: https://doi.org/10.1007/s10615-015-0573-y.

Rohde, M.C. et al. (2006) "Rape and attempted rape in Aarhus County, Denmark: police reported and unreported cases," *Forensic Science, Medicine and Pathology*, 2(1), pp. 33–38. Available at: https://doi.org/10.1385/FSMP:2:1:33.

Rossi, A. et al. (2012) "Burnout, compassion fatigue, and compassion satisfaction among staff in community-based mental health services," *Psychiatry Research*, 200(2–3), pp. 933–938. Available at: https://doi.org/10.1016/j.psychres.2012.07.029.

Scanlan, J.N. and Still, M. (2019) "Relationships between burnout, turnover intention, job satisfaction, job demands and job resources for mental health personnel in an Australian mental health service," *BMC Health Services Research*, 19(1), p. 62. Available at: https://doi.org/10.1186/s12913-018-3841-z.

Sherman, D.W. (2004) "Nurses' stress & burnout: how to care for yourself when caring for patients and their families experiencing life-threatening illness," *American Journal of Nursing*, 104(5), pp. 48–56. Available at: https://doi.org/10.1097/00000446-200405000-00020.

Sinclair, S. et al. (2017) "Compassion fatigue: a meta-narrative review of the healthcare literature," *International Journal of Nursing Studies*, 69, pp. 9–24. Available at: https://doi.org/10.1016/j.ijnurstu.2017.01.003.

Skakon, J. et al. (2010) "Are leaders' well-being, behaviours and style associated with the affective well-being of their employees? A systematic review of three decades of research," *Work & Stress*, 24(2), pp. 107–139. Available at: https://doi.org/10.1080/02678373.2010.495262.

Sprang, G. et al. (2019) "Defining secondary traumatic stress and developing targeted assessments and interventions: lessons learned from research and leading experts," *Traumatology*, 25(2), pp. 72–81. Available at: https://doi.org/10.1037/trm0000180.

Stamm, B.H. (2010) *The Concise ProQOL Manual: The Concise Manual for the Professional Quality of Life Scale* (2nd ed). Eastwoods, LLC.

Turgoose, D. and Maddox, L. (2017) "Predictors of compassion fatigue in mental health professionals: a narrative review," *Traumatology*, 23(2), pp. 172–185. Available at: https://doi.org/10.1037/trm0000116.

Vogt, D. and Mangan, E. (n.d.) *Research on Women, Trauma, and PTSD, PTSD: National Center for PTSD*. Available at: https://www.ptsd.va.gov/professional/treat/specific/ptsd_research_women.asp (Accessed: 23 August 2025).

Williamson, V., Stevelink, S.A.M. and Greenberg, N. (2018) "Occupational moral injury and mental health: systematic review and meta-analysis," *The British Journal of Psychiatry*, 212(6), pp. 339–346. Available at: https://doi.org/10.1192/bjp.2018.55.

Yates, M. and Samuel, V. (2019) "Burnout in oncologists and associated factors: a systematic literature review and meta-analysis," *European Journal of Cancer Care*, 28(3). Available at: https://doi.org/10.1111/ecc.13094.

5

Other Factors

In addition to factors directly related to the traumatic event and its management, several other elements can contribute to the risk of employee strain. Notable amongst these are the societal status of the profession, the presence of complaints or media coverage related to the incident, and the role of digital tools in the workplace. How digital tools affect strain in the workplace is both a complex and rapidly evolving question, which is why it is explored in greater detail than the other contributing factors. Nevertheless, elements such as social status, public scrutiny, and media coverage remain equally important for understanding work-related strain.

Social Status of the Job

How other people perceive your job has an impact on your risk of secondary traumatisation. Having a job that is socially appreciated, involves helping a group of people that others generally sympathise with, or a job that enjoys high social status, all constitute protective factors against work strain (Canfield, 2005).

Conversely, jobs with low social status and low social gratitude are a risk factor (Canfield, 2005). The same applies to jobs where you often need to explain or even defend the target group's need for help.

Prejudice and victim blaming often take the form of attitudes such as 'it's probably their own fault' in relation to rape victims, addicts, the unemployed, or people who binge eat, or 'they chose it themselves' in reference to police or military personnel. As a result, professionals who work with these target groups may stop sharing their work experiences with others outside the organisation. When entire organisations or institutions fall silent and withdraw from public discourse, this sustains an unfortunate dynamic that can ultimately lead to professional stagnation and even abuse of power.

Similarly, silent and closed-off organisations that isolate themselves from society in self-defence risk existing in a kind of time warp—characterised by outdated practices and disconnected from current criticism and the valuable input that engagement with the outside world could otherwise provide.

Complaints About Possible Errors

Formal complaints about a helping professional's work are associated with increased vulnerability for the employee, regardless of whether a mistake has actually been made. The fear of being labelled—online or in the press—as someone who has either deliberately harmed a client, patient, or service user, or who lacks professional competence, can be deeply stressful. Prolonged case processing times can also be a significant source of strain.

> *I feel there has been a positive development from looking at the individual midwife who might have misheard a heartbeat to now looking at the whole team and their workflows.*

Most professionals are conscientious and strive to carry out their duties to the best of their ability. Nevertheless, due to inexperience, high workload, or other circumstances, mistakes may still occur. In such cases, professionals are sometimes referred to as *second victims*, as they may be profoundly affected by the fact that their actions have negatively impacted another human being. The concept of the second victim highlights how trauma can arise not only from the original incident but also from the emotional aftermath of perceived failure, guilt, or public scrutiny.

If a mistake has been made and the organisation treats it solely as an individual failure—rather than acknowledging its shared responsibility—the helping professional involved faces an increased risk of traumatisation. This approach also closes off opportunities for learning and systemic accountability.

Media Coverage

Media coverage of a traumatic event is a double-edged sword that can generate stress both for the victims and for the professionals supporting them.

On one hand, sensitive reporting on a violent or distressing event—such as a natural disaster—can be valuable, helping to connect those affected with a broader community capable of offering understanding and compassion. On the other hand, insensitive coverage can make professionals in vulnerable or high-pressure situations feel exposed, violating their privacy and leading to psychological overload.

Moreover, direct media presence at an accident scene, where professionals are actively performing their duties, can add further pressure. Similarly, inaccurate accounts from bystanders—particularly if emotionally charged—can misrepresent the work of emergency responders and contribute to public misunderstanding or mistrust.

The Impact of Digitalisation and Technology

> *Sometimes it feels like I spend more time clicking boxes than looking my patient in the eye.*

Digital tools are present in nearly every corner of the helping professions. From teletherapy and virtual consultations to digital documentation and artificial intelligence (AI), the screen has become a second—or even primary—workplace. These tools promise reach, flexibility, and efficiency. And often they deliver. But they also reshape how care is given, how connection is formed, and how professionals experience their own role in the work.

Increasingly, the nature of professional strain is shaped not only by the work itself, but by the tools, systems, and expectations that surround the work. In this section, we take a closer look at how digitalisation and technology may affect the emotional strains professionals experience in their work. On one hand, clients and patients arrive burdened by new layers of existential anxiety—eco-worries, future dread, and despair that cannot be easily soothed. This phenomenon is sometimes called digital strain—the emotional toll of working in highly digitised, screen-driven environments.

Flexibility and Fatigue

Technology is no longer just a tool—it is fundamentally ingrained in the work of many helping professions. Since COVID-19, professionals are increasingly asked to offer services via video calls, respond to messages through portals, and complete records in electronic record systems.

These digital platforms offer several important advantages. For clients, patients, and service users, they may improve access to care. For professionals, especially those working in remote areas or small-scale organisations, the tools offer the possibility of connecting with colleagues, engaging in collaborative reflection, and receiving guidance from others who otherwise would be out of reach. This may reduce isolation and create a sense of belonging to a larger professional group.

Online encounters with clients, patients, or service users are now an expectation in many sectors. Telehealth, online therapy, and digital supervision all offer clear advantages. They remove geographical barriers with clients, allow for flexible scheduling, and make it easier to respond to urgent needs. Some professionals describe how working with clients online, rather than in person, may offer relief. Especially early-career practitioners and those working with severe or repeated trauma may experience the screen as a kind of psychological buffer—one that activates fewer senses (see Chapter 3), and thus shields against emotional overload, making it possible to stay attuned and in contact with the client (see p. 70).

However, these benefits come with significant challenges. For clients, patients, or service users who lack digital literacy—particularly older adults or those experiencing frailty—digitalisation can deepen existing inequalities in access to care (Bundsgaard Andersen et al., 2025). For helping professionals, it may introduce new sources of mental strain.

Research on videoconferencing fatigue (commonly referred to as 'Zoom fatigue') shows that constant eye contact, reduced physical cues, and the hyper-awareness of being on camera increase cognitive and emotional load (Wiederhold, 2020; Myronuk, 2022; Fauville et al., 2023). In one study, nurses exhibited the first signs of fatigue after just 10 minutes of virtual interaction (Khairat et al., 2025). Professionals often feel they need to work harder to develop emotional closeness and empathy with clients, when vital cues, such as body language, are removed. The overall effect of video consultations on providers' cognitive load is significant, with e.g., telepsychiatry estimated to demand 15–20% more mental effort and attentiveness from clinicians compared to in-person care (Myronuk, 2022). As one social worker in a study remarked:

> *1 hour on Zoom felt like 5 in person*
>
> *(McCoyd, Koller and Walter, 2021)*

Administrative Overload and Documentation

Digitalisation has transformed the documentation side of professional life. In many helping professions, practitioners now spend a growing share of their time navigating software systems designed by engineers, not practitioners.

Electronic record systems—now standard across many sectors—have clear benefits. They can streamline data collection, reduce errors, and enhance continuity of care. For vulnerable clients with multiple needs, better coordination means fewer gaps in care; for professionals it offers clarity and confidence that different teams are in sync.

When record systems are easy to use and match real life workflows, the decreased administrative burden can leave more mental energy for the human and ethical parts of care. Even small reductions of administrative work can, over time, help prevent mental tilting.

When Digital Tools Disrupt Care

A telling example occurred when the National Health Service (NHS) rolled out the electronic health record system, *Epic*, at Cambridge University Hospitals in the United Kingdom. Almost overnight, the quality of care deteriorated remarkably—prescription errors, delayed care, disrupted workflows, and clinician burnout spiked—and a subsequent report identified the new electronic system as the 'root cause' of the problems (Hirsch, 2015). More than 10 years later, the NHS continues to face ongoing failures and manual workarounds due to flaws in the same electronic system (Sollof, 2025).

Such examples are not isolated incidents. They reflect how poorly integrated digital systems may increase strain by forcing professionals to divert attention away from care—and into managing the tool itself.

(Hirsch, 2015; Sollof, 2025)

In practice, however, many professionals describe the opposite: clunky systems, disjointed workflows, and a growing sense that documentation no longer supports the work—it *is* the work.

A particular challenge arises when professionals are required to conduct sensitive interviews or clinical assessments in person while simultaneously entering data into digital systems. In many hospitals and clinics, it is now standard practice to have conversations with patients while facing a screen, navigating menus, and typing notes. This setup is not incidental—it is often how new electronic documenting systems are designed to be used: in real time, during the encounter. Yet many professionals report that this configuration splits their attention, diminishes presence, and provides much additional strain. The client may feel unseen; the professional, divided.

Many studies confirm a link between poor electronic record usability and professional burnout (Alobayli et al., 2023; Wu et al., 2024). The constant toggling between tabs, alerts, passwords, and incomplete data sets can feel like 'death by a thousand clicks' (Schulte and Fry, 2019). Over time, it may not just feel like time lost, but meaning lost. This loss of meaning is a contributing factor in what is increasingly described as technology-induced burnout—where the tools meant to support care become a source of exhaustion. The Big WHY, the essence of the work, may begin to fade from view.

AI in the Helping Professions

AI has begun to influence core aspects of helping work. AI offers speed, consistency, and expanded access. When used wisely and ethically, the new technology helps in predictive diagnostics and detecting early warning signs amongst clients and users—making it possible for professionals to intervene preventively and effectively.

But as AI moves deeper into workspaces, professionals raise important questions: what happens to human empathy when some aspects of care are outsourced to algorithms? How does working alongside AI affect one's professional identity and purpose? Concerns about the erosion of professional identity are especially prominent in fields where empathy, relational presence, and human judgement are core to practice.

Research suggests that while AI tools can reduce cognitive burden and assist with routine tasks, they may also distance professionals from direct human engagement. Helping professionals express ambivalence—they appreciate the gains in efficiency, but they also worry about emotional disconnection and loss of nuance in care delivery (Cross et al., 2024; Deepti and Rashmi, 2024).

Other ethical considerations also arise: AI systems reflect the biases of their training data, and professionals are often left with the responsibility for decisions shaped by systems they did not design and cannot fully examine. This not only introduces clinical risk—it also creates moral strain (see Chapter 10).

The Myth of Constant Availability

Another hidden cost of digitalisation is the collapse of boundaries. With smartphones, messaging platforms, and email alerts, many helpers feel perpetually reachable. This expectation of constant availability—often self-imposed but reinforced by organisational norms—creates a state of low-grade hypervigilance. Even off the clock, your mind remains in work mode. Rest may become something you have to schedule—and justify.

Helpful Digital Tools

The question, then, is not simply whether digitalisation helps or harms—but how, when, and to what extent it supports the work of helping professionals. Digitalisation is here to stay, but *how* we integrate it matters. When tools are used to support relationships and ease administrative workload, they amplify care and reduce strain. When tools become the focus, they amplify strain and reduce care. Helping professionals need systems that strengthen—not replace—the human core of their work.

References

Alobayli, F. et al. (2023) "Electronic health record stress and burnout among clinicians in hospital settings: a systematic review," *Digital Health, 9*, p. 20552076231220241. Available at: https://doi.org/10.1177/20552076231220241.

Bundsgaard Andersen, L. et al. (2025) "Quantitative evaluation of patients' digital capability evaluated in an emergency department setting: a cross-sectional study," *Emergency Medicine Journal*, p. emermed-2024-213999. Available at: https://doi.org/10.1136/emermed-2024-213999.

Canfield, J. (2005) "Secondary traumatization, burnout, and vicarious traumatization: a review of the literature as it relates to therapists who treat trauma," *Smith College Studies in Social Work, 75*(2), pp. 81–101. Available at: https://doi.org/10.1300/J497v75n02_06.

Cross, S. et al. (2024) "Use of AI in mental health care: community and mental health professionals survey," *JMIR Mental Health, 11*, p. e60589. Available at: https://doi.org/10.2196/60589.

Deepti, S. and Rashmi, R. (2024) "AI-driven mental health counseling: opportunities, challenges, and ethical implications," *Revista Electronica de Veterinaria*, pp. 550–558. Available at: https://doi.org/10.69980/redvet.v25i1S.765.

Fauville, G. et al. (2023) "Video-conferencing usage dynamics and nonverbal mechanisms exacerbate Zoom Fatigue, particularly for women," *Computers in Human Behavior Reports, 10*, p. 100271. Available at: https://doi.org/10.1016/j.chbr.2023.100271.

Hirsch, M.D. (2015) Problems with new Epic EHR contributed to U.K. hospitals' drop in care quality. FIERCE Healthcare. Available at: https://www.fiercehealthcare.com/ehr/problems-new-epic-ehr-contributed-to-u-k-hospitals-drop-care-quality (Accessed: 23 August 2025).

Khairat, S. et al. (2025) "Association of virtual nursing and task completeness: an observational study," *SAGE Open Nursing, 11*, p. 23779608251363667. Available at: https://doi.org/10.1177/23779608251363667.

McCoyd, J.L.M., Koller, J.M. and Walter, C.A. (2021) *Grief and Loss Across the Lifespan: A Biopsychosocial Perspective* (3rd ed). New York, NY: Springer Publishing Company. Available at: https://doi.org/10.1891/9780826149640.

Myronuk, L. (2022) "Effect of telemedicine via videoconference on provider fatigue and empathy: implications for the Quadruple Aim," *Healthcare Management Forum, 35*(3), pp. 174–178. Available at: https://doi.org/10.1177/0840470 4211059944.

Schulte, F. and Fry, E. (2019) Death By 1,000 clicks: where electronic health records went wrong. *KFF Health News.* Available at: https://kffhealthnews.org/news/death-by-a-thousand-clicks.

Sollof, J. (2025) Guy's and St Thomas' has 'reporting issues' with £450m Epic EPR. *Digital Health.* Available at: https://www.digitalhealth.net/2025/02/guys-and-st-thomas-has-reporting-issues-with-450m-epic-epr (Accessed: 23 August 2025).

Wiederhold, B.K. (2020) "Using social media to our advantage: alleviating anxiety during a pandemic," *Cyberpsychology, Behavior, and Social Networking*, 23(4), pp. 197–198. Available at: https://doi.org/10.1089/cyber.2020.29180.bkw.

Wu, X. et al. (2024) "The influence of big five personality traits on anxiety: the chain mediating effect of general self-efficacy and academic burnout," *PLOS One*, 19(1), p. e0295118. Available at: https://doi.org/10.1371/journal.pone.0295118.

6

Global Crises and Cumulative Strain—Helping in a Time of Permacrisis

In our times, the human mind and body must navigate a world where crises and strain no longer arrive one at a time, but pile upon one another. Global crises—pandemics, climate change, mass migration, armed conflicts, economic instability, and social unrest—shape the lives of individuals and entire communities in ways both visible and hidden.

When Crises Collide

When a hunter-gatherer community in Greenland was struck by a tsunami triggered by melting glaciers, the devastation was immediate—but its deeper consequences, such as diminished hunting opportunities, unfolded quietly in the months and years that followed. When COVID-19 spread across the globe, hospitals were overwhelmed, professionals were forced into impossible decisions, and policymakers delivered a flood of contradictory or confusing messages. The invasion of Ukraine displaced millions overnight and set off a wave of geopolitical instability that continues to ripple through international relations and everyday lives.

Such crises do not occur in isolation. They accumulate, overlap, and interact—shaping the world helping professionals now live and work in. Vulnerable populations are often the hardest hit, yet no one remains untouched. Each layer of crisis—climate change, armed conflict, social unrest, pandemics—erodes basic assumptions about stability, justice, and trust. The world feels less secure, less predictable, and less fair.

This state of chronic emergency does not just impact those directly present in scenes of crisis—it reshapes the very soil that all helping professionals work in. In this chapter, we explore how living and working in this state of constant crisis affects the mental resilience and emotional health of those whose task is to help others navigate an increasingly turbulent world.

Living on the Fault Line

On one hand, clients and patients arrive burdened by new layers of existential anxiety—eco-worries, future dread, and despair that cannot be easily soothed. These fears are grounded in the direction in which the world is developing, and in a constant feeling of unpredictability. On the other hand, helpers are not immune themselves. Healthcare workers, journalists, reporters, social workers, and other helping professionals face their own quiet reckoning: What kind of future are we working towards? And what happens if our helping systems collapse under the weight of crisis?

If strain psychology was a weather report, it would no longer be forecasting the occasional storm. It's no longer an occasional storm—we're living under a permanent weather warning. In fact, we may be living through what has been named a *permacrisis*—a state of ongoing and overlapping global crises. It is like navigating life on a fault line: even if the earth seems momentarily still, tremors are always threatening just beneath the surface.

The Crisis on Repeat: Understanding Permacrisis

It feels like I am trying to patch holes in a dam with my hands, and the water just keeps rising.

The term *permacrisis*—a blend of 'permanent' and 'crisis'—was Collins Dictionary's word of the year in 2022 (Bushby, 2022). And it is easy to see why. Gone are the days when crises came with clear beginnings and ends. Today, we are navigating simultaneous unrest: COVID-19 may have introduced us to emergency mode, but climate anxiety, economic shocks, armed conflict, and political instability have kept us there. Climate anxiety—a persistent fear of environmental collapse—is especially widespread amongst younger generations and those deeply engaged with science or activism.

Historically, crises have occurred occasionally, demanding immediate responses from individuals, communities, and institutions to support those most affected. However, when a crisis becomes prolonged, triggers subsequent crises, or converges with others to create widespread disruption that threatens basic survival, this changes the terms of our existence (Pawar, 2023). What distinguishes a permacrisis from ordinary crises is not just its scale—but its persistence. Global crises once felt like disruptions; now, they are conditions. This sustained exposure can create what psychologists call collective trauma—a shared psychological impact that affects entire populations over time, eroding a basic sense of safety and stability.

From a psychological standpoint, each crisis adds a new weight to the scales. The term *cumulative strain* describes how exposure to repeated or simultaneous stressors—especially those involving risk, loss, or moral conflict—can gradually wear down even the most resilient professional groups (see also Chapter 7 on sustainability).

The Helpers on the Front Lines

I used to believe I could make a difference. Now, I just try to survive the shift.

As we have seen, direct victims of crises and disasters are not the only ones who suffer psychological consequences. A considerable degree of strain also falls on those who step forward to help: nurses treating patients in chaotic COVID wards, therapists supporting clients through climate grief, journalists witnessing war and despair, emergency responders laying out sandbags during floods, relief workers establishing refugee camps, and soldiers in UN missions to civil war zones. Even those who research, write, or teach about wars, pandemics, and climate change are not immune. Their work exposes them repeatedly to the grim realities of a world weighed down by overlapping crises (Pivovarchuk, 2024).

In recent years, both media and research have increasingly documented how all these groups experience rising psychological strain. Whether first-line responders or second-line helpers, many now report high levels of burnout, PTSD symptoms, and frustration in the face of political inertia to the crises and the perceived lack of public recognition. As one distressed journalist said: 'I love my job, but my job is destroying me'. (Papadopoulou et al., 2024).

Research consistently shows that in these conditions, helpers experience:

- Higher rates of burnout and compassion fatigue
- Increased anxiety, sleep disturbances, and emotional detachment
- A sense of futility or existential strain, especially when systems seem beyond repair

Just like direct exposure, indirect exposure to the world's crises does more than exhaust. It can lead to impaired judgement, troubles in regulating emotions, and a breakdown in the helper's sense of meaning as protective anchors under pressure—The Big WHY (see Chapter 16).

Yet helping professionals—whether caregivers, researchers, or journalists—often find support in strong professional communities anchored in shared values. This sense of working for an important cause provides a vital protective factor. A value-driven professional identity can protect against psychological harm—but it also creates new vulnerabilities. When those values are under threat, or when the scale of the crises they confront undermines hope for the future, existential anxiety can arise.

As the emotional toll accumulates, even small stressors can begin to feel overwhelming—creating a new landscape of emotional risk that helping professionals must navigate daily. To understand the mental toll of permacrisis, think of emotional resilience as a bank account. Each crisis makes a withdrawal. If there is no time—or support—to replenish the account, even small stressors start to feel overwhelming. This is where emotional exhaustion begins, and where the risk of mental tilting rises.

Following the crises of COVID-19, many countries have introduced austerity policies, which have only sharpened the edge. Helping systems are often stretched to the breaking point—underfunded, understaffed, and structurally brittle. The so-called 'big quit'—a term used to describe the widespread wave of voluntary job resignations by skilled professionals during and after the COVID-19 pandemic—has created a vacuum not only in the workforce, but also in terms of accumulated experience and institutional knowledge. At the same time, we are perhaps more preoccupied with managing risks than ever before, as we live in what some sociologists have termed a *risk society* (Beck, 1992).

Helping in a Risk Society

Sociologist **Ulrich Beck** has described the modern world as a *risk society*—a society increasingly consumed with preventing and managing potential future catastrophes—rather than merely handling their consequences, when they occur.

This shift trains individuals to live in a state of constant anticipatory vigilance. Healthcare workers, climate scientists, journalists, and social workers are not only dealing with the aftermath of crises—they are expected to foresee and adapt to risks that have no clear endpoint.

This orientation towards a future that always seems under threat may foster a chronic state of hyper-responsibility, which feeds into the broader strain dynamics explored in this book. But when every day demands preparation for disasters yet to come, emotional reserves may be drained long before any crisis actually arrives.

This deepens the emotional burden: how do you care for others when you, too, are living in the fault lines of the same unstable world?

From Paralysis to Possibility

I was feeling completely despondent because of the climate crisis. Then someone told me to stop trying to solve the planet and start by creating changes in my small corner.

A key insight from research on emotional resilience is that action, even small, meaningful action, is an antidote to despair (Snyder, 2002; Ojala, 2012). These studies indicate that *hope* is crucial; not false hope or denial of problems, but *constructive hope*—a belief that one's efforts count.

Constructive hope doesn't mean pretending everything will turn out fine. It means believing that even in the midst of crisis, something meaningful can still be done. It's the refusal to give up on connection, the belief that broken systems can heal, and that people can still find purpose in the aftermath. As hope researcher C.R. Snyder noted, hope is not wishful thinking—it is a framework of motivation built on agency (Snyder, 2002). This means that even small, meaningful action can restore a sense of direction and competence. In the face of cumulative crises, helping professionals do not necessarily need entire solutions, but a belief that their work still matters, that they are not alone, and that systems are listening.

Snyder's theory offers a practical, goal-oriented lens on hope—focused on pathways and action. Yet hope also has a deeper, more existential dimension. As discussed later in this book, Václav Havel describes hope not as optimism, but as a spiritual orientation—a belief in meaning regardless of outcome (see page 124). Together, these views remind us that hope can be both a mindset for action and a sustaining force of meaning, especially in uncertain or high-risk work.

Regardless of whether we understand hope as an action mindset or a source of meaning, it is fundamentally built in relationships. Hope is not developed in isolation, but in shared practices: collective reflection, collaborative problem-solving, mutual recognition. Studies in relational resilience show that people regain strength not through acts of individual 'toughness' (Hartling, 2008), but through mutual recognition and honest connection (Gittell et al., 2006; Hernández, Gangsei and Engstrom, 2007; Hartling, 2008). Teams that cultivate routines for collective reflection, shared decision-making, and moral repair tend to preserve emotional endurance—even under long-term pressure.

When the System Feels Broken

Organisations are not passive bystanders in this. They can either act as strain multipliers or as buffers. Sadly, the former is more common. Healthcare systems often respond to crises with what might be called *policy noise*—an excess of guidelines, contradictory updates, and bureaucratic language that overwhelms rather than clarifies (Chiolero, 2023; Leung, Chew and Caltabiano, 2024). Additionally, adjustments to new crises may create new types of dilemmas, new inter-relational conflicts, mistrust of management, as well as enforcement of crises-management strategies without involving employees (Gensby and Andersen, 2025).

True transparent communication—by contrast—means not pretending to have all the answers. It means acknowledging uncertainty, updating staff regularly, and involving professionals in shaping decisions. It also means listening not only to outcomes but to emotional climate. What are people feeling? Who is exhausted, and who needs time to recover?

Mutual care between management and professionals is not just about 'being nice'. It is fundamental to organising work in the face of accumulating crises. As studies from the COVID-19 pandemic have shown, the presence of trusted, responsive leadership significantly decreases psychological strain—even in high-risk settings (Dickson et al., 2022; Ball et al., 2023; De Vos et al., 2024). Evidence from UK front-line healthcare during COVID-19 further highlights that unaddressed moral injury—feeling betrayed by leadership or system—predicts poorer mental-health outcomes, underscoring the need for visible and values-based leadership (Greenberg et al., 2020).

In Chapter 17, on the roles and responsibilities of the organisation and its leadership, you will learn how to build ethical and responsive leadership and develop more resilient structures that help buffer crises and accumulated strain. This has become increasingly important, particularly as global crises continue to intensify local pressures. Chapter 21, *In Times of Crisis*, focuses on what to do when crises occur, outlining key principles for effective crisis management. For now, we leave you with this reflection:

Final Thought: Remember to Breathe

If we expect people to carry others through crisis after crisis, we must also carry them. Permacrisis may be the new normal—but empathy, structure, and shared responsibility can still be our compass.

And sometimes, in the middle of the permanent storm, it is enough to say to a colleague: 'I see you. I am here. Let us breathe together before we go back in'.

References

Ball, J. et al. (2023) "The impact of COVID-19 on nurses (ICON) survey: nurses' accounts of what would have helped to improve their working lives," *Journal of Advanced Nursing*, 79(1), pp. 343–357. Available at: https://doi.org/10.1111/jan.15442.

Beck, U. (1992) "From industrial society to the risk society: questions of survival, social structure and ecological enlightenment," *Theory, Culture & Society*, 9(1), pp. 97–123. Available at: https://doi.org/10.1177/026327692009001006.

Bushby, H. (2022) Permacrisis declared Collins Dictionary word of the year. *BBC*. Available at: https://www.bbc.com/news/entertainment-arts-63458467 (Accessed: 20 August 2025).

Chiolero, A. (2023) "Academic framing as a cause of eco-anxiety," *Epidemiologia*, 4(1), pp. 60–62. Available at: https://doi.org/10.3390/epidemiologia4010006.

De Vos, J. et al. (2024) "Tackling the academic air travel dependency. An analysis of the (in)consistency between academics' travel behaviour and their attitudes," *Global Environmental Change*, 88, p. 102908. Available at: https://doi.org/10.1016/j.gloenvcha.2024.102908.

Dickson, K.S. et al. (2022) "Characterization of multilevel influences of mental health care transitions: a comparative case study analysis," *BMC Health Services Research*, 22(1), p. 437. Available at: https://doi.org/10.1186/s12913-022-07748-2.

Gensby, U. and Andersen, M.F. (2025) "Klimakrise og samarbejde om grøn omstilling i et arbejdspladsperspektiv: – Kan den danske model både leve og levere grønne bæredygtige løsninger?," *Tidsskrift for Arbejdsliv*, 27(1), pp. 65–71.

Gittell, J.H. et al. (2006) "Relationships, layoffs, and organizational resilience: airline industry responses to September 11," *The Journal of Applied Behavioral Science*, 42(3), pp. 300–329. Available at: https://doi.org/10.1177/0021886306286466.

Greenberg, N. et al. (2020) "Managing mental health challenges faced by healthcare workers during covid-19 pandemic," *BMJ*, p. m1211. Available at: https://doi.org/10.1136/bmj.m1211.

Hartling, L.M. (2008) "Strengthening resilience in a risky world: it's all about relationships," *Women & Therapy*, 31(2–4), pp. 51–70. Available at: https://doi.org/10.1080/02703140802145870.

Hernández, P., Gangsei, D. and Engstrom, D. (2007) "Vicarious resilience: a new concept in work with those who survive trauma," *Family Process*, 46(2), pp. 229–241. Available at: https://doi.org/10.1111/j.1545-5300.2007.00206.x.

Leung, H.-T., Chew, P.K.H. and Caltabiano, N.J. (2024) "Do pandemics trigger death thoughts?," *Journal of Humanistic Psychology*, p. 00221678241273422. Available at: https://doi.org/10.1177/00221678241273422.

Ojala, M. (2012) "Hope and climate change: the importance of hope for environmental engagement among young people," *Environmental Education Research*, 18(5), pp. 625–642. Available at: https://doi.org/10.1080/13504622.2011.637157.

Papadopoulou, L., Angelou, I. and Katsaounidou, A. (2024) "'I love my job, but my job is destroying me'. Permacrisis' toll on journalistic practice and perceptions about journalism in Southern Europe," *Journalism*, p. 14648849241272219. Available at: https://doi.org/10.1177/14648849241272219.

Pawar, M. (2023) "Poverty, policy and the poor," *The International Journal of Community and Social Development*, 5(2), pp. 137–145. Available at: https://doi.org/10.1177/25166026231179075.

Pivovarchuk, A. (2024) 'Scared as hell': climate scientists risk jobs, jail to save dying planet. *Climate Crisis News*. Al Jazeera. Available at: https://www.aljazeera.com/features/2024/6/16/what-grief-for-a-dying-planet-looks-like-climate-scientists-on-the-edge-2 (Accessed 20 August 2025).

Snyder, C.R. (2002) "TARGET ARTICLE: Hope theory: rainbows in the mind," *Psychological Inquiry*, 13(4), pp. 249–275. Available at: https://doi.org/10.1207/S15327965PLI1304_01.

Part II

The Reactions

7

Mental Tilting and Sustainability

When you are exposed to either sudden or persistent mental strain, it is common—and natural—to react.

These reactions manifest in the body, emotions, thoughts, or in our relationships with others. Their purpose is twofold: to protect both yourself and those around you, and to help process the experience—paving the way for recovery, regaining balance, and returning to a stable state.

In a sense, these reactions can be understood as a kind of emergency mode—a built-in survival response that helps you power through a demanding situation. Once the immediate pressure has passed, the system needs time to decompress and return to baseline. This transition back to normal functioning is gradual and involves a series of both physical and psychological adjustments.

While the time it takes to return to normal may vary, the aftereffects typically resolve within a few days or weeks. It is only when they persist for an extended period that it becomes important to take action. If this occurs, the reactions lose their original function and begin to take a toll on your psychological well-being.

Mental Tilting

As mentioned in the introduction, the term *psychological* or *mental tilting* is used as a general reference to the psychological imbalance that may develop in mentally high-risk professions. Just as a ship can become physically unstable and begin to tilt if its cargo is not properly balanced, people can become mentally unbalanced and begin to tilt if their psychologically demanding work is not organised in a balanced, purposeful—or sustainable—way (Cieslak et al., 2014; Rabenu, Yaniv and Elizur, 2017).

The 20 symptoms or warning signs described in Chapter 8 may indicate that a helping professional is at risk of developing—or has already developed—mental tilting. If the imbalance is not recognised in time, the affected individual may go on to develop a strain condition or a traumatic mental disorder. When the ship begins to tilt, it is time to rebalance—to right the vessel before it tips further. The more warning signs that are present, the greater the risk of emotional collapse.

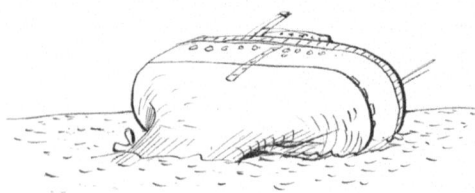

An improperly loaded ship is at an increased risk of tipping over and capsizing.

Building resilience and preventing mental tilting is about organising work in a sustainable way.

> **Sustainability** refers to a balance between using and protecting resources. Here, resources are broadly understood as time, finances, or individuals' or teams' professional and human competences.

Sustainable Organisation of Work

Sustainability is defined as a balance between using and protecting resources. Here, resources should be broadly understood as time, finances, and individuals' or teams' professional and human competences. Organisations or individuals who unscrupulously use resources, without considering a sustainable balance, risk unhappiness, stress-related illnesses, and high staff turnover (De Lange et al., 2003; Grawitch, Ballard and Erb, 2015). An exclusive focus on preservation—at the expense of sustainable balance—can lead to demotivation and psychological strain. In such cases, employees may feel under-challenged, as their skills and capacity are not being fully utilised. Moreover, organisations that become overly protective of their resources risk falling behind in a competitive environment.

Key Challenges

Invisible Symptoms

A common challenge across all mental disorders is that most symptoms of mental tilting—a precursor to these disorders—are not readily apparent. Therefore, it is crucial that organisations are aware of these symptoms and react quickly when they are identified. Mature organisations communicate explicitly that they know the reactions are due to the stressful nature of the work, rather than an employee's general abilities or individual strength.

Model 3: The Sustainability Model

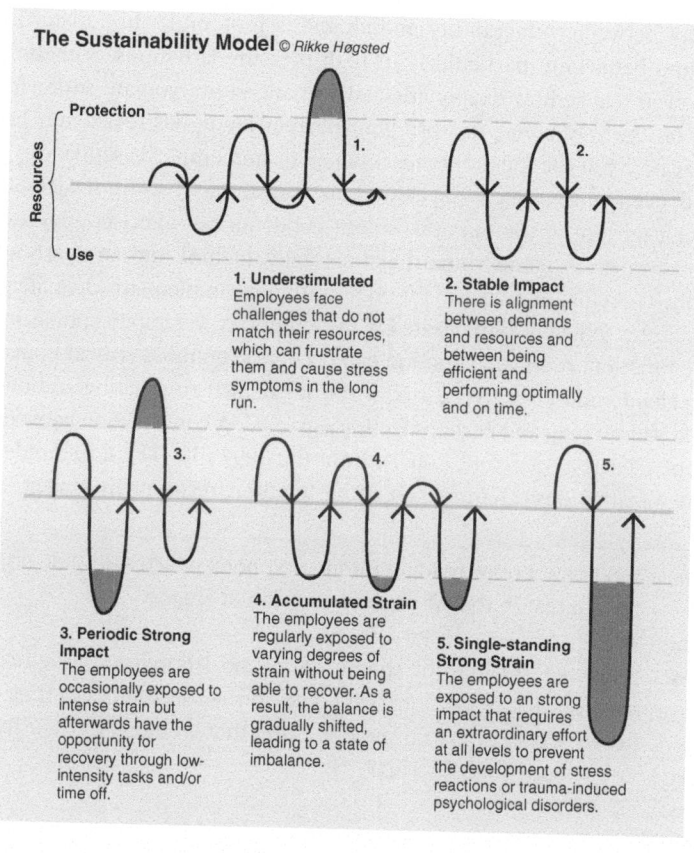

The Sustainability Model © *Rikke Høgsted*

Protection

Resources

Use

1. Understimulated
Employees face challenges that do not match their resources, which can frustrate them and cause stress symptoms in the long run.

2. Stable Impact
There is alignment between demands and resources and between being efficient and performing optimally and on time.

3. Periodic Strong Impact
The employees are occasionally exposed to intense strain but afterwards have the opportunity for recovery through low-intensity tasks and/or time off.

4. Accumulated Strain
The employees are regularly exposed to varying degrees of strain without being able to recover. As a result, the balance is gradually shifted, leading to a state of imbalance.

5. Single-standing Strong Strain
The employees are exposed to an strong impact that requires an extraordinary effort at all levels to prevent the development of stress reactions or trauma-induced psychological disorders.

Distancing

Another challenge is that helping professionals may distance themselves from a traumatic event by acting as though nothing has impacted them. Even if a workplace implements well-crafted preventive measures, employees under pressure tend to try to appear in control. It is almost reflexive to project an image of being unaffected and in control of the situation.

The link between vulnerability and shame is profound, often distorting perception and behaviour, particularly in high-pressure situations. Sometimes you may not even realise how deeply affected you are—until you are sitting alone in your car on the way home, or until your partner lovingly strokes your hair and you freeze or cry at the touch. Bosses, managers, and employees alike can appear unmoved, even without meaning to, and distance themselves from each other.

Regular exposure to trauma and violent incidents can affect employees, managers, and even entire teams, impairing their ability to think and act clearly and professionally. Therefore, it is crucial for organisations to implement adequate policies and procedures that will compensate for any temporary, yet imperceptible, lapses in cognitive function. A critical situation can become even more critical if, instead of thinking clearly and proactively, a person finds herself ruminating and obsessing over what went wrong and perhaps feeling ashamed. A conversation between three characters, Charles, Alec, and Robert, from the 1997 film *The Edge*, underscores how difficult situations can impair cognitive function, resulting in danger:

Charles:	You know, I once read an interesting book which said that, uh, most people lost in the wilds, they, they die of shame.
Stephen:	*What?*
Charles:	Yeah, see, they die of shame. 'What did I do wrong? How could I have gotten myself into this?' And so they sit there and they ... die. Because they didn't do the one thing that would save their lives.
Robert:	And what is that, Charles?
Charles:	*Thinking.*

See Part III for a full introduction to implementing preventive strategies to reduce the risk of *thinking* breaking down.

Getting Used to It

A final challenge is that many symptoms of mental tilting develop very gradually and in such small steps that you get used to them over time, failing to notice them in your daily life. This can be referred to as *habituation*. For example, it can be difficult to notice your own child's growth because you see them every day, whereas their cousin's growth is easy to spot—because you see them less often. Over the years, many helping professionals become accustomed to various warning signs—so that, in practice, they become blind and deaf to them (Kanno and Giddings, 2017; Branson, 2019). It is only upon retirement that they realise how they may have been chronically exhausted or sad for years—or the negative impact their work has had on their day-to-day life. No longer in a mentally high-risk job, they suddenly sleep through the entire night and wake up feeling refreshed and happy to rise. Suddenly, they enjoy engaging in creative activities again, or they enjoy seeing friends and have the energy to help them with their everyday problems.

> *One day, my adult daughter said she was so excited to have her old mum back. I asked her what she meant, to which she replied: 'Well, now you've become my mum again, who can laugh about everything and remind me that I shouldn't take everything so seriously, because it will all work out in the end'. It made me really happy, but it was also thought-provoking, because I knew she was right and that it was because I am no longer part of the busy everyday life in the maternity ward.*

References

Branson, D.C. (2019) "Vicarious trauma, themes in research, and terminology: a review of literature," *Traumatology*, *25*(1), pp. 2–10. Available at: https://doi.org/10.1037/trm0000161.

Cieslak, R. et al. (2014) "A meta-analysis of the relationship between job burnout and secondary traumatic stress amongst workers with indirect exposure to trauma," *Psychological Services*, *11*(1), pp. 75–86. Available at: https://doi.org/10.1037/a0033798.

De Lange, A.H. et al. (2003) "'The very best of the millennium': longitudinal research and the demand-control-(support) model," *Journal of Occupational Health Psychology*, *8*(4), pp. 282–305. Available at: https://doi.org/10.1037/1076-8998.8.4.282.

Grawitch, M.J., Ballard, D.W. and Erb, K.R. (2015) "To be or not to be (stressed): the critical role of a psychologically healthy workplace in effective stress management," *Stress and Health*, *31*(4), pp. 264–273. Available at: https://doi.org/10.1002/smi.2619.

Kanno, H. and Giddings, M.M. (2017) "Hidden trauma victims: understanding and preventing traumatic stress in mental health professionals," *Social Work in Mental Health*, *15*(3), pp. 331–353. Available at: https://doi.org/10.1080/15332985.2016.1220442.

Rabenu, E., Yaniv, E. and Elizur, D. (2017) "The relationship between psychological capital, coping with stress, well-being, and performance," *Current Psychology*, *36*(4), pp. 875–887. Available at: https://doi.org/10.1007/s12144-016-9477-4.

8

Warning Signs of Mental Tilting

A warning sign may also be called a symptom. A symptom is a physical or mental reaction that you can feel, or that others can detect. Not illnesses in themselves, symptoms can nevertheless be signs of an illness, particularly when there are several of them, or when they occur in a particular pattern.

20 Signs of Mental Tilting at the Individual Level

The different types of stress conditions and trauma-related mental disorders share several common features or symptoms, such as sleep problems. This can make it difficult for both the traumatised person and their carers to figure out what is wrong. The more warning signs are present, the greater the risk—and the more important it is to investigate the situation.

The 20 warning signs can be broadly divided into four groups:

- Five physical signals
- Five cognitive signals
- Five emotional signals
- Five signals in your behaviour and relationship to others

Five Physical Signals

1. Chronic hypervigilance
   The body's susceptibility to sensory input is heightened—creating a chronic state of alertness where abrupt sounds or sudden movements are interpreted as threats and can create a strong startle response (Maslach and Leiter, 2016; Kanno and Giddings, 2017).

The other day my son looked at me, totally puzzled, when I suddenly got startled and started scolding him—just because he accidentally turned the music up a bit too loud.

2. Psychomotor agitation

   Physical restlessness that manifests itself through small movements, such as tapping your foot, clicking a pen, or checking your phone every few moments. The person quickly becomes impatient, feels overwhelmed by a sense of urgency, and may be provoked by the calmness or slowness of others (Branson, Weigand and Keller, 2014; Kanno and Giddings, 2017).

   I eat quickly, cycle quickly—I do everything fast because I feel like I'm constantly behind and I have this uncomfortable feeling that something bad will happen if I don't hurry.

3. Sleep problems

   The person has trouble falling asleep, wakes up repeatedly during the night, or wakes up too early and cannot fall asleep again. The common features are waking up feeling unrested and having a sensation of being extremely tired and unwell during the day (Branson, Weigand and Keller, 2014; Kanno and Giddings, 2017).

"The other day at work we were joking about whether we should just call each other at night and have meetings then—since most of us can't sleep anyway, or wake up around four or five and can't get back to sleep."

The other day at work we were joking about whether we should just call each other at night and have meetings then—since most of us can't sleep anyway, or wake up around four or five and can't get back to sleep.

4. Altered desires or overuse of stimulants

   The appetite either increases or decreases, which will usually lead to weight changes (Branson, Weigand and Keller, 2014). Overall desire is reduced. This can also apply to a person's general desire to be physically active or desire for intimacy (van Dernoot Lipsky and Burk, 2009). Overconsumption of alcohol, cigarettes, drugs, or medication is also typical signs of psychological tilting and imbalance (Branson, Weigand and Keller, 2014).

For a while, I completely lost my sex drive. My wife—who's incredibly wise—said it might be tied to something else I was avoiding. She asked me what that could be, and said it was probably connected to my work. And yeah—she was absolutely right.

5. Exhaustion and physical discomfort
   A feeling of mental and physical exhaustion—and, in some cases, physical discomfort—may arise in the form of headaches, stomach aches, dizziness, dry mouth, impotence, increased heart rate, or sweating (Branson, Weigand and Keller, 2014; Kanno and Giddings, 2017). This state of exhaustion can occur even in the absence of sleep problems.

   Sometimes I feel like I can barely keep my eyes open and have to force them open just to focus on what's on the screen.

Five Cognitive Signals

1. Impaired concentration and memory
   Difficulties with maintaining an overview or remembering tasks, guidelines, appointments, and handling everyday activities (Sprang et al., 2019). The person may find it hard to read an article, follow a conversation, or keep track of a film's plot.

   These days I only read the captions in the newspaper and tell myself I'll read the article later. But I never do.

2. Reduced creativity and problem-solving skills
   A tendency to dichotomous or black-and-white thinking—and an inability to be explorative, playful, or creative, either professionally or privately (Bouchard, 2016). In a work context, this warning sign may be mistaken for being efficient or incisive—someone who quickly gets to the heart of the matter. This is especially true for experienced professionals, who may easily create a misleading impression of competence.

"My belief in professional improvements is now completely gone. On the outside, I smile and listen to the ideas of the management or younger colleagues, but inside me is an old, experienced man with his arms crossed, thinking that they're talking rubbish."

3. Involuntary and intrusive images

    Images of something previously seen or heard can suddenly enter the mind (Sprang et al., 2019). Flashbacks often take the form of visual, auditory, or olfactory impressions and may be triggered by stimuli that symbolise or recall the original stressful situation.

    > *Images from the house, where the children had clearly been fighting for their lives, just keep popping up.*

4. Mental clutter

    Thoughts spin out of control. They seem to queue, each demanding attention; no sooner is one thought completed than the next rushes in. This mental clutter—racing thoughts about work or other aspects of life—often emerges in the evening, around bedtime.

    > *Sometimes my thoughts just keep running, like a radio programme with no off button.*

5. Dissociation

    A sensation of disconnection between the senses, body, and mind, creating the feeling of being detached from oneself and one's own body. It can feel as though the individual is in a bubble, out of sync with time and place, and separated from themselves and those around them.

"The entire family had turned up for the funeral service, and several of them were in shock. The conversation started, but as it went on, their voices faded away and I could no longer hear what they were saying. I just saw their lips moving."

Five Emotional Signals

1. Helplessness, hopelessness, inadequacy, powerlessness, and omnipotence

    A feeling of helplessness and an acute realisation that no matter what one does, it will never sufficient. There are too many victims, too much suffering, and too few resources, and it feels like the traumatic situation will go on forever. This feeling of inadequacy frequently affects those helping professionals who see their work as a purpose or a calling in life, rather than 'just' a job.

There may also be a certainty that the incident will reoccur, and next time you will not be able to do enough. This can make the person question whether his or her efforts make a difference at all.

> Some days I feel like Cassandra from Greek mythology. She was given the gift of predicting the future, but when she rejected Apollo, he cursed her so that no one would ever believe her. And some days I just want to give up.

Feelings of helplessness can launch a pendulum swing between powerlessness and omnipotence. One moment you feel powerless: 'There is nothing I can do and my work is basically useless (Ashley-Binge and Cousins, 2020)'. The next moment you feel omnipotent: 'Only I can really do this job, and my work is the most important thing in my life'.

> Sometimes I catch myself thinking it's almost irresponsible to take a long holiday, like my colleagues won't be able to look after my clients properly if something comes up. That I'm the only one who really understands them, and that, on some very human level, I'm almost obliged to be there. I know it sounds a bit far-fetched, though—I've got some really good colleagues.

2. Fear, worry, and tears
   The person begins to sense dangers everywhere and out of proportion. Danger to their children, their clients or patients, their colleagues and themselves. The person feels vulnerable and always exposed, and all kinds of worries are constantly lurking at the back of the mind (Maslach and Leiter, 2016). Security measures may be reassuring for a short time before new threatening scenarios come to mind. Tears can easily come, and once one has started crying, it can be impossible to stop.

> One day, from the kitchen window, I saw my 13-year-old boy coming home from school on his bike without a helmet. I immediately rushed out the door launched into a long rant about all the cyclists I see every week in the emergency room with smashed skulls, chronic brain injuries, and so on. I only stopped when his older sister stepped in. She went over, grabbed her brother by the hand and pulled him away from 'the crazy woman', as she called me. It turned out he'd taken off his bike helmet because he wanted to impress a new girl in class.

3. Anger and revenge
   The person is overwhelmed by aggressive feelings that can be expressed either directly or indirectly (van Dernoot Lipsky and Burk, 2009). The anger can be directed at those the person is helping, in thoughts like 'they've brought it on themselves.' Or it may be directed towards a manager, who is perceived as not adequately appreciative.

Some may feel misunderstood and treated unfairly. A short temper can lead to situations where, instead of giving others the benefit of the doubt as before, one quickly jumps to the conclusion that the other person has negative intentions. The anger may also be directed towards individuals who have harmed a client, sometimes giving rise to thoughts or fantasies of revenge and vigilantism.

> *I almost hate myself when I lose my temper in front of the kids. The oldest gets angry, but the youngest just gets upset—his eyes well up. And those are the moments when I think about quitting my job. Or just calling in sick.*

4. Guilt and self-blame
   At times, professionals may feel personally responsible for conditions and situations that are impossible to resolve. Even when they recognise on a rational level that they are not truly responsible, it still feels that way. A gnawing sense of self-blame—disproportionate to their actual ability to influence the situation—may surface. This sense of responsibility can also be accompanied by feelings of guilt, as described in the preface (Kanno and Giddings, 2017).

> *I feel guilty because, at the end of the day, I can just go home.*

5. Trivialisation, denial, and cynicism
   At times, professionals begin to push the boundaries of what is perceived as a serious problem: '*It's not that bad*'. Stories that once stirred emotional responses no longer elicit a reaction. You might catch yourself questioning whether the person is exaggerating. Trivialisation and denial can pose a threat to both the professional's safety and that of the client, as critical situations risk being neglected—or entirely overlooked (Massey et al., 2019).

> *I noticed it was getting harder and harder to care for patients who didn't even have metastases—people who had a real chance of being cured. At times, I honestly felt like telling them to pull themselves together. Seeing so many incurably ill patients—especially dying parents of young children—had been pushing me to my limits for a long time.*

Five Signals in Your Behaviour and Relationships to Others

1. Reduced empathy towards others
   The person's ability to recognise and understand others' emotions—and to empathise with them—becomes diminished (Kanno and Giddings, 2017). Even when concentrating, you may find that you're not truly hearing what

the other person is saying. It can feel as if there is no room left in your system for more compassion. Previous feelings of curiosity and care are replaced by indifference, and some end up feeling completely *numb*.

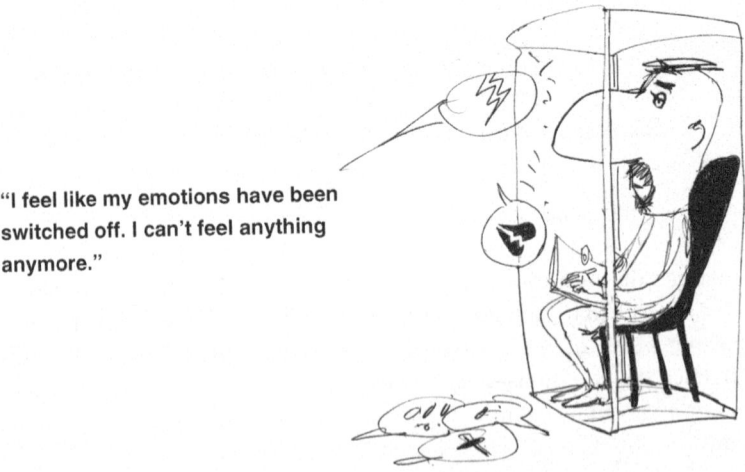

"I feel like my emotions have been switched off. I can't feel anything anymore."

2. Decreased desire for closeness

The person no longer desires closeness with others, whether physical or emotional (Jenkins et al., 2011). Intense eye contact may feel intimidating, and personal questions can become overwhelming. At night, there may be a preference for lying under one's own duvet rather than close to a partner. Caresses can feel demanding, and massages are no longer experienced as pleasant or relaxing.

> One day my sister said my hugs had become really mechanical, and asked what was wrong. I don't remember exactly what I said back. But I do remember realising that day that something had changed inside me—and it wasn't a good change.

3. Lack of social energy

Activities the person used to look forward to now feel more like a chore (Hersom, 2019). Other people's topics of conversation seem superficial, and you may feel alienated and disconnected from the community. Some may ignore phone calls and hope that the caller will just text instead.

"More and more often I find myself looking for a good excuse to cancel a party. Or at least get home early from it."

4. Changed worldview and self-image

The belief that the world is a safe and fair place, that others want the best for you, and that nothing bad will happen to you or your loved ones starts to unravel (van Dernoot Lipsky and Burk, 2009). The same happens to the belief that you have control over yourself and the situation (Denne, Stevenson and Petty, 2019).

> *I feel it most when it comes to my children. I just can't bring myself to tell them what I've learnt about the climate.*

The person's self-image may also change. Previously, some may have viewed themselves as robust and professionally competent. Now, however, they may feel fragile and vulnerable, and may develop semi-cynical or harsh thoughts about others.

> *When I was a student, I really believed I could help make things more just and reduce social inequality. Looking back, that was pretty ideal-istic—and a bit naïve.*

5. Avoiding talking about work—or talking about work non-stop

The person begins to brush off questions about work. When asked, they will often say that everything is fine and change the topic.

> *To be honest, I don't really talk about my work these days. A lot of people have strong opinions about refugees without much to back them up. It's often meant well, but I just can't take it anymore.*

Sometimes, it is the opposite—the person can't stop talking about work, even if no one asked about it.

> *In my first year of counselling, I talked about my work to anyone who would listen. I was so overwhelmed by all the lives and stories I encountered that it just kept pouring out of me.*

10 Warning Signs of Mental Tilting in Teams and Workgroups

Just as individual employees can be at risk of mental tilting due to the psychological strains of the job, entire work groups may also be affected.

---

10 Warning Signs in Teams and Work Groups

The following 10 warning signs may indicate that a group has developed a form of collective strain reaction—such as collective compassion fatigue or caregiver fatigue:

1. Loss of motivation and a general lack of initiative in the group.
2. Difficulty making both large and small decisions; mental and emotional numbness.
3. Low productivity.
4. Team conflicts; clique formation.

---

5. Identifying scapegoats—amongst group members or the leader.
6. Poor relationships with external partners (e.g., devaluing their contributions).
7. A callous or patronising tone when talking about clients.
8. Increased sick leave and frequent staff turnover.
9. Anger, grumbling, and dissatisfaction.
10. Destructive humour.

Many of these warning signs may be embedded in the organisation's culture—and may have been present for so long that no one remembers it ever being different. However, that does not mean change is impossible, provided there is a genuine desire to address it.

Just as individuals can develop blind spots when adapting to gradual change, a work culture can also develop collective blind spots—a kind of shared inability to detect undesirable behaviours. One example is a hardened or condescending tone when talking to clients, without even noticing it. Such language is unprofessional and signals overload. It is a clear sign that help is urgently needed.

Most of the warning signs are self-explanatory and do not require further clarification. However, two of them deserve special attention: frequent anger, grumbling, and dissatisfaction—and humour, which can be a double-edged sword.

Anger, Grumbling, and Dissatisfaction

Groups exposed to high levels of psychological strain are at risk of developing what could be described as a *culture of complaints*. However, I deliberately use the word *grumbling* rather than *complaints* to highlight the kind of unproductive criticism made up of grumpy or negative remarks that are neither constructive nor solution-oriented. Grumbling—especially when coming from an agenda-setting team member—can spread quickly and foster a negative atmosphere. Just as enthusiasm is contagious, so is grumbling, and it can cost the team valuable time and energy.

When a group begins to exhibit persistent grumbling, it may be a symptom of overload or mental tilting that needs to be addressed before its impact grows too great. Regardless of the underlying cause, it's important to take this behaviour seriously and put an end to it early. Repeating the same negative story about a specific person or issue can eventually create its own version of reality.

Grumbling can also lead to self-fulfilling prophecies. For example, a team leader who is frequently—and destructively—criticised for not being responsive or empathetic may eventually shut down emotionally as a means of self-protection, thereby reinforcing the very narrative they were accused of: being distant and unresponsive.

Problem Shifting

Another common reaction to traumatic experiences or high psychological demands is *problem shifting*. This occurs when someone, in an effort to preserve a positive self-image, shifts the cause of a difficult or painful situation to someone or something else. For example, a helping professional might say that if it weren't for their manager, the work structure, collaborating partners, or family members, they would be able to cope just fine. Or that if only they received an extra grant, avoided a cutback, or got a new boss, the problem would be solved.

Of course, proper working conditions, good management, and clear leadership are essential for staff to carry out their duties professionally—whether in a hospital, prison, residential care facility, or criminal investigation.

However, in mentally high-risk professions, the psychological strain of the work can never be eliminated simply by hiring more staff or appointing a new leader. These measures may improve the conditions, but if the job involves routinely confronting social suffering, loneliness, or death, feelings of powerlessness are an unavoidable part of the role. These must be acknowledged and addressed (see Chapter 15, for further discussion on powerlessness, power, working conditions, influence, and control).

While problem shifting is a normal and human reaction, it is also a form of self-deception that diverts attention from the real pain, tragedy, or emotional cost of the work. Though blame can be directed anywhere in or outside the organisation, leaders are often the most frequent targets, as they are widely perceived as having the power to change potentially harmful conditions.

Humour

Humour can be energising and serve as a way to ease tension in heavy or emotionally charged situations (Martin et al., 2003). It can make a team smile—even laugh—and offer a moment of relief from a tragic or challenging reality. Shared laughter can be cathartic and strengthen group cohesion, enhancing a team's sense of solidarity and effectiveness (Frankl, 2008).

However, it is important to avoid using irony or humour towards colleagues who are in crisis. Crises increase sensitivity and make our thinking more concrete. This means a colleague in crisis might not understand an offhand joke—or might find it inappropriate or even hurtful. A good rule of thumb is to be receptive to a colleague's own humour about their situation, but cautious with your own.

Humour is also culturally specific and can easily be misunderstood across cultural backgrounds. What is funny to someone raised in Japan may not be funny to someone raised in the United Kingdom—just as humour may vary significantly between individuals from rural and urban communities. Humour, including dark humour, can be both constructive and destructive.

Victor Frankl, Austrian physician and Holocaust survivor, described humour as *a weapon of the soul in the struggle for self-preservation*, enabling one to rise above any situation—if only for a few seconds (Keysers and Gazzola, 2009).

Destructive Humour

Humour becomes destructive when someone finds a joke offensive or inappropriate—and is then labelled 'overly sensitive' or a 'snowflake' for saying so. Destructive humour denies group members the opportunity to express how a joke made them feel. Perhaps the remark caused anger, discomfort, or confusion. If this is met not with an apology—such as *'Oops, I didn't mean to offend or hurt you'*—but with comments like *'Pull yourself together'* or *'Learn to take a joke'*, then it is no longer humour, but a form of harm.

Constructive humour strengthens a group and improves collaboration. Destructive humour does the opposite—it undermines cohesion and impairs teamwork.

As social beings, we all strive to belong. Most people can recall a time they laughed at a joke they didn't really understand or didn't find funny, simply to avoid being excluded. If this happens once, we can usually brush it off and stay true to our values. But if it happens repeatedly, it can begin to erode our boundaries—until we ourselves start making inappropriate jokes and dismissing others as overly sensitive.

Finally, some people use humour as a form of apology or deflection. When their words provoke a negative reaction, they may try to escape responsibility by saying they were 'just joking'.

References

Ashley-Binge, S. and Cousins, C. (2020) "Individual and organisational practices addressing social workers' experiences of vicarious trauma," *Practice*, 32(3), pp. 191–207. Available at: https://doi.org/10.1080/09503153.2019.1620201.

Bouchard, L.A. (2016) *Exploring Compassion Fatigue in Emergency Nurses*. The University of Arizona.

Branson, D.C., Weigand, D.A. and Keller, J.E. (2014) "Vicarious trauma and decreased sexual desire: a hidden hazard of helping others," *Psychological Trauma: Theory, Research, Practice, and Policy*, 6(4), pp. 398–403. Available at: https://doi.org/10.1037/a0033113.

Denne, E., Stevenson, M. and Petty, T. (2019) "Understanding how social worker compassion fatigue and years of experience shape custodial decisions," *Child Abuse & Neglect*, 95, p. 104036. Available at: https://doi.org/10.1016/j.chiabu.2019.104036.

Frankl, V.E. (2008) *Man's Search for Meaning: The Classic Tribute to Hope from the Holocaust*. Translated by I. Lasch. London: Rider.

Hersom, C. (2019) Using humour to build psychological and mental capacity. Available at: https://implementconsultinggroup.com/dk/en/using-humour-to-build-psychological-and-mental-capacity (Accessed: 21 August 2025).

Jenkins, S.R. et al. (2011) "The counselor's trauma as counseling motivation: vulnerability or stress inoculation?," *Journal of Interpersonal Violence*, 26(12), pp. 2392–2412. Available at: https://doi.org/10.1177/0886260510383020.

Kanno, H. and Giddings, M.M. (2017) "Hidden trauma victims: understanding and preventing traumatic stress in mental health professionals," *Social Work in Mental Health*, 15(3), pp. 331–353. Available at: https://doi.org/10.1080/15332985.2016.1220442.

Keysers, C. and Gazzola, V. (2009) "Expanding the mirror: vicarious activity for actions, emotions, and sensations," *Current Opinion in Neurobiology*, 19(6), pp. 666–671. Available at: https://doi.org/10.1016/j.conb.2009.10.006.

Martin, R.A. et al. (2003) "Individual differences in uses of humor and their relation to psychological well-being: development of the Humor Styles Questionnaire," *Journal of Research in Personality*, 37(1), pp. 48–75. Available at: https://doi.org/10.1016/S0092-6566(02)00534-2.

Maslach, C. and Leiter, M.P. (2016) "Understanding the burnout experience: recent research and its implications for psychiatry," *World Psychiatry: Official Journal of the World Psychiatric Association (WPA)*, 15(2), pp. 103–111. Available at: https://doi.org/10.1002/wps.20311.

Massey, K. et al. (2019) "Staff experiences of working in a Sexual Assault Referral Centre: the impacts and emotional tolls of working with traumatised people," *The Journal of Forensic Psychiatry & Psychology*, 30(4), pp. 686–705. Available at: https://doi.org/10.1080/14789949.2019.1605615.

Sprang, G. et al. (2019) "Defining secondary traumatic stress and developing targeted assessments and interventions: lessons learned from research and leading experts," *Traumatology*, 25(2), pp. 72–81. Available at: https://doi.org/10.1037/trm0000180.

van Dernoot Lipsky, D. and Burk, C. (eds.) (2009) *Trauma Stewardship: An Everyday Guide to Caring for Self While Caring for Others*. San Francisco, CA: Berrett-Koehler Publishers (A BK life book).

9

Mirror Neurons and the Red–Green–Blue Model

Professionals are human beings—with heartbeats, breath, and body heat. We naturally empathise with others—in fact, we cannot help it, thanks to our mirror neurons.

The human nervous system is designed in such a way that we automatically perceive other people's emotions and behaviours. 'Perceive' is a better word than 'register' here, since 'register' implies that we are consciously aware of the act—which is usually not the case (Heyes, 2018). Most information we receive about others does not appear as conscious thought but is instead immediately translated into action—for example, when we walk down a crowded street without bumping into others.

Mirror Neurons

Our ability to pick up on emotional and behavioural cues stems from mirror neurons—specialised cells in the cerebral cortex that enable us to evoke in ourselves the emotional states we observe in others. Our nervous system automatically connects us to each other, much like a device that links to Wi-Fi without needing a password.

Put simply, mirror neurons make emotions ripple from one person to another. Through empathic resonance, they allow us to 'read' others and share in their joys and sorrows (Gleichgerrcht and Decety, 2013). Without mirror neurons, we would lose our ability to be empathetic and compassionate.

Numerous experiments have demonstrated that 'mirroring' happens quickly and unconsciously. For instance, people exposed to a photograph of a smiling face for just half a second often begin to smile themselves—unless they actively suppress the reaction (Dimberg, Thunberg and Elmehed, 2000).

This means that when a client expresses an emotion through tone of voice or body language, the helping professional will automatically sense that emotion. And it works both ways: just as the professional picks up on the client's emotional state, so too does the client pick up on the professional's.

Italian researcher Giacomo Rizzolatti discovered the brain's mirror neurons in the mid-1990s, offering a neurobiological explanation for the experience of being 'on the same wavelength' with another person—i.e., mirroring each other and having interpersonal chemistry.

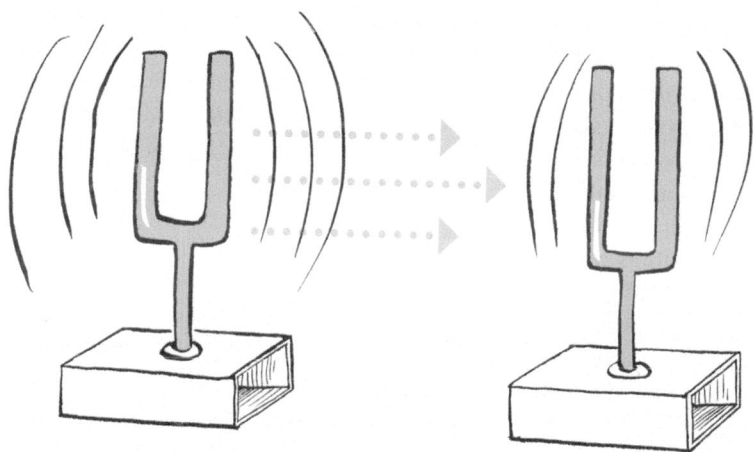

Just like vibrations from one tuning fork automatically propagate to another tuning fork through the air, emotional 'vibrations' propagate between people.

The Downside of Mirror Neurons

First-line responders routinely empathise with frightened or desperate individuals in pain or shock, or witness brutal scenes at crime scenes or in war-torn regions. Second-line responders often mirror the emotions of victims or relatives affected by trauma, for example during treatment or in the course of a criminal investigation.

These intense emotional demands—along with the threat of personal danger—leave a neurobiological imprint that helping professionals must carry day in and day out, year after year. Imagine how different the job would be if it involved mirroring the joy of a child receiving a puppy!

While mirror neurons enable empathy and compassion, they also leave professionals vulnerable to emotional overload. When overwhelmed, a professional may lose clarity, disrupt client contact, and impair their decision-making. To function effectively, helping professionals must remain connected to both their emotions and their thoughts. Emotions allow us to care; thoughts help us act (MacRitchie and Leibowitz, 2010).

Compassion is the heartfelt empathy and concern for others' suffering, accompanied by a genuine desire to alleviate it. It is the act of feeling and showing kindness towards those in distress.

When emotions become too intense, a helper may over-involve or under-involve themselves. Though expressed differently, both are responses to powerlessness. The *over-involved* professional moves closer, hoping that more commitment will solve the problem. The *under-involved* professional pulls away to protect themselves from emotional overload. Over-involvement can lead to emotional confusion and compromised judgement; under-involvement can result in denial and minimisation of problems.

Both reactions are human—but risky. Either may lead to poor professional judgement and increase the risk of mental tilting or breakdown.

Psychotherapists must be especially mindful of emotional contagion. Unlike oncologists who treat with medication or surgery, psychotherapists treat with their own thoughts and feelings (Warr, 1994); this requires clear boundaries. Without them, the professional risks absorbing the trauma, stress, and grief they encounter.

I use the terms 'attuned' and 'in contact' to describe the optimal state in which the professional remains emotionally present without being overwhelmed. The following section introduces the Red–Green–Blue model, a visual tool illustrating different levels of involvement.

OVER-INVOLVEMENT ATTUNED AND IN CONTACT UNDER-INVOLVEMENT

The Red–Green–Blue Model

This model consists of three zones on a horizontal line:

- **Green Zone (Centre):** Represents balanced, professional engagement—involving a feeling of competence and efficiency.
- **Red Zone (Left):** Reflects over-involvement—becoming too emotionally entangled.
- **Blue Zone (Right):** Indicates under-involvement—distancing or detachment.

Which zone you lean towards depends on the specific case, your role, coping style, team dynamics, and organisational culture.

Model 4: The Red–Green–Blue Model

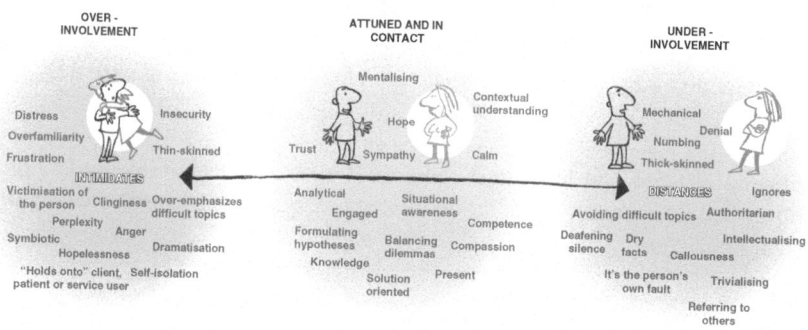

Being *attuned* and *in contact* involves using the capacity to mentalise and empathise, while remaining professionally grounded. It means allowing oneself to feel what is present in the situation, without becoming overwhelmed. This is possible because the professional trusts their ability to influence the situation in an appropriate way, drawing on professional judgement, experience, and available resources (see the middle of the image).

Contact means staying in touch with yourself despite the emotional impact of the situation. This includes being aware of your body, thoughts, and feelings (cf. 'The Principle of Self-awareness' on page 167).

Staying Attuned and in Contact

In the green zone, the professional focuses on solutions and can balance dilemmas, while remaining calm and attentive. This creates trust and allows them to quickly obtain the information required to deliver a solid, professional analysis, along with efficient treatment and action plans. You apply your professional and emotional intelligence to your work, and you use your situational awareness to navigate. You feel qualified and trust that your skills and experience are sufficient and can be applied suitably.

Staying attuned and in contact is essential for sustainable, high-quality practice in helping professions. It ensures that professionals maintain a healthy balance between using and protecting both their professional skills and human capacity (Jones, Smith and Johnston, 2005). This applies to all levels of the organisation and across professions. CEOs must be attuned and in good contact with their managers, who in turn must be attuned to their employees, who must then be attuned to each other and themselves (Fuertes, Toporovsky and Reyes, 2017); without these elements, key risks emerge:

- Senior management becomes unaware of departmental needs, **misallocating resources.**
- Team leaders fail to monitor team well-being, **mismanaging tasks.**
- Teams overlook **struggling colleagues.**
- Individuals disconnect from their own emotions, **impairing care delivery.**

Staying attuned and in contact requires the ability to **MENTALISE**: to infer other people's mental states (thoughts, needs, goals, and reasons) based on their behaviour.

Attuned and in contact

For self-employed professionals, it is important to be in regular contact with others who can help maintain the balance. This could be a supervisor, coach, or close business partner.

Many professionals in mentally high-risk jobs have direct contact with the person they are hired to help, and sound professional judgement requires obtaining a vast amount of data from that person. For instance, in cases of violence, the data may concern what happened and who did what. Or, in the case of physical illness or mental distress, the data concerns current symptoms, past medical history, or hopes and fears.

The helping professional's ability to stay attuned to the client is essential because:

- The person receiving help will feel themselves **treated with respect and dignity.**
- They gain confidence that the helping professional **understands them and their situation.**
- As a result, they feel able and willing to share **relevant information.**
- The professional is then able to make a sound **professional assessment** and propose a **viable action plan.**

In short, **mentalisation and emotional empathy** lead to *trust*, which enables *information sharing*, which supports *professional analysis* and *intervention* (Turner, 1999).

> *There's nothing worse than finding out a patient hasn't been taking their medication for a long time because they weren't comfortable with it, but didn't say anything.*

Other employees in high-risk jobs do not have a direct relationship with a specific person but rather with an entire group of people. This is the case, for example, for journalists and photographers who are out in emergency regions covering famine or civil war. They also need to be attuned to others to do a professional job.

> *We visited a lot of refugee camps over the years, and after a while we started comparing them—judging whether the camp we were in was better or worse than the ones we'd seen before. And we could always find examples of something we'd seen that was worse. We completely lost the sensitivity you need to do a proper news report.*

Being Over-involved

In the Red–Green–Blue model, the red zone corresponds to *over-involvement*, which typically occurs in cases of strong emotional identification with the person you are helping. When that happens, you are in danger of being 'contaminated' by the other person's feelings of helplessness, frustration, anger, despair, or powerlessness. As a helping professional, you may feel indignant and perceive the person as a victim in need of saving. The emotional intensity may cloud your judgement in the moment and make it hard to reflect afterwards.

Over-involvement often leaves the helping professional emotionally fragile and vulnerable. Whether consciously or unconsciously, this can lead the patient, client, or service user to question the professional's ability to handle their pain, despair, frustration, or anger (West, 2015).

Over-involvement can also lead the professional to create a symbiotic dynamic or foster such an intensely personal and confidential relationship that the client feels intimidated.

Over-involvement

Being Under-involved

The opposite of over-involvement in the Red–Green–Blue model is *under-involvement*—the side helping professionals may resort to when experiencing powerlessness in the face of emotionally intense situations. Under-involvement involves emotionally distancing oneself from the patient, client, or service user, and can present as either an overly intellectualised or indifferent attitude, or alternatively, as emotionally cold, irritable, or impatient behaviour. An under-involved professional will often deny or downplay the client's problems, or attempt to 'offload' the issue by referring the person elsewhere.

Under-involvement

Under-involvement can lead to becoming emotionally thick-skinned. As a result, the professional may appear authoritarian or insensitive. It can also manifest in the form of trivialisation, denial, or intellectualisation—attempts to create distance from the emotional weight of the situation. When in the blue zone, the professional may begin to think the client is to blame for their own situation.

Indeed, many complaints from patients, clients, or service users in the healthcare sector concern poor communication with under-involved staff.

On the surface, under-involvement can be mistaken for being in control—a trait widely valued in professional settings and often associated with competence and status. However, under-involvement is, in fact, a sign that the professional has lost their emotional balance. Like over-involvement, it signals a loss of control.

Which side a person tends to lean under pressure—over- or under-involvement—will often depend on the organisational culture, the individual's role in the group, and their personal coping style (Newell and MacNeil, 2010).

Company Culture

The culture of a company is an intangible quality—something that can be felt but not seen. It is a bit like the wind. Company culture encompasses rituals, norms, traditions, unwritten rules, and implicit expectations that shape how things are done in the organisation. These behaviours often go unnoticed because they are simply considered 'normal'.

Company culture also reflects core values—those things that make sense to employees simply because 'that's the way we do things around here'. The culture is constantly shaped by employees, managers, leadership, and external influences. It has a rhythm, a 'pulse', of its own.

Importantly, culture sets the unspoken rules for how psychological demands and strain are handled. Are employees expected to take sick leave after a traumatic event—or to show up to work the next day as usual?

Gender and Roles

A company's culture also reflects assumptions about gender and roles. In professions where women are in the majority, there has historically been a tendency to favour over-involvement strategies. Conversely, in male-dominated professions, under-involvement strategies have been more common.

For instance, a culture of over-involvement might be reflected in comments like: 'It's just great that she stayed and also took the evening shift, now that the patient's family was in such need of support, and she knows them best.' In an under-involved culture, on the other hand, one might hear: 'Well done, you couldn't tell he was affected at all. He just took it in his stride.'

> Sometimes I'm just so jealous of doctors. They come in, do a quick assessment, start the treatment, and then they're off—no one questions it. But us nurses, we're expected to sit there with the little kids on our laps, holding them, comforting them, over and over again. In the end, I just couldn't take it anymore.

Group Dynamics

The behaviour of each helping professional is also shaped by the group they work in. In most groups, there is a tendency to maintain a kind of internal balance. If some members begin to tilt towards emotional over-involvement, others may unconsciously respond by withdrawing emotionally and adopting a more theoretical or intellectual approach to their work with clients.

> At some point, I started noticing that I was becoming more matter-of-fact and a bit insensitive in what I was saying during the meetings, especially when one particular colleague wasn't there. She was usually the one who made those kinds of comments, and when she was absent, I realised I'd slipped into her role.

Group dynamics can be powerful. Once you have taken on a role—whether over- or under-involved—it can be difficult to shift away from it, especially if that role has become part of the group's established, if unspoken, balance.

We have a deep need for validation and often seek out those who share our emotional reactions and worldview. In such emotional echo chambers, perspectives are reinforced rather than questioned. Over time, this can distort a group's sense of reality, making alternative viewpoints harder to recognise—and less welcome. In high-strain work environments, these dynamics can create professional blind spots and reduce a group's ability to reflect, adapt, and course correct when necessary.

Individual Preferences

We have all experienced moments when we had to choose between following our emotions or our reason. When dealing with complex challenges, some people tend to lean towards the emotional side, while others favour a more rational approach. For most individuals, this preference remains relatively stable throughout life (MacRitchie and Leibowitz, 2010).

However, helping professionals may notice a shift over time. Some report that, after years of being over-involved and emotionally sensitive, they gradually—or suddenly—begin to withdraw emotionally from their work. They may feel emotionally thick-skinned, no longer affected by situations that once moved them deeply. Conversely, others may find that, after many years of under-involvement, they become increasingly affected by their work and feel more emotionally vulnerable and thin-skinned.

Recent graduates often tend towards over-involvement. This tendency may stem from a desire to compensate for their limited experience by demonstrating strong commitment and enthusiasm. Additionally, they may draw a deep sense of purpose and meaning from their new roles.

Personal life circumstances also play a role. Helping professionals who have small children, ill relatives, or other significant personal responsibilities naturally have less emotional capacity to invest in their work.

References

Dimberg, U., Thunberg, M. and Elmehed, K. (2000) "Unconscious facial reactions to emotional facial expressions," *Psychological Science*, 11(1), pp. 86–89. Available at: https://doi.org/10.1111/1467-9280.00221.

Fuertes, J.N., Toporovsky, A. and Reyes, M. (2017) "The working alliance in psychiatric care: agreement communication and trust in action," *Psychiatric*

Quarterly, 88(4), pp. 711–720. Available at: https://doi.org/10.1007/s11126-017-9492-0.

Gleichgerrcht, E. and Decety, J. (2013) "Empathy in clinical practice: how individual dispositions, gender, and experience moderate empathic concern, burnout, and emotional distress in physicians," *PLoS One*, 8(4), p. e61526. Available at: https://doi.org/10.1371/journal.pone.0061526.

Heyes, C. (2018) "Empathy is not in our genes," *Neuroscience & Biobehavioral Reviews*, 95, pp. 499–507. Available at: https://doi.org/10.1016/j.neubiorev.2018.11.001.

Jones, M.C., Smith, K. and Johnston, D.W. (2005) "Exploring the Michigan model: the relationship of personality, managerial support and organizational structure with health outcomes in entrants to the healthcare environment," *Work & Stress*, 19(1), pp. 1–22. Available at: https://doi.org/10.1080/02678370500065325.

MacRitchie, V. and Leibowitz, S. (2010) "Secondary traumatic stress, level of exposure, empathy and social support in trauma workers," *South African Journal of Psychology*, 40(2), pp. 149–158. Available at: https://doi.org/10.1177/008124631004000204.

Newell, J.M. and MacNeil, G.A. (2010) "Professional burnout, vicarious trauma, secondary traumatic stress, and compassion fatigue," *Best Practices in Mental Health*, 6(2), pp. 57–68. Available at: https://doi.org/10.70256/607490pbruec.

Turner, M. (1999) "Involvement or over-involvement? Using grounded theory to explore the complexities of nurse-patient relationships," *European Journal of Oncology Nursing*, 3(3), pp. 153–160. Available at: https://doi.org/10.1016/S1462-3889(99)80737-6.

Warr, P. (1994) "A conceptual framework for the study of work and mental health," *Work & Stress*, 8(2), pp. 84–97. Available at: https://doi.org/10.1080/02678379408259982.

West, A.L. (2015) "Associations amongst attachment style, burnout, and compassion fatigue in health and human service workers: a systematic review," *Journal of Human Behavior in the Social Environment*, 25(6), pp. 571–590. Available at: https://doi.org/10.1080/10911359.2014.988321.

10

From Warning Signs to States of Strain

In this chapter, we explore a range of psychological states that may emerge in high-risk professions—some clinical, others not, but all important to take seriously. If a helping professional exhibits warning signs or symptoms to a certain degree and for an extended period, it may indicate a state of strain or even a trauma-related mental disorder.

The most common psychological reactions associated with psychologically high-risk work include stress, burnout, mild anxiety, mild depressive symptoms, mild traumatisation, and increased use of stimulants. Importantly, these also include moral stress and moral injury. The terms *moral stress* and *moral injury* describe the distress experienced when professionals feel pressured to act in ways that conflict with their core moral values or ethical standards.

Moral injury is a more complex and less widely known phenomenon than the others. It has received growing attention in recent years, particularly in the wake of the COVID-19 pandemic, where healthcare and front-line workers were often placed in ethically challenging situations. For that reason, this chapter devotes more space to explaining moral injury than to the more familiar reactions, which the reader may already recognise. However, each of the reactions is important to understand and recognise in its own right.

Furthermore, despite their differences, all of these states of strain share one key feature: if the exposure continues over time or professional support is not provided, they can each develop into trauma-related mental disorders (Wilhelm et al., 2004).

The progression from experiencing typical after-effects to displaying isolated warning signs or symptoms typically unfolds gradually, potentially leading to a genuine stress state characterised by acute strain or the onset of a trauma-related mental disorder.

This chapter reviews the most common states of psychological strain that generally do not meet the criteria for a diagnosis. These are not classified as mental disorders but rather normal psychological or physiological reactions to stress (Hensel et al., 2015).

Chapter 11 provides a brief overview of trauma-related mental disorders and their official diagnostic criteria.

Stress

Stress is a state of emotional or mental strain that arises when external or internal demands exceed the resources available to the individual or team. Stress symptoms can be both physical and emotional.

Stress is conventionally divided into short-term and long-term stress. Short-term stress is a healthy response that enables a person to react quickly to particularly demanding situations. The mechanisms involved in a stress reaction prepare the body to perform optimally—both physically and mentally. The body goes on high alert, preparing itself for either fight or flight. In other words, stress is a kind of survival mechanism that is both appropriate and harmless, provided it lasts only for a short time and the person has the opportunity to recover afterwards. Problems only arise when we are exposed to prolonged and continued stress, and there is no opportunity to recover. Persistent stress reactions can lead to both mental and physical illnesses.

Stress can result from both physical and emotional demands and pressures. These may be work-related but are not always so (Jovanović et al., 2016). For many years, there has been an ongoing debate about whether the high incidence of stress in the Western world is due to increasing demands in the labour market or to pressures from private life and society in general. In this book, the focus is on work-related demands and strains faced by professionals in mentally high-risk jobs—strains that must be managed sustainably to avoid dissatisfaction, illness, and mental injuries (Sodeke-Gregson, Holttum and Billings, 2013).

Burnout

Burnout is a specific type of stress. The World Health Organisation (WHO) defines burnout as a chronic work-related phenomenon characterised by feelings of emotional exhaustion, increased mental distance or cynicism, and reduced professional efficacy (WHO, 2019). The reaction can occur when workload has long exceeded a person's resources and ability to cope. Apart from exhaustion, typical symptoms include an increased need for rest after completing tasks, sleeping difficulties, impaired concentration, fatigue, physical weakness, reduced tolerance for demands, and unusual emotional reactions (Lee et al., 2015).

Burnout is prevalent in professions where work primarily involves helping people with specific problems or needs. The recipients of help are not necessarily in crisis or traumatised, as is the case with secondary traumatisation. Rather than a sudden breakdown, burnout tends to develop gradually. In the early stages, employees often show high levels of commitment and idealism; over time, this may shift into frustration, disillusionment, withdrawal, and ultimately cynicism or emotional detachment (Maslach and Leiter, 2016).

Mild Anxiety

Anxiety is a natural reaction to an unexpected danger that usually disappears once the threat is over. When a person experiences anxiety for no reason, it can be considered a pathological reaction (Drury et al., 2014).

If only some of the symptoms of anxiety listed in the WHO's diagnostic manual (ICD-11, International Classification of Diseases) are present, or if they manifest in a mild form, the anxiety is considered subclinical. This is what is referred to in this book as 'mild anxiety'. If external stressors continue, the mild anxiety resulting from external stressors can develop into a constant state of anxiety (Jacobson et al., 2013). The most common anxiety symptoms and different types of anxiety are listed on page 92.

Mild Depressive Symptoms

Just as it is natural to experience anxiety when faced with an unexpected danger, it is natural to feel sad and lose energy when confronted with, for example, illness, death, dismissal, or an unwanted divorce. However, after some time, most people find their energy returning and their sad thoughts disappearing, regaining appreciation of life (Jacobson et al., 2013).

Similarly to mild anxiety, mild depressive symptoms are a subclinical condition. This means that the person meets some, but not all, of the criteria for a diagnosis of depression (Figley, 2013). Mild depressive symptoms can develop into a clinical depression, which you can read more about in Chapter 10.

Mild Post-traumatic Reactions

Finally, let us address mild post-traumatic reactions, where the person has some, but not all, symptoms of post-traumatic stress disorder (PTSD) (Figley, 2013). A mild traumatisation can be triggered by either first-line exposure, also referred to as *primary traumatisation*, or by second-line exposure, referred to as *secondary traumatisation*. The symptoms of primary or secondary trauma are the same (Jovanović et al., 2016; Jarrad et al., 2018). More information on the symptoms of post-traumatic reactions is provided in Chapter 10.

Increased Stimulant Consumption

When under pressure, some people react by increasing their consumption of stimulants such as alcohol, tobacco, medication, sugar, or caffeinated drinks (Killian, 2008). In short-term stress, many people tend to consume less food, while the opposite is true for long-term stress. In long-term stress, a person will typically consume more calories, resulting in overeating or bingeing.

Moral Stress and Moral Injury

A war reporter who could not intervene. A prison worker compelled to carry out an order they knew was wrong. A mental health nurse who sent someone home— only to learn they later took their own life.

These moments may not involve physical danger, but they can leave behind a deep and lasting mark—one that quietly unsettles our sense of who we are.

Moral injury refers to the profound emotional distress that may arise after taking part in or witnessing events that violate one's moral beliefs or expectations (Litz et al., 2009; Williamson et al., 2021). It often occurs when a professional recognises the ethically right course of action but is unable to pursue it.

Moral Stress: The Strain Before the Injury

Not every ethically difficult moment leaves a lasting wound. For many professionals, the first response is something quieter: a sense of frustration, inner tension, or unease—a feeling of being pulled away from what felt right. This is sometimes described as *moral stress*. It arises when we know what ought to be done but find ourselves unable to act on it—because of time pressure, rules, competing duties, or structural constraints.

Moral stress is not the same as moral injury. It may pass, or be resolved through reflection, conversation, or support. But when these situations repeat—especially in environments where there is little space to process them, or where leaders fail to acknowledge ethical weight—the stress may begin to harden. And over time, it can deepen into something more enduring: not just stress, but a deeper wound to the moral core.

> *I wanted to hold his hand as he died. But I was the only one there and I had three other patients I needed to attend to. I left him alone. I think about it every night.*

In this way, moral injury emerges not only from the strain of the event itself—but from the *meaning* we make of what we have done, failed to do, or been forced to witness. And crucially, it often arises when we feel let down—by systems, leaders, or even ourselves.

Moral Injury and PTSD

The term 'moral injury' was introduced by psychiatrist Jonathan Shay, based on his work on Vietnam war veterans. He described moral injury as a betrayal of what is right, by someone in legitimate authority, in a high-stakes situation (Shay, 1995). While originally used to describe military trauma, the concept has since expanded well beyond the battlefield. Brett Litz and colleagues broadened the definition to any act that violates one's deeply held moral beliefs—whether the individual committed, failed to prevent or witnessed them (Litz et al., 2009). This broader understanding has made moral injury increasingly relevant across other high-pressure professions.

During the COVID-19 pandemic, moral injury was consistently cited by healthcare workers as one of their most severe strains—especially when they were forced to choose between 'two evils' (Molendijk et al., 2022). Similar themes are echoed by war correspondents, humanitarian staff, and asylum officers, many of whom describe this as the hardest part of the work (Williamson et al., 2021).

While moral injury and PTSD may overlap, they are not the same. PTSD typically results from exposure to life-threatening or terrifying events, whereas moral injury stems from a violation of conscience (Williamson et al., 2021). PTSD is primarily about fear and survival; moral injury is about *guilt, shame, betrayal*, and a rupture in identity. Where PTSD tends to affect the nervous system, moral injury affects the *moral compass*. Some professionals describe this as a kind of 'lost innocence' (Molendijk et al., 2022).

Moral injury may involve:

- Intense self-blame or guilt.
- A deep erosion of trust—towards oneself or others.
- A feeling of being *irreversibly changed* by the event.
- Disconnection, disillusionment, or loss of meaning.

While PTSD models typically focus on *internal, psychological processes*, the concept of moral injury points to the *interconnection* between the individual professional and the broader context of their work. It highlights the systemic dimensions of moral stress: organisational blind spots, unsafe work cultures, structural constraints, insufficient supervision—or simply the lack of time and resources (Molendijk et al., 2022). Potentially morally injurious events may also occur when professionals unknowingly tilt towards the *blue zone*—becoming distant or less responsive to the needs of clients.

> *The worst part wasn't what happened. The worst part was living with the fact that I let it happen. (Høgsted, 2026)*

The Three Roads to Injury

Moral injury often arises through three distinct, overlapping pathways:

- **The injury of self**: 'I failed morally'—perhaps I overlooked something, made a mistake, or turned someone away who needed help.
- **The injury of inaction**: 'I saw something harmful and did nothing'—for example, witnessing unprofessional conduct but staying silent.
- **The injury of betrayal**: 'I was abandoned by leadership'—for instance, when help was promised but never came, or when the system prioritised bureaucracy over integrity.

Many professionals in high-risk settings recognise these paths. What hurts is not only *what happened*—but the sense that it *should not have happened*.

Responsibility and Its Shifting

> *I kept feeling like my manager should have done something and it was all her fault. And then I remembered ... her hands were tied. And maybe she was overwhelmed too.*

Moral injury often generates blame. Especially in hierarchical settings, the pain of a situation is often focused on those just above: leaders, supervisors, managers, as the ones having the final responsibility. Sometimes this may be justified. But at other times, it becomes a coping mechanism—what psychologists call *responsibility displacement* or *problem shifting* (cf. Chapter 8). It allows us to outsource the pain by simplifying the story: '*If only they had done their job*'. Whether we blame ourselves or management, moral injury often arises from simplified narratives about blame and guilt—stories that fail to consider circumstances, context, and structures. But the truth is often more complex. Perhaps *no one* had real agency in the moment. Perhaps the leader, too, was acting from constraint.

Making room for these nuances does not excuse direct cruelty—but it helps us distinguish between systems that are abusive and systems that are *overloaded*. Without that space, resentment may solidify—preventing the injury from healing. Recognising this complexity is not about letting go of responsibility—it's about making space for understanding and, ultimately, for healing. And that space is what many professionals need most.

Existential Pain

Repeated exposure to potentially morally injurious events increases the risk of injury and pain (Hegarty, Andrews and Tarzia, 2022). When isolated, such events may be attributed to situations or circumstances. However, when they accumulate, they form a kind of *moral crescendo*—where each new event evokes memories of previous powerlessness or failure (Hegarty, Andrews and Tarzia, 2022).

Some forms of moral injuries extend the boundaries of professional identity. They are existential wounds. The question becomes not only 'Why did this happen?' but 'Who am I, now that it has?'

This is especially true for those whose work is rooted in *values*: nurses, aid workers, and crisis responders. When those values are violated—the pain is not just psychological, it is *spiritual*.

Moral injury is not always loud. It can sit quietly beneath the surface—reshaping how we show up in our work and how we see ourselves. Over time, it may quietly harden into cynicism, numbness, or despair. Or it may remain a quiet pain that colours every decision with doubt.

In Chapter 17, we will explore what organisations and educational institutions can do to prevent and address moral injury in a meaningful way. For now, it is enough to say this: for professionals in helping roles, feeling wounded by a broken promise, a failed system, a human mistake, or a moment of helplessness is a sign of care; not a sign of weakness, and it is proof that your conscience is still alive.

References

Drury, V. et al. (2014) "Compassion satisfaction, compassion fatigue, anxiety, depression and stress in registered nurses in Australia: Phase 2 results," *Journal of Nursing Management*, 22(4), pp. 519–531. Available at: https://doi.org/10.1111/jonm.12168.

Figley, C.R. (2013) *Compassion Fatigue: Coping with Secondary Traumatic Stress Disorder in Those Who Treat the Traumatized*. Hoboken: Taylor and Francis (Routledge Psychosocial Stress Series).

Hegarty, K.L., Andrews, S. and Tarzia, L. (2022) "Transforming health settings to address gender-based violence in Australia," *Medical Journal of Australia*, 217(3), pp. 159–166. Available at: https://doi.org/10.5694/mja2.51638.

Hensel, J.M. et al. (2015) "Meta-analysis of risk factors for secondary traumatic stress in therapeutic work with trauma victims," *Journal of Traumatic Stress*, 28(2), pp. 83–91. Available at: https://doi.org/10.1002/jts.21998.

Høgsted, R. (2026) *Fundamentals of Psychological First Aid and Crisis Management*. Wiley (in preparation).

Jacobson, J.M. et al. (2013) "Risk for burnout and compassion fatigue and potential for compassion satisfaction among clergy: implications for social work and religious organizations," *Journal of Social Service Research*, 39(4), pp. 455–468. Available at: https://doi.org/10.1080/01488376.2012.744627.

Jarrad, R. et al. (2018) "Compassion fatigue and substance use among nurses," *Annals of General Psychiatry*, 17(1), p. 13. Available at: https://doi.org/10.1186/s12991-018-0183-5.

Jovanović, N. et al. (2016) "Burnout syndrome among psychiatric trainees in 22 countries: risk increased by long working hours, lack of supervision, and psychiatry not being first career choice," *European Psychiatry*, 32, pp. 34–41. Available at: https://doi.org/10.1016/j.eurpsy.2015.10.007.

Killian, K.D. (2008) "Helping till it hurts? A multimethod study of compassion fatigue, burnout, and self-care in clinicians working with trauma survivors," *Traumatology*, 14(2), pp. 32–44. Available at: https://doi.org/10.1177/1534765608319083.

Lee, W. et al. (2015) "Who is at risk for compassion fatigue? An investigation of genetic counselor demographics, anxiety, compassion satisfaction, and burnout," *Journal of Genetic Counseling*, 24(2), pp. 358–370. Available at: https://doi.org/10.1007/s10897-014-9716-5.

Litz, B.T. et al. (2009) "Moral injury and moral repair in war veterans: a preliminary model and intervention strategy," *Clinical Psychology Review*, 29(8), pp. 695–706. Available at: https://doi.org/10.1016/j.cpr.2009.07.003.

Maslach, C. and Leiter, M.P. (2016) "Understanding the burnout experience: recent research and its implications for psychiatry," *World Psychiatry*, 15(2), pp. 103–111. Available at: https://doi.org/10.1002/wps.20311.

Molendijk, T. et al. (2022) "Contextual dimensions of moral injury: an interdisciplinary review," *Military Psychology: The Official Journal of the Division of Military Psychology, American Psychological Association*, 34(6), pp. 742–753. Available at: https://doi.org/10.1080/08995605.2022.2035643.

Shay, J. (1995) *Achilles in Vietnam: Combat Trauma and Undoing of Character*. New York: Simon & Schuster.

Sodeke-Gregson, E.A., Holttum, S. and Billings, J. (2013) "Compassion satisfaction, burnout, and secondary traumatic stress in UK therapists who work with adult trauma clients," *European Journal of Psychotraumatology*, 4. Available at: https://doi.org/10.3402/ejpt.v4i0.21869.

WHO (2019) *Burn-out an "occupational phenomenon": international classification of diseases*. Available at: https://www.who.int/news/item/28-05-2019-burn-out-an-occupational-phenomenon-international-classification-of-diseases.

Wilhelm, K. et al. (2004) "Work and mental health," *Social Psychiatry and Psychiatric Epidemiology*, 39(11), pp. 866–873. Available at: https://doi.org/10.1007/s00127-004-0869-7.

Williamson, V. et al. (2021) "Moral injury: the effect on mental health and implications for treatment," *The Lancet Psychiatry*, 8(6), pp. 453–455. Available at: https://doi.org/10.1016/S2215-0366(21)00113-9.

11

Trauma-related Mental Disorders

When psychological strain is prolonged or left unaddressed, it may escalate into a diagnosable mental disorder. As described in Chapter 10, this escalation often begins with milder signs of emotional overload or early symptoms of mental tilting.

In this chapter, we explore the trauma-related disorders that can emerge when such strain goes untreated. The chapter introduces two widely used mental health screening tools that can help identify early signs of mental distress. Both tools support a proactive approach to helping professional well-being, encouraging early conversations about support needs.

Mental health disorders can be triggered by a single traumatising event or, as described in Part I of this book, by the indirect impact of such an event. As we have discussed, secondary traumatisation may manifest itself in the same way as post-traumatic stress (American Psychiatric Association, 2013). Other common strain-related mental disorders are anxiety and depression, which can often be trauma-induced or exacerbated by strain or trauma. This is also the case for various forms of substance use. Many trauma-related disorders are accompanied by emotional exhaustion, which may affect empathy, concentration, and interpersonal relationships.

Adjustment Disorder

Adjustment disorder refers to a strain-related condition characterised by emotional or behavioural symptoms in response to a significant life change or stressor. These symptoms arise within three months of the onset of the stressor and cause marked distress that is out of proportion to the severity or intensity of the event—or significant impairment in social, occupational, or other areas of functioning.

Unlike trauma-related disorders such as post-traumatic stress disorder (PTSD), adjustment disorder is not triggered by extreme or life-threatening events. Instead, it typically follows significant but non-catastrophic stressors—such as job loss, divorce, the death of a colleague or loved one, interpersonal conflicts, or threats to personal or professional stability.

The individual's response is influenced by personal vulnerability, coping capacity, and contextual factors. While the stressor may not be severe enough to elicit a trauma diagnosis, its psychological impact must be significant—and the presence of a stressor is a prerequisite for the diagnosis.

Post-traumatic Conditions

Both direct and indirect exposure to trauma can lead to post-traumatic reactions. According to the American Diagnostic and Statistical Manual of Mental Disorders, the *DSM-5*, PTSD results from exposure to actual or threatened death, serious injury, or sexual violence. This includes direct experience, witnessing the event, learning it happened to a close other, or repeated exposure to traumatic details—such as in the work of helping professionals.

Secondary traumatic stress, also called *secondary traumatisation*, refers to distress from indirect exposure, especially through empathic engagement with trauma survivors. While not a separate *DSM-5* diagnosis, it can lead to symptoms similar to direct exposure. If the indirect exposure meets *DSM-5* trauma criteria and symptoms are significant, a diagnosis of PTSD or another stress-related disorder may be appropriate (American Psychiatric Association, 2013).

Post-traumatic Stress Disorder—PTSD

According to *DSM-5*, PTSD can result from both direct and indirect exposure to trauma. This includes directly experiencing a traumatic event, witnessing it in person, learning that it occurred to a close family member or friend (in cases of violent or accidental death), or repeated exposure to stories of aversive details of trauma experienced by others—common amongst helping professionals.

This broader view contrasts with WHO's diagnostic manual, the ICD-11, which limits the PTSD diagnosis to direct or witnessed traumatic events. However, research has shown that symptoms of direct and indirect trauma exposure are often similar—and distinctions may become less relevant in future diagnostic systems (Friedman, 2013; Kelty et al., 2023).

Qualifying traumatic events typically involve actual or threatened death, serious injury, or sexual violence—such as accidents, assaults, war, rape, torture, natural disasters, or violent crime. These symptoms often lead to significant distress or disruption. They typically emerge within three months, although delayed onset later in life is also recognised. Core symptoms include (WHO ICD-11, 2019):

- Intrusive symptoms, such as flashbacks, nightmares, or vivid, involuntary memories.
- Avoidance of reminders related to the trauma.
- Negative alterations in mood or cognition, such as emotional numbing, detachment, memory gaps, or diminished interest in life.
- Increased arousal, including sleep disturbances, irritability, hypervigilance, or concentration problems.

Individuals with PTSD may withdraw from others, struggle to express affection, and experience significant disruptions in daily life. They may also have difficulties remembering all aspects of the event. While PTSD often begins soon after the trauma, symptoms may also surface months or even years later, especially when triggered by new, often less severe, forms of strain.

Secondary Traumatisation

The terms 'secondary traumatic stress' or 'secondary traumatisation' refer to what is also known as *compassion fatigue* or *caregiver fatigue* (Jarrad et al., 2018). These reactions may occur in professionals working closely with traumatised individuals, as well as in family members or friends of those affected by trauma. The condition may arise gradually over time or be triggered suddenly by a single event. In severe cases, symptoms can progress into full PTSD, particularly when exposure meets diagnostic criteria outlined in the *DSM-5* (Hensel et al., 2015).

The use of terms like compassion fatigue or caregiver fatigue highlights the empathic strain involved—often marked by a reduced capacity for empathy or emotional responsiveness. These labels are sometimes preferred as they are perceived as less pathologising—especially in professional settings where acknowledging psychological strain can carry stigma.

While there is no simple solution to the issue of pathologisation, the reluctance to be seen as 'ill' is understandable. As a helping professional, it is important to recognise that such responses—though not always fully healthy—are often natural reactions to repeated exposure to suffering and trauma. Still, many find it invalidating when serious psychological strain is dismissed as mere 'tiredness' or 'fatigue'.

For clarity and consistency, we use the term 'secondary traumatisation' as an umbrella term throughout this book, in line with the work of many psychologists.

Secondary traumatisation occurs when caregivers become psychologically affected through indirect exposure to the trauma of others—typically in the course of supporting, treating, or witnessing the suffering of traumatised individuals.

This traumatisation may develop suddenly, in response to a single intense incident, or gradually, through cumulative exposure over time. It often leads to a shift in how caregivers view themselves, their clients, and the world.

Like those directly exposed to trauma, caregivers may experience symptoms such as anxiety, intrusive thoughts, emotional numbing, and social withdrawal.

As mentioned, the American diagnostic system for mental disorders, the *DSM-5*, recognises the possibility of being secondarily traumatised through professional work when it involves repeated or extreme exposure to unpleasant details of a traumatic event. This criterion is intended for professionals who have never been in direct danger themselves, but who experience the consequences of traumatic events in their daily work. Secondary traumatisation can thus be considered PTSD if the diagnostic criteria are otherwise met.

Complex PTSD

Complex post-traumatic stress disorder (C-PTSD) is a condition that may develop following prolonged or repeated exposure to traumatic events of an extremely threatening or catastrophic nature—such as chronic abuse, torture, prolonged domestic violence, or captivity.

In addition to the core symptoms of PTSD—including intrusive memories, avoidance, and heightened arousal—complex PTSD involves:

- Persistent difficulties in emotional regulation (e.g., sudden anger, sadness, or emotional numbness);
- A negative self-concept, such as chronic feelings of guilt, shame, or worthlessness; and
- Ongoing problems in relationships, including difficulty feeling close to others, trusting others, or maintaining stable interpersonal connections (ICD-11).

ICD-11 (World Health Organization, 2019) formally recognised Complex PTSD as a distinct diagnosis in 2019, separate from PTSD. It requires that core PTSD symptoms are present along with the three additional symptom clusters: affect dysregulation, negative self-concept, and relational disturbances. The *DSM-5* by contrast, does not have a separate diagnosis for Complex PTSD (WHO ICD-11, 2019). Instead, it includes many of these symptoms under PTSD, especially in its broader symptom clusters (e.g., negative alterations in mood and cognition). As a result, individuals who might qualify for C-PTSD in ICD-11 are typically diagnosed with PTSD and one or more comorbid disorders in *DSM-5* (e.g., borderline personality disorder, depression, or dissociative disorders).

Anxiety

Anxiety disorders are characterised by persistent feelings of fear, unease, or worry—often out of proportion to the situation or arising without a clear external trigger. Symptoms can vary widely, from mild nervousness in specific situations to more generalised states of tension and even intense panic.

Physically, anxiety may show up as heart palpitations, shortness of breath, dizziness, trembling, or digestive discomfort. The body reacts as if facing acute danger—even when none is present.

On a psychological level, people may experience restless thinking, sleep disturbances, difficulty concentrating, or a sense of being constantly on alert. Over time, anxiety can lead to avoidance of behaviours that affect daily routines, work participation, and social life.

Anxiety may arise from long-term psychological strain, unresolved trauma, or appear alongside other conditions such as depression, PTSD, or substance use. While anxiety is often treatable, it can be deeply distressing. Recognising early signs—and making it easier to talk about anxiety without stigma—helps prevent escalation and supports mental well-being.

Depression

Depression is a persistent state of sadness that, similarly to anxiety, can occur without an obvious external cause, though it may also follow exposure to chronic psychological strain or traumatic events (WHO ICD-11, 2019). Burnout in care professions has been identified as a major contributor to strain-induced depression, particularly in emotionally demanding roles. A large Danish study found that professionals exposed to high emotional demands at work had a 19–31% increased risk of hospital-treated depression (Madsen et al., 2022).

Depression varies in severity, from feeling low and lacking energy for a few weeks to experiencing severe, long-term symptoms, lasting months or years. In addition to low mood, depression often includes fatigue, loss of interest, poor concentration, sleep disturbances, and a pessimistic outlook. The condition often impacts self-esteem and self-confidence, and may involve feelings of guilt or remorse. In its most severe form, depression can lead to psychosis, where the person loses touch with reality, becoming withdrawn, overwhelmed by self-blame, and experiencing suicidal ideation or intent.

Suicide

Suicidal thoughts, attempts, and suicide itself are amongst the most serious consequences of trauma-related mental health challenges—including PTSD, depression, and substance use difficulties.

While personal vulnerability plays a role, research shows that suicidal behaviour is also shaped by environmental and structural conditions. Work-related factors can contribute—such as chronic emotional pressure, job insecurity, bullying, traumatic events in a professional role, or distress following work-related injury or illness. In some fields—like healthcare, law enforcement, veterinary practice, or agriculture—easy access to lethal means such as firearms, medications, or pesticides can further increase the risk.

Depression remains one of the strongest predictors of suicide. But post-traumatic conditions can also raise risk levels, especially when combined with shame, emotional numbing, hopelessness, or social isolation. For professionals in helping roles, repeated indirect exposure to trauma—secondary traumatisation—has been linked to elevated suicide risk, particularly in workplaces where support is limited or stigma makes it harder to reach out (LaMontagne et al., 2024).

It is important to remember that suicidal thoughts are not always a sign of mental illness in themselves. Often, they reflect a deep psychological crisis—a response to overwhelming strain, the loss of meaning, or the painful belief that one is a burden to others. This makes early recognition and timely support crucial—not just on an individual level, but in how organisations and systems respond (LaMontagne et al., 2024). These findings underscore the urgent need for systemic attention to occupational mental health, particularly in professions exposed to repeated trauma or sustained emotional demands.

Substance Use and Addiction

Substance use can take many forms—from low-risk or occasional use to more harmful patterns, and, in some cases, full-blown dependency or addiction with long-term psychological and physical effects. It may involve alcohol, prescription medication, or other mood-altering substances.

Not all use is problematic. But for some, it gradually begins to interfere with daily life—affecting well-being, relationships, or the ability to function. In such cases, substance use may also serve as a way to cope with emotional strain, traumatic experiences, or psychological pain (National Institute on Drug Abuse, 2021).

Recognising signs of problematic use early makes a difference. It can reduce harm, prevent escalation, and make it easier for individuals to access the right kind of support—without stigma or judgement.

Assessment of Well-being and Mental Tilting

Recognising whether you, a colleague, employee, or manager are thriving—or struggling with significant mental strain—is sometimes straightforward. Does the person appear happy, energised, relaxed, and generally well? Or are the warning signs so prominent that it is clear they are overwhelmed and in need of support?

At other times, assessment is more difficult. This is especially true when signs of strain have been present for so long that they are mistaken for stable personality traits. It becomes even more challenging if several colleagues show similar patterns, making these warning signs seem like a general workplace culture rather than indicators of someone needing help.

People naturally vary in temperament, which is important to keep in mind when evaluating someone's mental state. Observations should always be compared to the person's usual behaviour. For example, concern is warranted if someone who is normally outgoing and engaged begins to isolate themselves—whereas the same behaviour may not be unusual for someone who is typically introverted.

WHO-5

There are many tools that can help assess whether a person is in good mental health or begins to tilt psychologically, as seen in conditions such as stress, anxiety, depression, PTSD, and others.

A simple yet reliable measure of well-being is the WHO-5 Well-Being Index, developed by Professor Per Bech (Boxall, Guthrie and Paauwe, 2016). This test is freely available and included on page 202. It consists of five short questions about how a person has felt over the past two weeks, focusing on positive emotional experiences.

Although the WHO-5 is not a diagnostic tool, it serves as a useful barometer of well-being (Topp et al., 2015). Low scores may indicate a need for support, reflection, or further evaluation. Any assessment of whether professional help or treatment is needed should be carried out by a qualified healthcare provider, such as a doctor or psychologist.

Professional Quality of Life Scale

Another useful tool for tracking well-being—and potential exhaustion in caring professions—is the Professional Quality of Life Scale (ProQOL) (Stamm, 2010). Originally developed by Charles Figley and now freely available in an adapted version by B. Hudnall Stamm, the ProQOL consists of 30 questions measuring three key areas: compassion satisfaction, burnout, and secondary traumatic stress. A summary of the full test is provided in the Appendix on page 203.

As with most assessment tools, the ProQOL should not be used in isolation. A full understanding of the individual's mental state requires a face-to-face conversation. However, the scale serves as a valuable screening instrument and can support meaningful discussions with colleagues, employees, or others in the workplace.

References

American Psychiatric Association (eds.) (2013) *Diagnostic and Statistical Manual of Mental Disorders: DSM-5* (5th ed). Washington, D.C.: American Psychiatric Association.

Boxall, P., Guthrie, J.P. and Paauwe, J. (2016) "Editorial introduction: progressing our understanding of the mediating variables linking HRM, employee well-being and organisational performance," *Human Resource Management Journal*, 26(2), pp. 103–111. Available at: https://doi.org/10.1111/1748-8583.12104.

Friedman, M.J. (2013) "Finalizing PTSD in DSM-5: getting here from there and where to go next," *Journal of Traumatic Stress*, 26(5), pp. 548–556. Available at: https://doi.org/10.1002/jts.21840.

Hensel, J.M. et al. (2015) "Meta-analysis of risk factors for secondary traumatic stress in therapeutic work with trauma victims," *Journal of Traumatic Stress*, 28(2), pp. 83–91. Available at: https://doi.org/10.1002/jts.21998.

Jarrad, R. et al. (2018) "Compassion fatigue and substance use among nurses," *Annals of General Psychiatry*, 17, p. 13. Available at: https://doi.org/10.1186/s12991-018-0183-5.

Kelty, S. et al. (2023) "Assessment of occupational stress," in Houck, M.M. (ed.) *Encyclopedia of Forensic Sciences* (3rd ed). Oxford: Elsevier, pp. 209–220. Available at: https://doi.org/10.1016/B978-0-12-823677-2.00017-9.

LaMontagne, A.D. et al. (2024) "Work-related suicide: evolving understandings of etiology & intervention," *American Journal of Industrial Medicine*, 67(8), pp. 679–695. Available at: https://doi.org/10.1002/ajim.23624.

Madsen, I.E. et al. (2022) "Emotional demands at work and risk of hospital-treated depressive disorder in up to 1.6 million Danish employees: a prospective nationwide register-based cohort study," *Scandinavian Journal of Work, Environment & Health*, 48(4), pp. 302–311. Available at: https://doi.org/10.5271/sjweh.4020.

National Institute on Drug Abuse (2021) *Words Matter: Preferred Language for Talking About Addiction*. National Institute on Drug Abuse.

Stamm, B.H. (2010) *The Concise ProQOL Manual: The Concise Manual for the Professional Quality of Life Scale* (2nd ed.). Eastwoods, LLC.

Topp, C.W. et al. (2015) "The WHO-5 Well-Being Index: a systematic review of the literature," *Psychotherapy and Psychosomatics*, 84(3), pp. 167–176. Available at: https://doi.org/10.1159/000376585.

World Health Organization (2019) *ICD-11: International Classification of Diseases* (11th ed.). WHO.

Part III

The Strategies

12

HR Policy Framework

Working in a mentally high-risk job can feel deeply meaningful. What you do makes a real difference—simply showing up matters.

But—just as the term suggests—it also comes with risk. Working with death, suffering, violence, or threats inevitably involves danger. There is no way to make these roles entirely safe. Being exposed repeatedly to traumatic events, whether as a first responder or second-line helper, comes with an inevitable psychological cost.

Preventing mental strain and injury is therefore a matter of mental risk management. In practice, this means identifying the workplace factors that increase or reduce vulnerability to psychological harm. These factors were described in the first part of the book and are now translated into concrete ideas and strategies in Part III.

As stated in the introduction, it is always the organisation that carries the overall responsibility—both legally and ethically—for creating a safe psychological and physical work environment. This responsibility must be taken seriously by any organisation that chooses to operate in the mentally high-risk space—whether in healthcare, social work, the media world, emergency response, or professions often described as helping roles.

Developing Strong HR Policies

One way to fulfil this responsibility is to develop strong HR policies that attract, retain, and support the development of employees. An HR policy—also sometimes referred to as a human resource management (HRM) policy—provides the overarching framework for the workplace environment.

It outlines the principles guiding how managers should treat employees, and how employees should treat each other (Weinberg et al., 2019). The goal of an HR policy is to contribute to effective and sustainable staff management, while supporting the organisation's core services and strategic goals around development, well-being, and productivity.

Organisations operating in mentally high-risk sectors have a particular need for a clear HR policy framework that helps ensure all risks are handled as thoroughly as possible.

An HR policy is a living document. It should be revised regularly, based on the organisation's real life experiences. It must align with the organisation's culture and include strategies for both daily stability and crisis preparedness—reducing the risk of cumulative strain in everyday operations and minimising traumatic aftereffects during critical events (Ericsson and Pool, 2016).

Standard Operating Procedures (SOPs)

An HR policy defines the overall framework for a safe and functional work environment. Within this framework lie the organisation's more specific systems and procedures.

In some sectors, these are referred to as SOPs—a term borrowed from English. An SOP is a set of step-by-step instructions developed by the organisation to ensure high-quality performance and safety for both helpers and the people they assist.

SOPs simplify daily operations. When employees know what to do, they don't need to evaluate every case from scratch. However, SOPs should avoid unnecessary complexity or detail, so they don't waste employees' time or mental resources.

Organisational Maturity

Most organisations working in mentally high-risk environments already have HR policies in place that include both preventive practices and formal procedures for managing incidents when harm occurs.

In some organisations, these policies are used actively and are an integrated part of daily routines. In others, they may sit forgotten in a folder somewhere—though staff fondly remember the engaging discussions that took place when they were created.

Some organisations may not have written procedures at all but instead operate based on established traditions and informal norms that successfully distribute workloads and protect employees. Finally, there are newer or growing organisations that are only just beginning to recognise the importance of addressing mental health risks in a structured way.

Regardless of where an organisation is on this spectrum, it is vital to continually review and adjust policies and practices. This is a dynamic process that requires regularly checking whether current approaches still meet the demands placed on employees—and reflect the realities of their working conditions.

A well-crafted HR policy enables managers to lead and allocate work effectively across a variety of situations. For example, if a workplace offers a senior scheme, the policy must ensure that funding is available to support it when employees decide to use it.

Turning Preventive Procedures into Practice

It may sound obvious, but a preventive SOP only works if it's actually followed.

It's one thing to spend time identifying focus areas and writing them down in a procedure. It's quite another to turn them into meaningful, lasting habits in a busy workday.

Even if a manager or employee fully agrees with the procedure—or helped write it—it's still easy, in a moment of stress, to think: *'Today, let's just do what we usually do. It's easier'.*

This illustrates one of the key challenges of policy implementation: turning written intentions into lived organisational practice. This can apply to anything: scheduling difficult conversations at a certain time of day, attending a supervision session, or ensuring two people are on duty during a night shift under specific conditions. Under pressure, it's often easy to justify making an exception—*just this once*—especially if the decision is made alone.

When introducing new preventive practices, it's essential to support each other in implementing them consistently. Track each completed activity—and celebrate when you reach 10 or 100 completions. Just as importantly, track when the procedure wasn't followed, and investigate why.

Changing behaviour takes practice (Polanyi and Sen, 2009).

Tacit Knowledge

Many mentally high-risk jobs are old, traditional professions. Generations of professionals have walked the paths that today's workers now follow.

Some of that experience has been formalised and written into HR policies and SOPs. But in other cases, important knowledge lives on as tacit knowledge—the kind of knowledge that is hard to put into words or write down in a manual.

Tacit knowledge is what is passed on when one colleague shows another how to handle a specific task or situation (Diehm, Mankowitz and King, 2019). When people know and trust each other well, tacit knowledge can be transferred remarkably quickly.

Often, people are not even aware of the tacit knowledge they possess—or how valuable it might be to others.

In reality, any HR policy will always go hand in hand with the tacit knowledge embedded in the organisation's everyday life.

References

Diehm, R.M., Mankowitz, N.N. and King, R.M. (2019) "Secondary traumatic stress in Australian psychologists: individual risk and protective factors," *Traumatology*, 25(3), pp. 196–202. Available at: https://doi.org/10.1037/trm0000181.

Ericsson, K.A. and Pool, R. (2016) *Peak: Secrets from the New Science of Expertise.* Boston, New York: Houghton Mifflin Harcourt.

Polanyi, M. and Sen, A. (2009) *The Tacit Dimension.* Chicago; London: University of Chicago Press.

Weinberg, A. et al. (2019) "Organizational uptake of NICE guidance in promoting employees' psychological health," *Occupational Medicine (Oxford, England),* 69(1), pp. 47–53. Available at: https://doi.org/10.1093/occmed/kqy148.

13

Psychological Safety as a Shared Resource

In demanding professions, safety often refers to physical protocols, protective equipment, or risk procedures. But in recent years, another form of safety has become increasingly central to how we understand sustainable professional life: psychological safety.

Psychological safety refers to the shared sense that it is possible to speak up, ask for help, show doubt, or express emotion—without fear of rejection, punishment, or ridicule (Edmondson, 2019). It is not a personal quality or a leadership technique, but a shared relational condition built over time.

This chapter focuses on psychological safety as a key element in how professionals experience and process strain. Not as a solution to pressure, but as a condition that shapes how pressure is lived, shared, and recovered from. Safety and strain can coexist—but psychological safety is what makes strain bearable and shareable.

Psychological Safety in Emotionally Demanding Work

In the professions explored in this book—including healthcare, firefighting, social work, journalism, spiritual care, and education—professionals are regularly exposed to high-responsibility situations marked by emotional complexity, unpredictability, and intensity.

In these settings, people need to be able to say:

- That was difficult
- I'm unsure what to do here

- I need help
- This doesn't feel right

But these small, honest sentences are often difficult to say—unless the surrounding culture actively supports them. In environments with low psychological safety, professionals may hold back, pretend, or keep their doubts to themselves. This is rarely a question of motivation or skill. Rather, it reflects a lack of relational permission—the subtle signals that tell us whether honesty is welcome or risky (Høgsted, 2024).

Psychological safety does not remove strain. But it changes how strain is carried—whether it becomes isolated or shareable, silenced or speakable.

Signs of Psychological Safety in Practice

Psychological safety often becomes visible in small moments:

- People speak openly about mistakes or doubts
- Colleagues check in after difficult situations
- Emotions are acknowledged, not dismissed
- Feedback is shared with care—and received without fear
- Team members ask each other, 'How are you holding up?'

These small behaviours reflect the broader condition of team psychological safety—the shared sense within a group that it is safe to speak up, disagree, or ask for help without negative consequences.

Where psychological safety is low, professionals may:

- Stay silent when something feels wrong
- Avoid giving or receiving feedback
- Downplay or suppress emotional reactions
- Withhold doubts or questions
- Feel disconnected—even when surrounded by others

In treatment meetings, when we're talking about service users, I sometimes feel completely cut off from the rest of the team—especially when I disagree with something or understand someone's distress differently. It's almost like we're living in different worlds, but I don't feel able to say that. I honestly never know what to say, so I just stay quiet.

A Shared Condition—Not an Individual Trait

Psychological safety is not something a person has or lacks. It is not the same as confidence or resilience. It is a shared property of the group. It grows when people repeatedly experience that their thoughts, questions, and emotions are met with openness rather than judgement.

It is shaped through daily interactions—in tone, timing, pauses, reactions, and follow-up. Psychological safety is never static. It shifts over time, can change quickly, and varies between teams. No one can create psychological safety alone. But everyone contributes to it. Some contributions, however, have more weight than others.

The Leader's Role—From Framework to Response

While psychological safety is co-created by all, leaders carry a distinct responsibility in shaping the conditions for openness, reflection, and emotional honesty—especially under pressure. This is often described in the literature as inclusive leadership, where leaders actively invite and value diverse perspectives and emotional expression. Psychologist and researcher Amy Edmonson (Nembhard and Edmondson, 2006; Edmondson, 2019) identifies three essential leadership behaviours that help build psychological safety in teams:

Setting the Stage

The leader defines the task and clarifies that the environment is one where uncertainty, learning, and mistakes are expected. This creates a frame that reduces fear and guesswork, allowing professionals to focus and engage with greater confidence. The leader can say:

- *These cases are never straightforward—and it's okay to feel unsure. What matters is that we talk about it. No one should carry ethical doubt or emotional strain alone. If something feels off, bring it up. We'll figure it out together.*
- *We will likely discover things that don't work as intended—and that's not a sign that anyone did something wrong. It's how we learn. If something feels off, or if you ever felt unsure in a situation, say so. For me, mistakes and friction points are useful feedback, not signs of failure.*

Inviting Participation

The leader actively invites input, questions, concerns, and emotional reactions. This invitation can be verbal ('What's your view?'), behavioural (pausing and making space), or cultural (normalising debriefs and shared reflection). It signals that everyone's voice matters—not just the confident or senior ones. The leader can say:

- *This is a situation where it's easy to miss something important. Are there any concerns or perspectives we haven't heard yet? Even if it feels small or uncertain, please share it.*
- *Last time, we touched on some difficult topics—and that's okay. Big conversations sometimes bring silence, or very quick reactions. If you've had second thoughts, or just needed more time to reflect, you're very welcome to bring it up now. I'd love to hear what's still on your mind.*

Responding Productively

Perhaps the most decisive moment is how the leader reacts when someone dares to speak openly. A sharp or defensive reaction can shut down trust quickly. But a constructive, even imperfect response can reinforce the signal: honesty is welcome here. The leader can say:

- 'Thank you for being honest. It sounds like this had some effects we didn't intend. Let's take a look at it together and see if there's anything we can adjust'.
- 'Thanks for sharing that. Many of us often think we're the only ones unsure—until someone says it, and others realise they feel the same. So really—thank you for putting it into words'.

While Edmondson lays out these three behaviours as core to psychological safety, I have previously studied how they take shape in emotionally demanding fields (Høgsted, 2024). From the standpoint of Strain Psychology, leaders are themselves affected by strain—and may react with fight, flight, freeze, or fawn. In times of strain and pressure, they may initially feel threatened by opposing viewpoints and employees' criticism. These are not failures—they are human responses to strain. What matters is whether the leader can recognise and initiate repairs after such moments—and protect the trust climate in the team.

Psychological Safety and Sustainable Strain Management

Psychological safety does not replace training, boundaries, or clear roles—but it strengthens them. It allows professionals to ask, reflect, and adjust before pressure escalates.

People can handle a great deal of emotional strain—but not in isolation, and not without spaces where it is safe to be real. When strain cannot be shared or named, it often accumulates quietly (see Chapter 7). Over time, this may lead to mental tilting, burnout, detachment, or injury to one's professional integrity. Psychological safety is not about removing difficulty. It is about creating the conditions where difficulty can be faced together—instead of alone (Høgsted, 2024).

> Even when I challenge something, my colleagues and team manager are curious rather than defensive. It feels like we all just want to learn, not just be right. It's the first time I experience that, and it makes me more willing to speak up—even when I'm unsure. Our team leader often reminds us that disagreement is part of good practice.

Final Reflections

Psychological safety is not a soft ideal. It is a core condition that shapes how professionals relate to themselves, each other, and the work they are here to do. It depends on culture, leadership, language, and practice—but above all, on human presence.

When psychological safety is present, professionals can bring more of themselves into the room. They can speak honestly, recover more easily, and remain connected in the midst of pressure. When it is absent, people may still carry out their duties—but with growing distance, hesitation, or protective silence.

Over time, this difference becomes cultural, structural, and ethical. And it shapes not only how pressure is endured—but whether it becomes something we survive alone or grow through together.

References

Edmondson, A.C. (2019) *The Fearless Organization: Creating Psychological Safety in the Workplace for Learning, Innovation, and Growth.* Hoboken, NJ: Wiley.

Høgsted, R. (2024) *Håndbog i Psykologisk Tryghed: Tør vi? Tør vi lade være? Psykologisk tryghed fra et belastningspsykologisk ståsted.* København: Forlaget Belastningspsykologi.

Nembhard, I.M. and Edmondson, A.C. (2006) Making it safe: the effects of leader inclusiveness and team psychological safety on performance in diverse work groups. *Journal of Organizational Behavior*, 27(7), pp. 941–966.

14

The Strain Square

There are a wide range of SOPs useful to incorporate into personnel policy for employees in mentally high-risk environments. These policies should also account for the individual vulnerabilities present in any staff group.

The strain square highlights key areas when working to prevent psychological overload and loss of balance. The model consists of an X-axis that depicts objective strains and a Y-axis showing individual employees' subjective vulnerabilities. The X-axis is deliberately longer than the Y-axis, as specific external events pose the greatest risk to employees' mental balance and, in the worst scenario, can cause a trauma. The strain square is divided into the following four fields:

1. The workday routine
2. The sore spot
3. Difficult tasks and collective crises
4. The worst moments

To build resilience and prevent injuries, an organisation's HR policy should include appropriate measures for all four areas.

X-axis—Objective Strains

The objective strains are described in Chapter 3. They are defined both by the duration of the incident and the nature of the incident. Was it a short-term acute strain, a series of prolonged challenges, or one persistent, ongoing burden? Was the employee's own life and well-being at risk? Is there a risk of the incident recurring—and is it over, or is it still ongoing? What was the threat level—and did the incident also involve casualties? Was it human-made or natural? Were children involved? How many people were involved and how strong sensory inputs have employees been exposed to? And finally, was the incident anticipated—or did it come out of the blue?

Model 5: The Strain Square

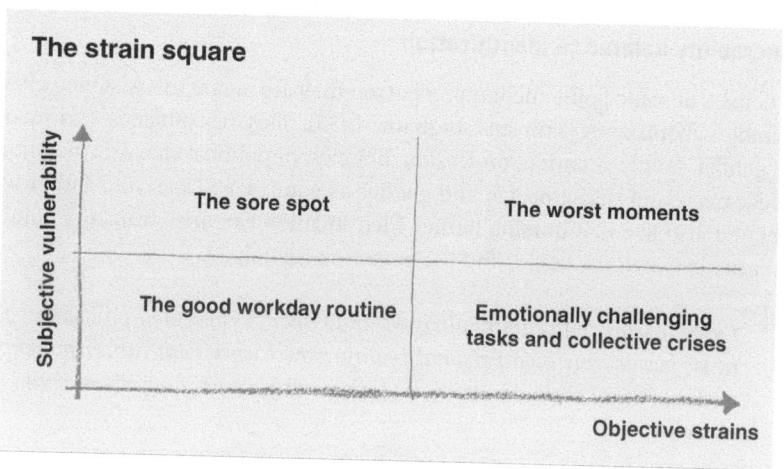

The strain square

- Subjective vulnerability (y-axis)
- Objective strains (x-axis)
- The sore spot
- The worst moments
- The good workday routine
- Emotionally challenging tasks and collective crises

Y-axis—The Subjective Vulnerability

Subjective vulnerability can be divided into four aspects:

- Vulnerability related to the past
- Vulnerability related to the present
- Vulnerability related to identification
- Vulnerability related to personally knowing those in need of your help

Vulnerability Related to the Past

This vulnerability is linked to past strains and traumas in your life, both personal and professional (Cetin et al., 2005; Hensel et al., 2015), e.g., growing up in a home with an abusive parent or losing your mother at a young age. Vulnerability may also consist of having once been assaulted on the job, having a patient, client, or service user commit suicide on your shift, or having lost a colleague on a job. This is referred to as re-traumatisation (Hensel et al., 2015).

Vulnerability Related to the Present

Current stresses in your personal or professional life are great vulnerabilities. You could be grieving over the loss of a loved one, be in the middle of a challenging divorce, or being evaluated for a potentially serious illness. Alternatively, you may have been overworking recently, leaving you feeling tired and exhausted (Rabenu, Yaniv and Elizur, 2017).

Vulnerability Related to Identification

All helpers at some point encounter a person they are meant to assist who closely resembles themselves (Luft and Ingham, 1955). This resemblance can involve age, gender, family situation, profession, hobbies, or political views. Is the injured or deceased child the same age and gender as your own? Does your father with dementia also live in a nursing home? Identification can arise from any point of similarity between the helper and the person being helped.

> *I used to work with children in care, and I always knew their problems would never become my own personal reality. Now I work with cancer patients— and that could easily be me—even tomorrow. Several of my clients could just as well be me.*

Vulnerability Related to Personally Knowing Those in Need of Your Help

This type of vulnerability (Broberg, Dyregrov and Lilled, 2005) is especially relevant in emergency work, where you often begin your shift not knowing whom you will be helping that day or night. If you live in a smaller community and work close to home, the likelihood increases that the person in need might be a neighbour, a former colleague, or one of your child's classmates.

Unlike the first three types of vulnerability, which can, to some extent, be considered when planning work, it is rarely possible for a manager to prepare for the risk that an employee might personally know the person they are helping. In such cases, it is vital to ensure that the experience is followed up on afterwards. Support and care should be offered to the affected employee, who, in this instance, is connected in some way to the injured, ill, or deceased person. At the same time, the employee should receive professional supervision and constructive feedback to help them process the experience and relate it back to their core professional role.

When organising tasks, it is important to be aware of employees' individual, subjective vulnerabilities, as these create particular working conditions. A professional who personally knows the service user will face greater challenges in maintaining solid contact and in keeping a healthy balance between over- and under-involvement.

Maintaining good contact is essential for performing the task professionally and sustainably.

The Four Fields

To reiterate, the strain square consists of the four fields:

- The good workday routine
- The sore spot
- Emotionally challenging tasks and collective crises
- The worst moments

In the following, I provide a brief description of each of the four fields, along with an overview of some of the strategies—or tools—that may be useful in different situations. The model on page 113 shows where you can find more detailed information about each of these strategies.

The Good Workday Routine

A good workday routine is one where there is a suitable balance between demands and resources, as well as between being efficient and maintaining the capacity to meet the patient, client, or service user in a caring and solution-oriented manner. The workgroup is able to provide safe and stable interventions while also having the energy to develop and learn new things (Grawitch, Ballard and Erb, 2015).

In such work, it is normal for employees to be emotionally affected on a regular basis. This is a natural and common human response to encounters with people in crisis or with traumatised individuals—or in response to verbal attacks and threats. Mentally high-risk jobs require employees to manage negative emotions such as pain, despair, fear, and anger.

The Sore Spot

The sore spot refers to an individual employee's personal vulnerability. This vulnerability may stem from past or present experiences, from identification with the person in need of help, or from personally knowing them. Some similarities between the employee and the person they are helping are immediately obvious; others are less visible or entirely hidden.

Some professionals are aware that certain types of cases affect them more personally than others. For instance, working with survivors of abuse may surface unresolved experiences from their own past. In other cases, it may be a colleague who first notices that a case is having a deeper emotional impact—perhaps even before the person themselves realises it.

Sometimes, personal experiences remain completely hidden until a particular situation unexpectedly triggers a strong emotional response. In other cases, a professional may quietly carry private life experiences—such as having a sibling with a similar diagnosis to a client—which subtly influences how they engage with their work and the responsibility they carry. Whether recognised or not, acknowledged or private, these experiences can deepen empathy but also heighten the risk of emotional strain if not handled with care.

Emotionally Challenging Tasks and Collective Crises

Emotionally challenging tasks involve severe tragedies, such as a parent killing their own children, a major accident resulting in numerous fatalities and widespread destruction, or a young person taking their own life.

When encountering such situations—whether as a first- or second-line professional—you are confronted with events so tragic, brutal, and horrifying that intense emotional reactions are a natural response. It is crucial to process these emotions in order to re-establish a sense of connection with the individuals you are helping, while also maintaining professionalism and a solution-focused approach.

A collective crisis refers to an acute incident that affects many employees at the same time. For such events, it is essential that an appropriate emergency plan is in place.

The Worst Moments

The worst moments arise when a professional is confronted with their own vulnerability while dealing with an especially challenging task or during a collective crisis.

For a police officer, it might be entering a home to find that a father has killed his two young sons—particularly harrowing if the officer is also a father of two young boys. For a care worker, it could be being assaulted again by a resident, echoing a previous traumatic incident. Or it may be a surgeon who loses a patient on the operating table due to a mistake, only to lose another soon after.

In these moments, personal vulnerability and professional responsibility collide, often leaving a lasting emotional impact.

Model 6: The Strain Square Strategies

The Strain Square
Overview of relevant preventive strategies you can read more about in this book

The sore spot
• Deliberate task sharing *page 141*
• Individual supervision *page 176*
• Trauma therapy *page 178*

The worst moments
• Deliberate task sharing *page 141*
• Psychological counselling *page 183*
• Full or partial sick leave *page 187*
• Trauma therapy *page 178*

The good workday routine
• Trauma training *page 138*
• Supervision *page 21 and 176*
• Leadership mentoring/coaching *page 178*
• Professional management and Professional development *page 140*
• Social support *page 146*
• Buddy system *page 177*

• Fisherman's bench *page 148*
• New hire mentoring programme *page 177*
• Clarity about tasks and roles *page 139*
• Strategic planning *page 140*
• Defusing guard *page 153*
• Systematic learning and development *page 135*
• Terms of employment *page 135*

Emotionally challenging tasks and collective crises
• Implementing the contingency plan *page 134*
• Crisis management *page 185*
• Psychological defusing *page 182*
• Psychological first aid *page 183*
• Psychological debriefing *page 182*
• Psychological counselling *page 183*
• Fisherman's bench *page 148*

Subjective vulnerability

Objective strains

Moved, Affected, and Shaken

Danish psychotherapist Susanne Bang distinguishes between three levels of emotional impact, which she describes as being *moved*, *affected*, and *shaken* (Bang, 2018).

The term *moved* refers to the natural and essentially human emotional response we feel when we encounter someone going through something painful or tragic—it is a sign of empathy and presence.

Affected refers to the helper's personal emotional reactions, often shaped by their own current life circumstances or unresolved past experiences—such as divorce, alcohol issues, or eating disorders.

Shaken refers to those moments when we are confronted with events so extreme or horrifying that we temporarily lose our emotional connection to the patient, client, or service user.

Model 7: Moved, Affected, Shaken

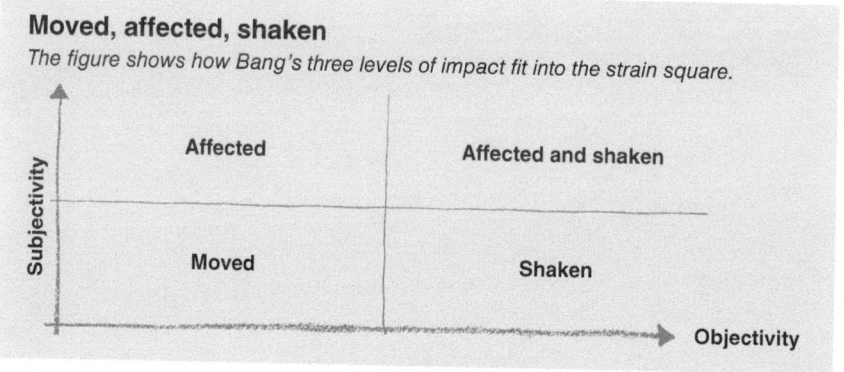

Moved, affected, shaken
The figure shows how Bang's three levels of impact fit into the strain square.

References

Bang, S. (2018) *Rørt, ramt og rystet: supervision og den sårede hjælper*. 1. udgave, 8. oplag. København: Hans Reitzel.

Broberg, A.G., Dyregrov, A. and Lilled, L. (2005) "The Göteborg discotheque fire: posttraumatic stress, and school adjustment as reported by the primary victims 18 months later," *Journal of Child Psychology and Psychiatry, 46*(12), pp. 1279–1286. Available at: https://doi.org/10.1111/j.1469-7610.2005.01439.x.

Cetin, M. et al. (2005) "Identification and posttraumatic stress disorder symptoms in rescue workers in the Marmara, Turkey, earthquake," *Journal of Traumatic Stress, 18*(5), pp. 485–489. Available at: https://doi.org/10.1002/jts.20056.

Grawitch, M.J., Ballard, D.W. and Erb, K.R. (2015) "To be or not to be (stressed): the critical role of a psychologically healthy workplace in effective stress management," *Stress and Health, 31*(4), pp. 264–273. Available at: https://doi.org/10.1002/smi.2619.

Hensel, J.M. et al. (2015) "Meta-analysis of risk factors for secondary traumatic stress in therapeutic work with trauma victims," *Journal of Traumatic Stress, 28*(2), pp. 83–91. Available at: https://doi.org/10.1002/jts.21998.

Luft, J. and Ingham, H. (1955) "The Johari window: a graphic model of interpersonal awareness," in *Proceedings of the Western Training Laboratory in Group Development*. Los Angeles, CA: UCLA Extension Office.

Rabenu, E., Yaniv, E. and Elizur, D. (2017) "The relationship between psychological capital, coping with stress, well-being, and performance," *Current Psychology, 36*(4), pp. 875–887. Available at: https://doi.org/10.1007/s12144-016-9477-4.

15

The TIC Model and the Powerlessness – Power Pendulum

Feelings of powerlessness are a pivotal issue in mentally high-risk work—and arguably the most critical. Yet it is often one of the most difficult emotions for helping professionals to manage.

Powerlessness is difficult to face—especially for those used to taking action in critical situations. However, if the powerlessness inherent in some situations is not acknowledged, you risk exhausting yourself in futile attempts to fix what cannot be fixed. Worse still, you may end up withdrawing—out of guilt or shame—leaving the person alone in their pain.

'Just Being' with the Other Person

As a helping professional, you must learn to accept that your work will place you in situations where your efforts may feel ineffective. Paradoxically, it is often through accepting this powerlessness that the opportunity to make a genuine difference emerges.

This is sometimes described as *just being* with the person—not doing something *for* them. The word *just* is misleading, as if this task were easy. In reality, nothing could be more demanding. Being present with someone in a devastating or absurd situation—one that you cannot change—requires considerable mental strength and energy.

Professionals regularly witness traumatic events, terminal illness, chronic injury, loneliness, or the loss of a loved one. Some face situations that painfully reflect their own lives: a paramedic or priest may find themselves responding to the very road accident that took a loved one's life. A doctor may receive the same diagnosis they once delivered to a patient. A psychiatric nurse may care for someone suffering in the same way as their own child. Each situation reminds the carer of their own mortality and personal vulnerability (see Chapter 14 for more on subjective vulnerability).

On a psychological level, 'just being' during moments of powerlessness takes immense courage—and a willingness to confront one's own limits and fragility. There is nothing 'just' about it—it demands presence, courage, and deep mental strength.

Instead of simply being present, many professionals understandably reach for words like, 'At least it's good that ...' or 'Well, you still have your ...'. But these well-meaning comments often offer little comfort—and may even cause the person to feel invalidated or alone.

> We often say to each other, 'I can't stand this.' But maybe what we really mean is, 'I can't stand just standing there, powerless.' Because a lot of the time, it's the powerlessness we can't bear. It takes a huge amount of mental energy to really be present with someone who's deeply unhappy. You just can't do that for forty hours a week.

Helping means embracing both the vulnerability of powerlessness and the strength of taking grounded professional action (see section *The Powerlessness–Power Pendulum* for more on this balance).

The TIC Model

The TIC model stands for *Terms*, *Influence*, and *Control*, and is inspired by the work of American author Stephen Covey (Covey and Covey, 2020). It is a framework for determining where to place your mental focus—and what to consciously keep out.

Model 8: The TIC Model

The model consists of three concentric circles:

- **The innermost circle** represents what you have **control** over—things you can decide for yourself without needing approval. This could include how you organise your day, your work methods, your attire, your vote, or your personal opinions.

The TIC model

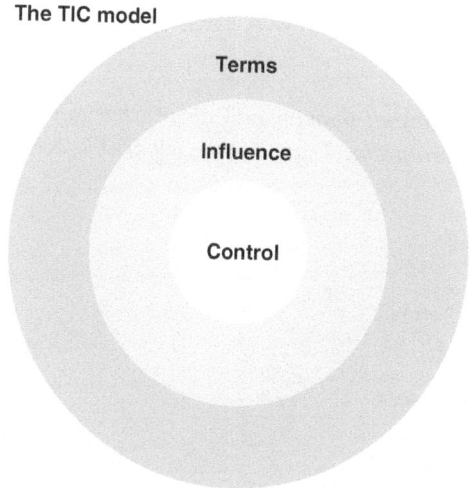

Terms

Influence

Control

- **The middle circle** encompasses what you have **influence** over—areas you can help shape alongside others. This includes professional methods, task prioritisation, teamwork, and organisational strategies.
- **The outer circle** represents the **terms and conditions** you must work under—factors you have little or no control over, such as legislation, policy changes, chronic illness, or budget constraints. This circle also includes existential conditions: that we are born and die alone, that we must continually make choices, and that we must create meaning in a world without an inherent one.

As a general rule, try to focus 80% of your energy on what you can influence or control, and no more than 20% on what you cannot. This fosters resilience and prevents burnout.

The Roman Emperor Marcus Aurelius (121–180 AD) is often quoted:

> *Give me the serenity to accept the things I cannot change, the courage to change the things I can, and the wisdom to know the difference. (Aurelius, 2002)*

As a helping professional, you might adapt the last line:

> *… and the wisdom and professionalism to know the difference.*

Organisational reforms, new regulations, and external pressures are ongoing—and require professionals to continuously assess what can realistically be changed—and what cannot. Sustainable work requires a shared understanding of when *good is good enough*.

> *When I'm under pressure, I catch myself thinking only about what can't be done anymore. And if no one interrupts me, I can't stop myself. It's like being stuck in quicksand.*

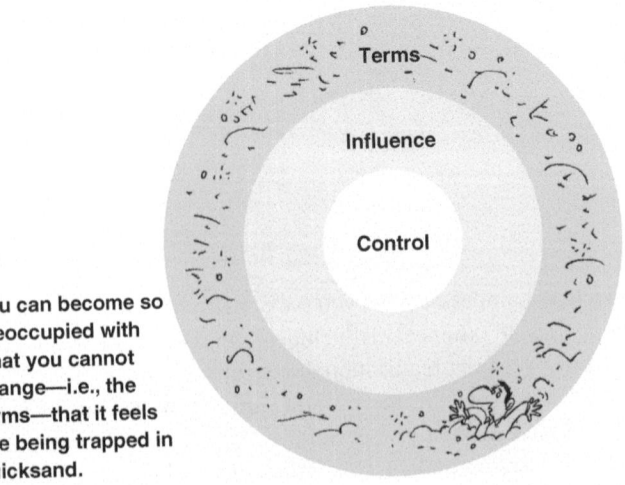

You can become so preoccupied with what you cannot change—i.e., the terms—that it feels like being trapped in quicksand.

To avoid this mental trap, the relationship between powerlessness and power must remain dynamic and fluid—like a pendulum.

The Powerlessness–Power Pendulum

Inspired by the grief researchers Margaret Stroebe and Henk Schut, the **powerlessness–power pendulum** draws from their two-track model of grief (Stroebe and Schut, 1999). According to their model, healthy grieving requires oscillation—shifting between confronting the loss and stepping back from it. Grief is exhausting, and people need breaks from the pain to continue functioning.

The same principle applies to helping professionals: they, too, must oscillate—between being *powerless* and *powerful*.

Model 9: The Powerlessness–Power Pendulum

The powerlessness–power pendulum © *Rikke Høgsted*

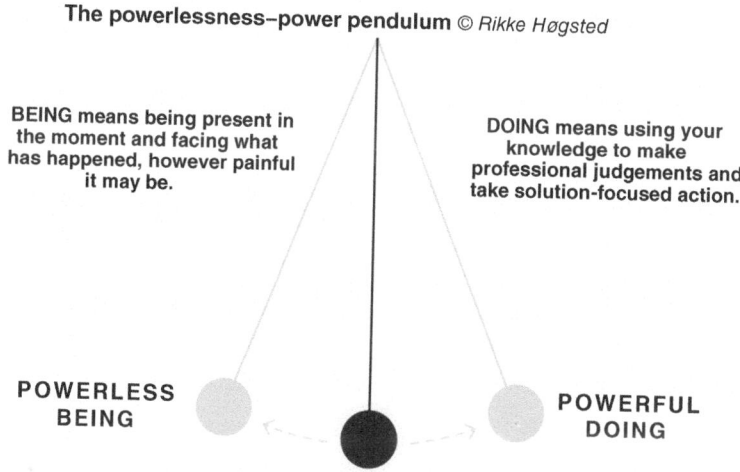

BEING means being present in the moment and facing what has happened, however painful it may be.

DOING means using your knowledge to make professional judgements and take solution-focused action.

POWERLESS BEING

POWERFUL DOING

Being can take many subtle but profound forms: it might involve silently holding the other person without speaking, listening attentively without offering analysis or solutions, or simply sitting beside them in stillness, sharing breath, and presence. It means tuning into the emotional atmosphere in the room and bearing witness to it without trying to change it. Being is not passive—it's an intentional and deeply respectful form of presence. It resembles the way we might experience nature: acknowledging the weather as it is, without trying to control it. As someone once put it, 'True consolation lies in realising that there is no consolation'.

Acting, by contrast, involves steps taken to offer structure, direction, or relief. It may include initiating a treatment, offering guidance, suggesting a small ritual, or even just standing up and getting the other person a glass of water. The aim of acting is to be solution-focused and to help create a sense of orientation for the individual or group, particularly when their ability to think clearly has been disrupted by trauma, loss, or chaos.

While these two approaches—*being* and *acting*—may appear distinct, they often overlap. In truth, being often contains an element of doing, and vice versa. They are two sides of the same coin. Yet in the moment, they can feel quite different, both for the one offering support and for the one receiving it.

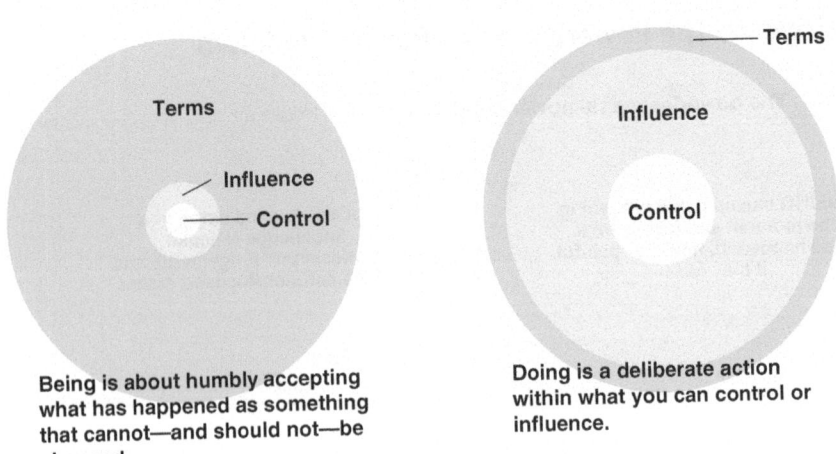

Being is about humbly accepting what has happened as something that cannot—and should not—be changed.

Doing is a deliberate action within what you can control or influence.

I think it's both incredibly hard and incredibly meaningful to step into someone else's pitch-black darkness. The first few times I let go of any sense of control and went into that darkness, I had no idea what would happen. But then something strange happened - I started to see.

It's hard to explain, but Elvis Costello puts it well in his song 'I Want You', where he sings,

'The truth can't hurt you, it's just like the dark. It scares you witless, but with time you see things clear and stark.'

Being there together - two people in the darkness - made it possible to start seeing again. And slowly, little paths began to appear. They were faint, but we could start taking careful steps along them, towards a life that, after everything that had happened, had felt completely meaningless.

References

Aurelius, M. (2002) *Meditations: A New Translation.* Translated by G. Hays. Modern Library.

Covey, S.R. and Covey, S. (2020) *The 7 Habits of Highly Effective People.* 30th anniversary edition; unabridged. New York: Simon & Schuster Audio.

Stroebe, M. and Schut, H. (1999) "The dual process model of coping with bereavement: rationale and description," *Death Studies*, 23(3), pp. 197–224. Available at: https://doi.org/10.1080/074811899201046.

16

The Big WHY?

At the core of everything lies the individual's reflection on WHY they chose the mentally high-risk profession they did. This introspection brings forward the core values that shaped their decisions about education and career path.

The Big WHY may be grounded in values such as justice, presence, freedom, courage, patience, flexibility, compassion, responsibility, solidarity, or a sense of adventure. Each individual has their own reasons for the choices they've made. These reasons should be revisited regularly throughout one's professional life to ensure that the work continues to align with and retain meaning on a deeply personal and value-based level. Choosing a high-risk profession is often an act of purpose-driven work—a decision rooted in personal conviction and the desire to contribute to something larger than oneself.

Everyone was sitting in a huddle at the meeting, and then one of the older members of the group exclaimed: 'Boss, why don't you jump up on the beer crate and say something?' And then she—our manager—grabbed the moment and spoke without a single 'uhm' for ten minutes straight about why she had chosen our profession in the first place. Why—despite all the cutbacks and pointless documentation requirements—she was actually happy with her job and the opportunities it gave her to stand up for what she believed in. And that she hoped the rest of us would persevere because she thought we were the right people for the job. I still remember that impromptu speech. I think the others do too. It was a really powerful moment.

Meaning and Compassion Satisfaction

Mentally high-risk professions are often imbued with meaning. For helping professionals, the meaning is frequently tied to the experience of making a difference in someone's life—or in the world. This duality makes helping professionals both strong and vulnerable. You feel strong because meaning gives you resilience and determination. But your passion also exposes you to emotional risk.

Professionals may feel deeply self-critical if they believe they have failed or were unable to provide adequate help. Moral stress can emerge when what can be offered falls short—not because of a lack of effort, but because of limited options (see Chapter 10 on moral stress and moral injury). The flip side of professional pride is professional shame, and this can be particularly acute in roles where your actions directly impact another person's well-being—or even survival (Kanno and Giddings, 2017).

As noted earlier, empirical research shows that employees who feel successful in their work—who gain satisfaction from supporting others—are less likely to suffer mental tilting, even when working under very challenging conditions (Yates and Samuel, 2019). This protective effect is known as *compassion satisfaction*. It raises an important question: what enables professionals, despite confronting tragedy and despair, to derive a sense of achievement from their efforts, even when the visible outcomes are small? One answer lies in a sustained sense of meaning in work—a belief that each action, no matter how small, contributes to something that matters.

This is an essential question for helping professionals to reflect on—individually, and with peers, supervisors, mentors, or coaches. The questions included in the 'Professional Quality of Life Scale' in Appendix 2 (see page 203) may serve as a useful starting point for such reflections.

Personal Experiences

For many professionals in mentally high-risk jobs, personal experience played a role in their career choice. Some may have admired a relative or mentor who worked as a paramedic, social worker, or lawyer. For others, the choice was part of a family tradition—as is often the case amongst doctors—though we no longer 'inherit' our parents' professions as directly as we once did.

Some are motivated by more personal experiences: living through an eating disorder, losing a parent at a young age, or growing up in an environment marked by addiction or violence. Perhaps a teacher, police officer, or therapist once helped them in a meaningful way. Or perhaps no one did—and their career choice reflects a determination to offer others the help they never received.

Professionals with personal experience may contribute valuable insights and empathy, as dual 'experts'—both professional and personal. While no one can fully understand another person's pain, or 'walk in their shoes', some may have a heightened awareness of what the path feels like.

Surprisingly, even in a time when patient- and service-user perspectives are increasingly valued, we often overlook the wealth of lived experience already present within the workforce. While some prefer to keep their stories private, others find that sharing them brings meaning—transforming personal struggles into strengths. Speaking from the perspective of a 'survivor' rather than a 'victim' can also be empowering.

However, personal experience can heighten emotional vulnerability. A professional may over-involve, driven by a subconscious desire to rescue, or under-involve to protect themselves from painful reminders. Unprocessed trauma presents a dual risk: that the person being helped does not receive optimal care, and that the professional suffers secondary trauma (La Mott and Martin, 2019; Massey et al., 2019).

> *I'd been working as a doctor with seriously ill and dying patients for years before it hit me that I was using all my energy to ease their pain so I wouldn't have to feel my own.*

By contrast, a lack of personal experience in the field can have different effects. On one hand, it may narrow a professional's perspective and reduce their sensitivity. On the other, it can enhance psychological resilience, allowing them to confront another person's pain without risking the activation of their own (Richardson, 2017).

The Professional WHY and the Personal WHY

Alongside the professional WHY, there is often a private or personal WHY. This concerns the values that guide a person in life—the beliefs they pass on to their children and apply in everyday decisions. These values are often shaped early in life and are sometimes referred to as core values.

Asking 'Why do I stay alive?' might feel too abstract or intense to answer. A better prompt might be: 'If I were seriously ill, why would I want to recover?' The answers to this often reflect love and responsibility for particular people, cherished places or activities, and a desire for more life.

> *Whenever I'm travelling, I meet other Westerners who just live and breathe their jobs. They don't really have a personal life anymore—it's all work.*

And when work goes wrong, everything goes wrong. That's when their tone hardens, they start drinking, and they take stupid risks. My job is dangerous, but I'm always careful because I've got a family at home—that's what I live for. I love my job, but at the end of the day, it's just a job.

It is important to stay connected to your personal WHY and to ensure your work doesn't take over or crowd out the rest of your life. When work becomes the sole focus, you risk losing balance—and becoming emotionally fragile in the face of setbacks or job loss. That's true whether you're a front-line worker, a manager, or a CEO.

Closely linked to meaning is hope. We hope that patients will recover, that our writing or actions will raise awareness, that traumatised people will heal, that help will arrive in time, and that wise decisions will be made to protect our planet. In this way, risk is intrinsically connected to meaning, and meaning is deeply intertwined with hope.

Hope

Every risk carries with it a possibility of harm—and thus, an uncertainty about outcomes. The opposite of risk is *certainty*—a term frequently discussed in prevention and safety plans. But certainty is a misnomer; no plan can ever guarantee success. With our professional choices, we can only strive to bring about desired outcomes or work to prevent undesired ones.

A risk reduced to zero is no longer a risk. Therefore, working with risk also means hoping.

Hope exists in many forms—from an abstract hope that your efforts will have a broader or even global impact to a concrete, intimate hope that your next patient, client, or service user will find your intervention helpful. Focusing on the immediate and tangible can be a powerful strength, grounded in the belief that the task at hand has meaning. And that the next one will too. And the one after that—forming a purposeful chain, like a string of pearls.

I always keep in mind that I can't and shouldn't fix the world. Small victories, you know ...

Another way to embrace hope is to imagine that your professional choices will lead to a meaningful outcome. Let yourself feel the joy of that imagined future—and allow it to illuminate the present moment. Former Czech writer and president Václav Havel described hope not as a 'state of the world', but as a 'state of the spirit'. He wrote: 'Hope is not prognostication. It is an orientation of the spirit, an orientation of the heart. It transcends the world that is immediately experienced and is anchored somewhere beyond its horizons'. (Havel, 1989)

Hope is, at its core, a steadfast belief that something holds meaning—regardless of the outcome (Franke, Felfe and Pundt, 2014).

The hardest part was sending a group out on a mission into an area where you had no idea who was friendly and who meant you harm. The enemy doesn't wear a uniform. Then there's the waiting—knowing it'll be three days before they're back, and all you can do is hope they all make it home. A plan based on hope is always frustrating and risky. But sometimes, it's the only plan—and the best one you've got.

Hope based on an either/or scenario—such as a military commander's natural hope that everyone returns safely to camp—involves profound vulnerability. There is a real risk that what you hope for may not happen. This kind of hope demands considerable mental strength and courage.

All forms of risk-related work—whether physical or mental—require courage and the ability to take calculated risks grounded in professional judgement; the alternative is recklessness. Unfortunately, whether someone in a high-risk role is seen as brave or foolhardy often depends on the outcome. If things end well, they're called brave; if not, they're labelled reckless.

Luck—both good and bad—plays a crucial role in these situations, and professionals must learn to live with that uncertainty. One way of doing so is to find clear, meaningful answers to the question of why you chose your profession and your role.

IGLO-E

If you have found your answer to the *why*—the reasons you chose to work in a mentally high-risk profession—the following chapters will offer suggestions on *how* you can manage it.

These chapters are structured around the IGLO-E model, which stands for *Individual, Group, Leadership,* and *Organisation*. The *E* represents *Educational institutions,* which bear the initial responsibility of preparing future professionals by raising awareness about the potential psychological risks of their chosen field—and by introducing strategies for building resilience and preventing traumatisation.

Model 10: The IGLO-E Model

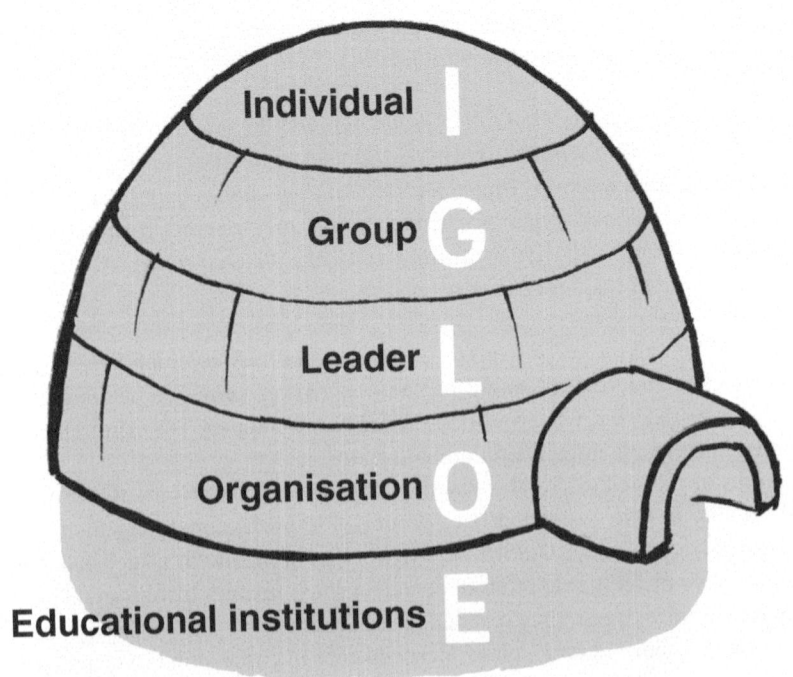

The model emphasises that preventing mental imbalance and creating well-being in the workplace is a shared task.

References

Franke, F., Felfe, J. and Pundt, A. (2014) "The impact of health-oriented leadership on follower health: development and test of a new instrument measuring health-promoting leadership," *German Journal of Human Resource Management: Zeitschrift für Personalforschung, 28*(1–2), pp. 139–161. Available at: https://doi.org/10.1177/239700221402800108.

Havel, V. (1989) *Or Living in Truth: Twenty-two Essays*. Translated by Paul Wilson. Faber & Faber.

Kanno, H. and Giddings, M.M. (2017) "Hidden trauma victims: understanding and preventing traumatic stress in mental health professionals," *Social Work in Mental Health, 15*(3), pp. 331–353. Available at: https://doi.org/10.1080/15332985.2016.1220442.

La Mott, J. and Martin, L.A. (2019) "Adverse childhood experiences, self-care, and compassion outcomes in mental health providers working with trauma," *Journal of Clinical Psychology, 75*(6), pp. 1066–1083. Available at: https://doi.org/10.1002/jclp.22752.

Massey, K. et al. (2019) "Staff experiences of working in a Sexual Assault Referral Centre: the impacts and emotional tolls of working with traumatised people," *The Journal of Forensic Psychiatry & Psychology, 30*(4), pp. 686–705. Available at: https://doi.org/10.1080/14789949.2019.1605615.

Richardson, K.M. (2017) "Managing employee stress and wellness in the new millennium," *Journal of Occupational Health Psychology, 22*(3), pp. 423–428. Available at: https://doi.org/10.1037/ocp0000066.

Yates, M. and Samuel, V. (2019) "Burnout in oncologists and associated factors: a systematic literature review and meta-analysis," *European Journal of Cancer Care, 28*(3), p. e13094. Available at: https://doi.org/10.1111/ecc.13094.

17

Educational Institutions, Organisations, and Leaders: Roles and Responsibilities

There are two essential points that everyone in the organisation must understand in order to support a sustainable workplace:

- If trauma exposure is not handled professionally, it can lead to mental tilting and increase the risk of strain and psychological disorders.
- Trauma exposure can affect *everyone* in the organisation—employees, managers, and even the organisational culture—which in turn can impair the group's collective ability to think clearly and act professionally.

Here's the manager who didn't understand their role and responsibilities.

Building resilience and preventing traumatisation must be prioritised at all levels—it's a team effort where everyone contributes. While the overall responsibility lies with the organisation and management, it all starts with the educational institutions responsible for preparing future generations of professionals for mentally high-risk jobs. This chapter discusses the roles and responsibilities of educational institutions, organisations, and leaders.

Educational Institutions: Roles and Responsibilities

There are several reasons why students training for a mentally high-risk profession should be introduced to strain psychology early in their studies.

One obvious reason is to give students a real chance to reflect on whether this is the right path for them. When informed of the psychological risks, some may decide they are not comfortable with the emotional demands associated with becoming, for example, a doctor, priest, police officer, prison guard, midwife, soldier, social worker, or journalist.

Another key reason is to support the professional and emotional maturation of students: to help them learn, from the outset, what it means to take responsibility for the people they are preparing to help—and how to care for colleagues, peers, and themselves along the way. By addressing these topics early, students gain the chance to test coping strategies, build psychological insight, and develop a sustainable mindset for their future work.

> *One of the experienced teachers in medical school talked about it every year and said, 'You're five years away from being responsible for losing a patient. Now you're four years away... Now three years...'. It was actually comforting—it helped us gradually come to terms with the fact that it might happen.*

Importantly, many students are already exposed to potentially traumatic situations during internships or student jobs—whether in healthcare, social services, or the media.

> *During Utøya, everyone in the editorial office was on holiday, so only the young people were left at the screens, watching the images pour in—completely unedited. As a war photographer, I've chosen to confront horror through a camera lens. But in the newsroom, they receive it unfiltered, with no preparation. It can be deeply disturbing.*

To better prepare students and reduce the risk of dropout or psychological injury, educational institutions can take proactive steps such as:

- **Including core teaching on strain psychology** as part of the curriculum for students in emotionally demanding professions.
- **Making participation in study or reflection groups mandatory**, to help students build peer support and habits of collaborative meaning-making.

- **Facilitating structured group conversations before, during, and after internships**, allowing students to share and process emotionally demanding experiences.
- **Designing bridging roles** between educational institutions and workplaces, to support smoother transitions and ensure that students are not left unsupported in high-stress environments.

From Preparation to Practice

While educational institutions lay the groundwork for sustainable working lives, the responsibility for mental well-being deepens once graduates step into the workplace. Research highlights the importance of *Psychosocial Safety Climate (PSC)*—the shared beliefs about how seriously psychological health and safety are prioritised in leadership, policies, and everyday practice. A strong PSC is linked to lower stress levels, higher employee engagement, and reduced risk of burnout in high-strain professions (Dollard, Dormann and Awang Idris, 2019).

The following section outlines how organisations can translate these principles into concrete responsibilities and actions that protect staff and foster a culture of professionalism and care.

Organisations: Roles and Responsibilities

A mentally sustainable organisation makes a commitment to its users to deliver work on a high professional level. They are also committed to preventing employees from being harmed by their work. While some organisations have thousands of employees across many countries, others are quite small. Regardless of the size of the organisation, each employee typically has one boss and a group of close colleagues with whom they collaborate. Organisations are responsible for the people they employ. Indeed, the organisation has legal responsibility to ensure that there is an up-to-date and well-implemented HR policy in place covering the four areas in the previously discussed strain square. This policy should include preventive practices to avoid injuries as well as procedures for accessing help if an injury occurs. This policy should also enable each leader to manage and distribute work in a sustainable way (Ashley-Binge and Cousins, 2020).

New Hires

When hiring, it is the organisation's responsibility to ensure that each applicant is informed about the psychological risks associated with the position. Applicants should also be made aware that the workplace has a coordinated approach in place to prevent trauma exposure from leading to mental injury or impaired judgement. It can also be helpful to encourage applicants to discuss these aspects with their personal network, supporting them in making a well-considered decision before accepting the role.

Building Your *Kintsugi* Team

The Japanese term *kintsugi* refers to a technique of using powdered gold, silver, or platinum to repair broken ceramics and porcelain. The purpose of this technique is not to hide the damage, but rather to create an aesthetic testimony to the history of the repaired object. *Kintsugi* is part of an over 500-year-old philosophical tradition, *Wabi sabi*, which can be loosely translated as 'finding the beauty in broken or old things'. This philosophy emphasises that life is not about the flawless and perfect, but about the genuine. Life is perfect in its imperfection.

Working in a mentally high-risk job for a long period of time may leave lasting marks—emotional and mental—on almost everyone and some also suffer

(Continued)

(Continued)

mental injury in the form of PTSD. What if organisations take inspiration from *kintsugi* and explore how to 'repair' PTSD with gold or silver?

Many professionals who have taken sick leave due to work-related stress later share how their breakdowns have provided them with valuable lessons: the ability to prioritise, gratitude for bosses' and colleagues' understanding, and awareness about warning signs from the body and the mind.

> *These days, I see myself as a canary in the mine—someone who senses when the air is running out before others do, and can raise the alarm when it's time to let some fresh air in.*

Many argue that the era of prestige tied to filling a home with eight identical designer chairs is behind us. Today, the focus has shifted towards authenticity, diversity, sustainability, and an appreciation for quality materials and craftsmanship with a story. Designers in the Nordic region often emphasise the tradition of highlighting raw materials, celebrating their natural beauty and imperfections. In this light, it is worth considering whether your team should metaphorically resemble eight pristine, matching designer chairs—or a collection of diverse chairs of varying ages and styles, each with its own unique character, even if a few show signs of wear.

Role Models

As role models, senior management have a significant influence on the organisation's culture. This influence extends across many areas—from something as simple as having lunch in the canteen, sending a signal that, despite a busy schedule, all employees should take time to pause and eat, to the way they speak about customers or business partners, patients, or service users.

Senior leaders carry both the responsibility and the privilege of shaping the tone and atmosphere at work to reflect the values they wish to define the organisation. They also play a crucial role in addressing unwanted or unhelpful behaviour within teams (see Chapter 8 for warning signs of mental tilting in teams and work groups).

As outlined elsewhere in this book, leaders operate under considerable pressure, being accountable for both the quality of the work and the well-being of employees. In mentally high-risk environments, leadership teams rely on a balanced and attuned senior leader—someone capable of restoring calm and clarity in a kind, caring, and effective manner. For this reason, it is essential that senior leaders themselves can thrive and maintain a healthy balance between over-involvement and under-involvement.

Responsibility for Your Own and Other Managers' Well-being

If you are a senior manager, you are responsible for the well-being of the entire organisation (Franke, Felfe and Pundt, 2014)—and that responsibility begins with yourself. If a senior manager is unhappy over an extended period, this can easily affect the well-being of the entire management team, which in turn impacts employees throughout the organisation. For this reason, it is essential that senior managers remain in good contact with themselves and quickly recognise any personal signs of unhappiness or mental tilting (White, 2006).

In day-to-day operations, senior management is, to some extent, better positioned to maintain balance than many others in the organisation. They are typically less exposed to the direct emotional strain of interacting with crisis-stricken or traumatised patients, clients, inmates, or service users. However, this distance can also pose a challenge: without regular contact with those at the frontline, it becomes more difficult to remain attuned to the emotional pressures faced by managers and staff. As a result, senior management may be perceived—fairly or unfairly—as thick-skinned or dismissive of concerns related to psychological safety and employee well-being. This is an important dynamic to keep in mind.

Referring to the Red–Green–Blue model discussed in Chapter 9, an employee once observed:

> *We're always met with blue from above, and then we just turn red. And that's a real shame, because people are much more open to what we're saying when we're able to speak from the green area.*

Although senior managers may not stand in the trauma-filled environments of an accident scene, a prison corridor, or a crisis-ridden newsroom, they face intense pressure from other sources: financial performance, political expectations, board demands, or directives from regional leadership. In the worst-case scenario, such pressures may threaten the organisation's very survival, putting jobs and livelihoods at risk. These demands can significantly challenge a leader's psychological balance.

Unlike many employees, who can turn to peers for informal support, senior managers often carry sensitive information that cannot be shared internally. This can be a deeply isolating experience (Bonnerup and Hasselager, 2019). Still, it comes with the territory—and underscores the importance of identifying one or more trusted sparring partners. These individuals can offer valuable perspective, honest feedback, and help ensure that your decisions remain balanced and sustainable.

When a manager senses that their superior does not prioritise well-being, they may assume that both their own and their team's well-being must be managed alone. Over time, this perception can contribute to a broader devaluation of well-being, placing it lower on the organisational agenda. Without meaningful dialogue, the manager may begin to adopt the myth of the all-powerful leader—leading to feelings of inadequacy or powerlessness, which often express themselves in unbalanced behaviour, including over-involvement:

> *By the end, I had given my private phone number to almost half of the employees in the team and told them that they could call 24/7 if they just needed to talk ...*

Or, conversely, under-involvement:

> *I sometimes feel the impulse to kick my employees in the arse and tell them to get their act together. It's probably my most important personal warning sign.*

These dynamics highlight the importance of prioritising manager's mental health—not just for the leader's sake, but for the overall psychological health of the organisation.

Physical Security

In workplaces where there is a risk of threats and violence, organisations must also address physical safety through careful attention to layout, escape routes, and alarm systems. It should be easy for employees to call for help and to exit the workplace quickly if needed. In some settings, it may be appropriate to provide physical shielding between employees and service users—for example, through the use of counters or shatterproof glass. Particular care should also be taken when employees work alone or carry out tasks in private homes, as these situations can present additional vulnerabilities.

Contingency Plans for Emergency Situations

All organisations can be affected by an acute crisis and should have a contingency plan in place. Such situations require clear and decisive leadership. The contingency plan should be activated in the event of a violent incident in the workplace, but it may also be relevant when a serious event occurs outside of work. After all, how can employees be expected to engage with service users or remain professional at the front desk if they have just learned that a group of colleagues has been involved in an accident or a terrorist attack?

Effective crisis management not only strengthens the organisation internally—by fostering a sense of unity and enhancing team cohesion—but also externally, by enabling clear communication about how the situation was handled. Ultimately, a crisis offers an opportunity for management to demonstrate calm, competence, and a genuine commitment to supporting their employees.

It is equally important for managers to remain self-aware during a crisis. Those deeply involved in managing the situation may initially believe that focusing on responsibilities and tasks will protect them from being personally affected. However, this can lead to underestimating their own vulnerability and overestimating their resilience—potentially resulting in intense emotional reactions later on.

> *I once worked on a job where, after days of huge pressure, the senior manager had a complete breakdown. He was so focused on looking after everyone else that he missed all his own warning signs and just went straight through a red light.*

Terms and Conditions of Employment

Policies around working time—such as reduced hours, leave of absence (including unpaid leave), or senior work arrangements—are part of the organisation's responsibility. Adjusting working time can be one way to regulate an employee's exposure to psychological strain, and temporary leave may offer the necessary distance from work, whether for a short or extended period.

However, adjustments to individual hours should not stand alone. In many cases, strain can be reduced not by stepping away from work, but by reconfiguring how the work is done. This might include redistributing tasks, offering flexible scheduling, or introducing job-swop arrangements—temporary role or responsibility exchanges between colleagues that help dilute exposure and bring new energy into established routines.

Such measures can help prevent overburdening any one individual, and also contribute to shared responsibility within teams. Practices and traditions vary widely across organisations, and it can be helpful to look to other workplaces for inspiration when developing or updating these kinds of supportive structures.

Systematic Learning and Development

Ultimately, it is the organisation's responsibility to foster a learning culture—both in general, and especially when it comes to the inevitable mistakes that employees will make from time to time. The focus must be on organisational responsibility: what the whole organisation—and perhaps even the wider field—can learn from an incident, rather than placing attention solely on the individual.

Such learning depends on a foundation of psychological safety—a climate where employees feel safe to speak up, share doubts, and reflect openly on what went wrong (see also Chapter 13 on psychological safety).

In the Armed Forces, we used to talk about 'Lessons Identified' and 'Lessons Learned.' These were established terms, long before I joined. That was comforting to me. It meant... well, generations before me hadn't always handled things perfectly either. It was a strong signal—not just that we can improve, but that we have a professional obligation to do so.

Creating a learning culture is not just a matter of professional development—it also plays a crucial role in safeguarding the emotional and ethical well-being of staff. How organisations respond to mistakes or difficult decisions can either build trust—or deepen distress.

If you single out the individual when something goes wrong, the rest of the team freezes. People become afraid to act. No one wants to end up on the front page of the tabloids just for doing their job.

Fostering a Learning Culture Also Means Acknowledging Moral Impact

Fostering a learning culture also means acknowledging the emotional and ethical impact that mistakes—or difficult decisions—can have on employees. When people feel blamed or isolated in the wake of an incident, the risk of moral injury increases. This makes it essential for organisations to approach such situations with care, clarity, and a shared sense of responsibility.

Preventing Moral Injury: The Role of Educations and Organisations

Organisations and educational institutions cannot prevent every injury. But they can shape cultures where ethical dilemmas are acknowledged, explored, and held with care. Professional practice is unavoidably moral: ideals and realities will inevitably clash, creating normative tensions that need to be recognised and discussed rather than solved once and for all (Brinkmann, 2011). To help prevent moral distress and moral injury, organisations and training programmes should:

- **Introduce the concept of moral injury early**—not just in crisis, but during onboarding and training. Make room for conversations about ethical grey zones and moral conflict as a normal part of the work.
- **Recognise the pressure of 'two-evils' choices**—and, where possible, make transparent the organisation's ethical priorities during particularly strained periods.
- **Normalise ethical reflection**: Create regular space for shared sense-making, even outside of acute crises.

- **Respond to moral distress and injury as a shared challenge—not a private problem**: The experience may belong to the individual, but the responsibility for meaning, care, and repair is collective.
- **Foster contextual thinking**: Instead of jumping to blame, help staff explore who actually had influence over what (see also Chapter 15 on the TIC model).
- **Meet moral pain with listening, not defensiveness**: The most important early response is not explanation—but presence.
- **Understand that trauma-focused interventions may fall short**: Traditional PTSD models often miss the deep feelings of guilt and the existential dimensions of moral injury, which may lead to poor outcomes. In these cases, support should not focus on 'acting' or 'fixing' but rather on 'being' and **bearing witness**—being with the person in their powerlessness, and gently reconnecting them to meaning, forgiveness, and belonging. A concrete example of such a measure is the *Fisherman's bench*, discussed in Chapter 18.
- **Sometimes, the most helpful thing to say is simply**: *That was not fair. You did your best. You are not alone.*

Managers: Roles and Responsibilities

Being a manager in a mentally high-risk workplace is often a delicate balancing act. When the daily work involves trauma, death, suffering, violence, neglect, or threats, there is a need for clear leadership—anchored in compassion and the ability to set priorities amid tragedy and complexity (Richardson, 2017). At the same time, employees need room to process the intense impressions their work brings.

Whether in hospital wards, emergency scenes, offices, or people's homes, helping professionals carry substantial responsibility for the well-being of others. They make themselves available, using their empathy to build trust—trust that forms the basis for sound professional judgement and effective action. To offer that trust to others, they must also feel trusted themselves.

The challenge is to offer clear structure while also meeting staff with autonomy and confidence in their judgement. While this may feel like a paradox, it is, in many ways, what good leadership is all about (Newton and Maierhofer, 2005).

Even though I've been a manager for years, it's still hard. If I try to help by stepping in and helping someone prioritise, I'm often told I should back off and trust they've got it. But if I pull back too much, I'm told I've left them alone with everything—and that really gets to me. One employee had a serious stress-related breakdown before any of us even noticed.

Recruitment

Hiring the right person for the job is always important—but in mentally high-risk work, it becomes essential. A mismatch between the role's demands and the employee's skills or experience may not only impair service quality; it may also increase the risk of psychological strain or mental overload.

These roles often require more than just technical and interpersonal skills; they also call for cultural competence. This is particularly relevant when working across cultural boundaries—either abroad or with people from different backgrounds at home.

It's hard as a manager to predict how an applicant will respond in a crisis, even if their CV is excellent. I once had to send an employee back home quickly. He had done well in a demanding job in Denmark, but he was completely unable to read the social cues in the foreign culture.

Trauma Training and Supervision

Once the right person is hired, managers are responsible for ensuring they receive a basic understanding of strain psychology. New employees should learn what affects helping professionals (Part I of this book), how people typically react (Part II), and what can be done to prevent harm (Part III).

This basic knowledge should be combined with an introduction to the organisation's own preventive practices—so that employees know exactly what is expected of them, both in terms of protecting themselves and supporting their colleagues.

Managers are also responsible for ensuring that staff regularly receive supervision or other forms of professional guidance, including structured space for reflection on the mental and emotional strains inherent in the work (Sprang, Craig and Clark, 2011; McFadden, Campbell and Taylor, 2015).

Meeting Strain with Professionalism

Working in a mentally high-risk job requires strong social skills. Keep in mind that a colleague under pressure may behave in ways that are difficult to interpret—but such reactions are best met with professionalism and care:

- A sceptical, critical, angry, or unreasonable person needs to be met by someone who doesn't take it personally.

- Someone who appears insecure or distrustful needs calm, credible guidance.
- Rigid thinking calls for patience and persistence.
- A person who struggles to listen needs clear, concise communication.
- A quiet or withdrawn colleague needs proactive support.
- Someone who is anxious or helpless needs care—and sometimes, someone who can temporarily take over responsibility.

Clarity About the Task and Defined Roles and Frameworks

A clear understanding of the task at hand, combined with well-defined roles within a work group, is one of the most effective preventive measures a manager can implement. When responsibilities, decision-making authority, and operational frameworks are explicitly stated, both individual employees and the team are better equipped to develop effective work plans and maintain realistic expectations (O'Connor, Muller Neff and Pitman, 2018).

Having this kind of clarity, along with shared expectations between managers and colleagues, significantly increases the likelihood of job satisfaction—an important protective factor.

It is the manager's responsibility to continuously foster this clarity, ensuring that each team member knows their role and shares an understanding of what constitutes a job well done. See also *The Principle of Honesty* on page 155 for more on groupthink and shared professional awareness.

Professional Language Use

Frequent exposure to mental strain at work—particularly when it leads to over- or under-involvement—can influence the way language is used. In fact, language is often where early signs of psychological tilting become apparent. Over-involvement may reveal itself through an anxious or irritable tone, dramatic or overly affectionate phrases, or frequent use of overly personal or over-familiar language. Conversely, under-involvement can be reflected in a detached or overly measured tone, judgemental remarks, or excessively formal language. When such imbalances persist over time—sometimes even across generations—language may become harsh, cynical, or stripped of nuance. Mental tilting can also be expressed through slang or jargon that distances professionals from the people they assist.

It is the manager's responsibility to ensure that the group uses professional language—language that is friendly and respectful, objective and solution-oriented. As a rule of thumb, professional communication ensures that any patient, client, or service user feels seen, heard, understood, and respected—even if they do not fully understand the technical terms used.

Often, organisations, teams, or individuals are unaware of their own language habits. Verbal and non-verbal expressions form part of the organisation's blind spot—behaviours that go unchallenged simply because 'that's what we usually call it'. However, inappropriate language is often quickly picked up—and potentially found offensive—by those outside the group, organisation, or profession.

When offering feedback on behaviour that falls within someone's blind spot, it is essential to use professional, respectful language. This helps ensure the message is received constructively, without the person feeling scolded or judged.

Professional Leadership and Development

Most employees in mentally high-risk jobs take pride in helping others and maintaining a high professional standard. They work hard to treat trauma, put out fires, report critical stories, maintain calm and safety in prisons, or bring children into the world. Yet, they do not always succeed—and when things go wrong, it is vital that they have a clear professional understanding of what happened. This is where subject-matter leadership becomes a crucial part of a manager's responsibility.

If the manager does not have a relevant professional background, it must be clearly defined who the subject-matter expert is—someone employees can turn to when they have questions or professional uncertainties. A helping professional who has lost their balance and has begun to over- or under-involve needs skilled professional guidance to refocus on the core task and regain their professional composure.

The manager is also responsible for ensuring that employees consistently have the right competencies, as well as access to ongoing development through peer training, courses, and further education.

Strategic Planning

Another responsibility of a manager is to allocate tasks in a way that makes the best possible use of the team's overall resources. The Job Demands–Resources (JD-R) framework (Demerouti et al., 2001; Bakker and Demerouti, 2017) offers a practical lens: high demands—time pressure, emotional load, role conflict—drain energy and raise burnout risk, whereas adequate resources—clear roles, autonomy, feedback, social support, and learning opportunities—fuel engagement and buffer strain. Task allocation is therefore not only about productivity; it is also an opportunity to rebalance demands and resources, so the team remains both effective and sustainable. The JD-R framework has since been extended to reflect this broader view of resources—from individual strengths to organisational structures.

How managers choose to fulfil this responsibility can vary across organisations. In some workplaces, helping professionals are accustomed to—and perhaps even comfortable with—the manager taking primary responsibility for task allocation. In others, there is a tradition of shared responsibility, where the team and manager jointly organise the work.

Regardless of the approach, six key principles should always be kept in mind, as they influence how deeply the work may affect you.

1. **The principle of teams**

   Being part of a well-functioning, supportive work group is one of the strongest protective factors when it comes to managing emotionally demanding tasks. For this reason, it is generally preferable to organise work in teams rather than assigning individuals to work alone (Ashley-Binge and Cousins, 2020).

2. **The principle that the hardest tasks belong to the team, by definition**

   The most difficult—say, 10%—of the tasks in a department should be regarded as a shared responsibility within the team. While one person may act as the gatekeeper or primary contact, the responsibility for fulfilling the task should rest with the team as a whole. It's *our* job—not *your* job.

   > *It's made a huge difference that we now help each other with the really difficult cases. Before, you could be unlucky enough to get several of them in a row, and then it was easy to feel like the worst social worker in the country.*

3. **The principle of variation**

   There is a risk of becoming professionally worn out if you are assigned the same type of task continuously, especially in high-strain roles. To help prevent this, it is important to create variation in tasks across the workday, workweek, and work year (Hensel et al., 2015).

   > *I always try to find tasks for the group that aren't too hard—for example, teaching assignments, participating in project groups, and things like that. We need something to dilute all the emotionally demanding tasks.*

4. **The principle of deliberate task sharing**

   By consciously sharing tasks, managers can help mitigate psychological strain on employees who may have specific vulnerabilities. These vulnerabilities may arise from past or present life experiences, personal identification, or familiarity with the individuals they are supporting. For further insight into subjective vulnerabilities, see Chapter 14.

   > *When I was pregnant and had just become a new mum, my manager made sure I didn't get the dying mums as clients.*

5. **The principle of spending the best part of your working hours on the hardest tasks**

As a human being, you are more vulnerable to strong impressions when you are tired or otherwise find it difficult to approach tasks with a professional and analytical mindset. It is therefore important to schedule the most demanding tasks at the time of day, week, or even year when you are at your freshest and have the most energy.

6. **The principle of deliberate transit**

The daily transition between personal and professional domains requires time and mental adjustment. An abrupt changeover can leave you especially vulnerable to the intense impressions encountered at work. This vulnerability is heightened when the workday or workweek begins or ends—whether intentionally or unexpectedly—with particularly challenging, critical, or otherwise demanding tasks.

All these principles apply not only to permanent staff, but also to those in temporary or external roles, who may face added vulnerabilities and require particular attention to ensure they are adequately supported.

Leadership Duties for Temporary and External Staff

Many professionals—such as substitutes, freelancers, volunteers, or external consultants—are asked to take on emotionally demanding work with little preparation and high responsibility. These temporary or peripheral roles are increasingly common and serve important purposes across healthcare, education, emergency services, and journalism.

Those working outside the core of an organisation may face uncertainty, limited access to support systems, and unclear responsibility for follow-up after difficult events. Emotional exposure without debriefing or feedback can leave individuals feeling isolated and unacknowledged. Even when professionals act responsibly and competently, the lack of psychological safety or organisational inclusion can lead to long-term emotional strain.

This issue is particularly acute when hiring substitutes. Temporary professionals—such as agency staff—often fall between two chairs. The regular employees may assume that the agency is responsible for supporting the substitute, while the agency assumes it is the hiring organisation's responsibility. Without clear agreements in place, no one takes ownership when something goes wrong. This creates a serious gap in protection—especially during or after critical incidents. In a time marked by labour shortages and growing demands for specialisation, organisations increasingly rely on short-term staffing rather than investing in upskilling permanent employees. This shift can leave temporary staff carrying significant responsibility without adequate support or follow-up.

Examples include a volunteer not being included in a team debrief, a freelance journalist returning from a conflict zone without follow-up, or a substitute teacher left out of the resolution of a crisis they helped manage.

Small, consistent actions—such as proper onboarding, access to debriefings, and inclusion in team practices—can make a significant difference. It is essential that the manager makes clear agreements with the temp agency from the onset, as to who holds responsibility for temporary staff in potentially critical situations. The manager should also ensure that psychological safety (see Chapter 13) is actively extended to all professionals, regardless of employment status. In doing so, the organisation helps prevent unnecessary strain and fosters a more resilient and inclusive workplace.

These elements are part of the organisation's broader staff support systems, which must actively include temporary and external professionals.

Creating psychological safety and a sustainable work environment for others is only possible when managers themselves feel secure and well-balanced. For this reason, responsibility for well-being in the workplace must begin with the manager's own state of mind and resilience.

Responsibility for Your Own and Your Employees' Well-being

As a manager, you may often become so preoccupied with your employees' well-being that you overlook your own. This is an unfortunate dynamic, as outlined in Part I: a manager's well-being can significantly affect both the team's performance and its overall health. For this reason, it is essential that you stay in close contact with yourself and speak up early if you begin to feel unhappy or unwell.

While dissatisfaction—your own or your team's—can stem from many external factors, the emotional demands of the job should always be taken seriously. Warning signs of strain may include loss of motivation, erosion of trust, dissatisfaction with leadership, difficulties in cooperation, or exhaustion. It is important to take the time to carefully investigate the underlying causes of dissatisfaction, so that any actions taken are appropriate and effective.

At my performance review, we talked about how I hadn't really had the spark I used to for years. My boss suggested a good—and fairly expensive—course, and I agreed to it. But it almost made things worse, because I didn't have the energy or motivation to commit to that either.

It wasn't until one day, when I was talking to a former colleague who bluntly told me I'd become a shadow of my former professional self, that it hit me: I'd developed a kind of work-related depression. I just didn't believe anymore that our smoking prevention work would actually make a difference.

References

Ashley-Binge, S. and Cousins, C. (2020) "Individual and organisational practices addressing social workers' experiences of vicarious trauma," *Practice*, 32(3), pp. 191–207. Available at: https://doi.org/10.1080/09503153.2019.1620201.

Bakker, A.B. and Demerouti, E. (2017) "Job demands–resources theory: taking stock and looking forward," *Journal of Occupational Health Psychology*, 22(3), pp. 273–285. Available at: https://doi.org/10.1037/ocp0000056.

Bonnerup, B. and Hasselager, A. (2019) *Love and Loneliness at Work: An Inspirational Guide for Consultants, Leaders and Other Professionals* (1st ed). New York: Routledge. Available at: https://www.taylorfrancis.com/books/9780429851094 (Accessed: 21 August 2025).

Brinkmann, S. (2011) *Psychology as a Moral Science: Perspectives on Normativity*. New York, NY: Springer. Available at: https://doi.org/10.1007/978-1-4419-7067-1.

Demerouti, E. et al. (2001) "The job demands-resources model of burnout," *Journal of Applied Psychology*, 86(3), pp. 499–512. Available at: https://doi.org/10.1037/0021-9010.86.3.499.

Dollard, M.F., Dormann, C. and Awang Idris, M. (eds.) (2019) *Psychosocial Safety Climate: A New Work Stress Theory*. Cham: Springer International Publishing. Available at: https://doi.org/10.1007/978-3-030-20319-1.

Franke, F., Felfe, J. and Pundt, A. (2014) "The impact of health-oriented leadership on follower health: development and test of a new instrument measuring health-promoting leadership," *German Journal of Human Resource Management: Zeitschrift für Personalforschung*, 28 (1–2), pp. 139–161. Available at: https://doi.org/10.1177/239700221402800108.

Hensel, J.M. et al. (2015) "Meta-analysis of risk factors for secondary traumatic stress in therapeutic work with trauma victims," *Journal of Traumatic Stress*, 28(2), pp. 83–91. Available at: https://doi.org/10.1002/jts.21998.

McFadden, P., Campbell, A. and Taylor, B. (2015) "Resilience and burnout in child protection social work: individual and organisational themes from a systematic literature review," *British Journal of Social Work*, 45(5), pp. 1546–1563. Available at: https://doi.org/10.1093/bjsw/bct210.

Newton, C. and Maierhofer, N. (2005) "Supportive leadership and well-being: the role of team-based value congruence," in Katsikitis, M. (ed.) *Past Reflections, Future Directions: Proceedings of the 40th Annual Conference of the Australian Psychological Society*. Australian Psychological Society.

O'Connor, K., Muller Neff, D. and Pitman, S. (2018) "Burnout in mental health professionals: a systematic review and meta-analysis of prevalence and determinants," *European Psychiatry*, 53, pp. 74–99. Available at: https://doi.org/10.1016/j.eurpsy.2018.06.003.

Richardson, K.M. (2017) "Managing employee stress and wellness in the new millennium," *Journal of Occupational Health Psychology*, 22(3), pp. 423–428. Available at: https://doi.org/10.1037/ocp0000066.

Sprang, G., Craig, C. and Clark, J. (2011) "Secondary traumatic stress and burnout in child welfare workers: a comparative analysis of occupational distress across professional groups," *Child Welfare*, 90(6), pp. 149–168.

White, D. (2006) "The hidden costs of caring: what managers need to know," *The Health Care Manager*, 25(4), pp. 341–347. Available at: https://doi.org/10.1097/00126450-200610000-00010.

18

Groups: Roles and Responsibilities

To reiterate, there are two essential points that everyone in the organisation must understand to support a sustainable workplace:

- If trauma exposure is not handled professionally, it can lead to mental tilting and increase the risk of strain and psychological disorders.
- Trauma exposure can affect *everyone* in the organisation—employees, managers, and even the organisational culture—which in turn can impair the group's collective ability to think clearly and act professionally.

Building resilience and preventing traumatisation occurs on all levels and can be viewed as a team sport where everyone involved must contribute actively. In this chapter, you can read about the role and responsibilities of the team.

As a group and as colleagues, you share a collegial and compassionate responsibility for one another, even though the formal legal responsibility lies with the group leader. As mentioned in the Prologue, responsibility is inherently tied to power. Those who hold power—and thereby influence—also carry responsibility. Within a team, your significant influence on each other's well-being translates into a meaningful shared responsibility.

Here's the group that hasn't understood its roles and responsibilities.

Being part of a well-functioning work group is one of the most effective protective factors against mental strain and psychological distress (Mathieu, 2012; Ashley-Binge and Cousins, 2020). This protective function is strongly supported in research on social support, which consistently identifies peer relationships as a key buffer against strain, trauma, and burnout.

As colleagues, you can offer each other different forms of social support. This chapter will explore the following types:

- Emotional support
- Feedback-oriented support
- Counselling or professional support
- Practical support

Emotional Support

The Principle of 'On Equal Terms'

Colleagues can offer a form of support that no one else can—no matter how kind, caring, or well-intentioned they may be. Sharing experiences with people who truly understand your reality creates a deep sense of connection. It helps ease the isolation that often accompanies emotionally intense work.

Colleagues know what it's like to sit beside a dying young mother or to be on the receiving end of a service user's frustration. They understand the weight of placing a deceased person into a coffin after witnessing their final moments, or the emotional impact of meeting the desperate gaze of a child in a refugee camp. They also understand, without needing explanation, how that kind of work can spill over into your personal life—how your patience with your own children may run short, or how you might wake from a nightmare about something that happened on shift. They know what it is like to stand in a supermarket and forget why you came, or to feel a sudden wave of guilt in a joyful moment, simply because others you encounter at work are facing unbearable pain.

> *Afterwards, I just felt like I wasn't allowed to be happy about my own children. Not when they'd lost theirs—especially since I felt partly responsible.*

Professionals in mentally high-risk jobs who work in close pairs or teams often develop exceptionally strong bonds. At times, these bonds can be so tight that the partners and children of helping professionals may feel left out—or even jealous.

> *There was a big accident in Afghanistan while my dad was home on leave. It was clear that he really wanted to go back to help. I understood—his friends were there. But I was hurt, too. We needed him at home. And I could tell my mum was really scared.*

The principle of on equal terms refers to the special kind of support colleagues can offer each other—support that is grounded in shared experience. When your emotional reality is mirrored by someone who understands intuitively, without long explanations, it can be profoundly affirming and healing.

> *One of the most powerful experiences of human connection I've ever had happened through work. I'd just spent the night covering a horrific bus crash, with many fatalities—most of them kids. It was cold, we were in a field, and I was driving home in the early hours, numb and overwhelmed. Then I got a text from an older colleague:*
>
> *'I just heard about the crash. I covered one like that once. It was unbelievably hard. Call me if you want.'*
>
> *I've never felt so understood.*

While intense experiences can forge strong bonds between colleagues, it's important not to withdraw from others. Even if friends or family can't fully understand the specific nature of your work, they can still provide essential forms of care, comfort, and grounding.

> *The harm of bringing it up is less than the harm of staying silent.*

Fisherman's Bench

The Fisherman's Bench is a simple method for creating a quiet, shared space amongst colleagues—not to analyse, solve, or evaluate, but simply *to be*. It offers an existential encounter that centres on *presence* rather than *performance.* You can read more about the difference between *being* and *doing* in Chapter 15.

Fishing is a dangerous profession, and Denmark—as a seafaring nation—has a long tradition of high-risk work. Throughout history, countless fishermen have lost their lives at sea, leaving partners widowed and children fatherless.

Many can picture the image of a small group of fishermen sitting together on a bench outside a weather-beaten shed—quiet, thoughtful, and safe. The catch has been landed, the nets have been repaired, and the boat is ready for its next voyage. Now the fishermen sit together, quietly absorbing the impressions from the day.

In much the same way, helping professionals can benefit from moments where they come together to share the emotional weight of their work—not to fix or evaluate, but simply to acknowledge what has made an impact.

We deal with so many dramatic stories at work. If we don't slow down occasionally, we risk bypassing the emotional impact—whether we want to feel it or not.

The Fisherman's Bench is not a replacement for professional supervision or defusing. It is a quiet, supplemental space for existential reflection—a place to sit with what has been painful, challenging, or hard to carry, and allow it to simply *be*.

We're actually quite good at doing defusing and debriefing at our workplace. But we're probably not so good at allowing ourselves to stay in that phase where you're just tired and sad.

You can use the Fisherman's Bench with trusted colleagues—within or across organisations. It is not about sharing advice or solutions, and it is not a forum for feedback. It is simply a shared pause—a collective moment to acknowledge what cannot be fixed, only *carried*.

Working with people in crisis inevitably leaves a mark on the professionals involved—whether they want it to or not. The Fisherman's Bench offers a time and place to give those impressions a voice—or even just a place to land. It can also be used to return to past events that still linger—the kind that ebb and flow in the body over time.

Some cases just stay with you. And every now and then, they come back. You get that oh no—that was awful feeling again. Then it fades. And one day, it rolls back in. It really does come in waves. At first, I kept wondering whether I'd made the right call—like, was it too much to bring such a young psychologist into the room with me? Had it been too tough on her? But now it's more of a quiet memory of something deeply, deeply sad.

How to use the Fisherman's Bench

Find a quiet spot—either outdoors or indoors—where people can sit on a bench or in a row of chairs, side by side. If possible, choose a place with a view, so your eyes can drift naturally. Everyone should face the same direction. Eye contact is appropriate in dialogue, but can be distracting when you are trying to turn inward.

(Continued)

(Continued)

Begin with a few deep breaths together. Calm bodies are contagious—just like tense or agitated ones. Once a sense of calm is present, the first person begins by sharing an experience that left an impression since the last time you met. Some stories will be short. Others may be longer. The task of the group is to listen openly and without judgement—like listening to a piece of music.

When the story ends, the storyteller thanks the group for listening, and the group thanks the person for sharing. Then the floor passes to the next person. If someone has nothing to share, they simply say 'pass' and the turn moves on. There is no pressure to speak—only a shared responsibility to hold what is shared with care and confidentiality. What is said on the bench stays on the bench.

Before starting, agree on how long the session will last, and decide who will be the 'skipper'—the person responsible for keeping track of time and gently bringing the session to a close.

The Principle of Sharing

As professionals, we often offer well-meaning advice to those we help: Get some fresh air. Eat something nourishing. Get some rest. Laugh when you can. Don't be so hard on yourself. And—most importantly—don't carry it all alone. Find someone to talk to.

We encourage them to share their thoughts and feelings with loved ones, so others can understand and offer care. Or to connect with peers in similar situations—because being met with recognition and resonance can be deeply reassuring. It reminds us: *It's not just me.*

Yet, for all our emphasis on openness, many of us don't do the same. We stay quiet. Closed. Caught in the idea that *we* should be able to handle it.

The principle of sharing is about turning the tables— gently holding ourselves to the same advice we often give to others. It means allowing ourselves to open up to colleagues when something has affected us, even if we don't have the perfect words to explain it.

When one person shares honestly, it creates space for others to do the same. And in that shared space, we stop being alone with what we're carrying.

Go ahead and take them - we don't use them ourselves anyway

A light reminder that even helpers need to take their own advice.

The Principle of Dark Humour

Dark humour can sometimes arise as a reflex within a group—and in the right setting, it can be an effective way to restore balance during intense or emotionally charged moments. Laughter helps strengthen group cohesion by building emotional bridges between colleagues, and it is also a powerful way to release muscle tension (Martin et al., 2003).

A group is a safe space where you can joke and just relax.

That said, dark humour should be used with care. It can become destructive if left unchecked. It is also important to consider others who may not share the same perspective or history—such as new colleagues, interns, or people outside the team—who may not fully understand the pressure that humour is responding to.

Dark humour must never stand alone as a coping strategy. Organisations must ensure that their standard operating procedures also include other processing tools and structured support methods, such as those described in Part III of this book. If dark humour becomes the dominant way to handle difficult experiences, it can gradually desensitise the group. People may begin to search for the ironic or amusing in the tragic—while losing touch with vital emotional cues like sadness, anger, disgust, or despair. These reactions are important. Being attuned to them is essential for good, ethical professional work.

> I once told my supervisor I didn't know whether to laugh or cry. She said, 'Do both.'
>
> Sometimes, after a tough shift, I just put on some sad music and cry. I guess I need to let the sadness out of my system.

You're not alone. Others frequently feel the same way you do.

The Principle of Not Overburdening One Another

Colleagues can easily, albeit unintentionally, place strain on one another during day-to-day work, especially when deeply affected by what they've just seen or heard. While spontaneous sharing of such experiences, as previously mentioned, is an effective strategy for preventing mental overload—it can be helpful to process the day's intense impressions with someone before returning home to family and friends. However, it is important to share in a way that allows the listener to absorb the story without becoming emotionally overwhelmed. Otherwise, colleagues risk 'tertiary traumatizing' one another (Beck and Beck, 2021).

> She asked if I wanted to spar with her, but then she just unloaded a horrible story and ran out the door, saying she had plans with her kids. I was left there, stuck with the awful story all by myself. Thanks for that, I'm just saying!

This highlights the importance of *mindful sharing*—not only to protect the listener, but to preserve trust and psychological safety amongst colleagues.

End-of-day Defusing Duty

Some workplaces have established a structured defusing system in which one specific colleague is on duty during the final hour of the workday. This person keeps their calendar free of meetings and makes themselves available to coworkers who may need to decompress after a difficult shift.

The setup is simple: a quiet office, a few minutes to talk, and someone who is present, prepared, and emotionally available. The defusing duty provides a transitional space—a kind of psychological airlock—that helps colleagues let go of the day's emotional residue before stepping back into private life.

The conversation might be brief, perhaps even quiet. But having a dedicated person available creates safety. Sometimes, the person on duty simply listens. Other times, they might offer perspective, a helpful suggestion, or just affirm that the day really was demanding. The support may also take a practical form—such as helping the colleague get a quick overview of unfinished tasks, jotting down a few notes for the next day, and then drawing a line under the day.

It's not a replacement for everyday peer support—spontaneous conversations and small moments of solidarity still matter. But assigning one person to hold this space sends a clear message: emotional follow-up is not optional or individual—it's a shared, structural responsibility.

To support this kind of space, colleagues are also encouraged to use slow approaches—starting the story from a broader context and gradually moving into the more intense or emotional moments. This helps prevent overwhelm and supports a shared sense of pacing and presence.

Slow Approach

Do you have a moment? I'd like to share something from today that left a real mark on me. It's a bit heavy, but I just need to say it out loud before I head home.

Give your colleague a real chance to opt in

A father called the drop-in counselling service today. He had just lost his teenage son—the situation was still very fresh.

The death was sudden and deeply distressing. The father was overwhelmed with grief and guilt.

(Continued)

(Continued)

Without going into all the details, what really stayed with me was how he kept asking, 'Did I miss something? Should I have seen it coming?'

I sat with him through the conversation and tried to hold space for his pain. Since the call, it's just stayed with me.

The Principle of Taking Good Care of Each Other

Many professionals understand that they need to take care of themselves. It is a familiar message and hard to disagree with. Remembering to leave work on time, seek help from colleagues during busy periods, take a proper lunch break with something nutritious, and maintain a good working posture are all essential reminders. Yet time and time again, you put the needs of a current patient, client, or service user ahead of your own needs and forget about all the above.

Individuals in mentally high-risk professions often feel driven by a strong sense of calling. As a result, advice to 'take care of yourself' is frequently disregarded. However, when helping professionals are encouraged to look out for their colleagues, the response is often much more positive.

A father whose son was going to be a combat soldier in Afghanistan once told me:

> *Actually, I never told him to look after himself. I told him to look after his mates ... I thought it was important to emphasise that it was the camaraderie and the others in the group that would determine whether things would go well or badly.*

The principle of looking after one another emphasises supporting preventive measures. In practice, this includes attending supervision sessions even when there is no immediate crisis you need to resolve, keeping lunch breaks free of heavy discussions about patients by focusing on lighter topics like weekend activities, and maintaining task variety and diversity, even if it means letting go of some 'favourite' responsibilities. Naturally, looking after each other is also about caring for each other.

> *I still remember clearly what it was like to perform a caesarean section on a woman who had died, although it was many years ago.*
>
> *There was a more experienced doctor who wrote me a real letter afterwards. She wrote that life is like that sometimes. And that she thought I was a good doctor. That helped me.*

Feedback-oriented Support

Your colleagues are the people you interact with most throughout your workday. They see you in action, understand the daily pressures of the job, and are often the ones best placed to notice changes in your behaviour, energy, or performance. While a manager may be responsible for your professional development, they might not always be present on-site or involved in the everyday workflow. This makes colleagues a vital source of feedback-oriented support—offering timely observations, sharing constructive input, and helping you reflect on how you carry out your role.

Being part of a group offers professionals many advantages, as explored throughout this chapter. However, group membership also comes with challenges—including destructive and, unfortunately, all-too-common dynamics such as bullying, scapegoating, and groupthink. While this book does not delve into a full analysis of these phenomena, it is worth briefly highlighting groupthink. This particular dynamic illustrates how a group can collectively fail to correct a shared bias, even when individual members are aware of the issue.

The Principle of Being Honest—And the Risk of Groupthink

Groupthink occurs when individuals suppress their own professional or personal values to preserve harmony or social acceptance within the group (Gilbert and Simos, 2022). As a result, problematic behaviour—especially from formal or informal leaders—may go unchallenged, even when it clearly violates professional standards.

You might wonder why highly competent professionals sometimes fail to speak up. Often, the desire to belong and maintain group cohesion outweighs the discomfort of witnessing behaviour they know is wrong. Over time, they may stop noticing the discomfort altogether. This can happen because the group is seen as 'above critique' due to the difficult nature of the work—or simply because the problematic behaviour has become normalised.

To stay in the group, people may unconsciously engage in self-deception: offering justifications and explanations that locate the cause of the problem outside the group's control. Fear, misguided loyalty, respect for authority, or conflict avoidance may all contribute to silence. But silence has consequences—not only for professional quality, but also for the psychological work climate.

Psychological safety is the foundation that allows professionals to speak honestly—especially when they disagree. In a psychologically safe group, team members feel able to express concerns, doubts, or ethical discomfort without fearing ridicule, punishment, or exclusion (see Chapter 13 for more on psychological safety).

> *We all talked about psychological safety in theory—but it wasn't until someone challenged our manager in a meeting, and the group backed them up respectfully, that I realised what it actually looks like in practice.*

To reduce the risk of groupthink, teams should regularly reflect on the quality of their professional language, their workload distribution, decision-making processes, and how they treat one another. When shared values are visible and alive in the group, it becomes easier to act on them—and to speak up when something contradicts them.

A small but powerful step is for managers to speak *last* in group decision-making. This simple change signals that all voices matter and encourages more honest contributions.

Ultimately, the principle of speaking honestly is about staying rooted in your professional and ethical values—and let them support not just you, but your colleagues as well.

The Principle of Focusing on the Incident—Not the Individual

As this book has repeated many times: working in high-strain environments leaves an impact. That is how it is—and how it should be. If a professional is able to handle tragic, violent, or deeply distressing situations year after year without occasionally being affected, it may be a sign that they have grown too emotionally numb.

When a doctor, priest, teacher, journalist, police officer, prison guard, midwife—or any helping professional—is visibly shaken by a particular event, they need colleagues who respond with trust and respect.

They need to hear:

> *I can see that this has really shaken you. It must have been a brutal case—for someone as experienced and grounded as you to react like that.*

Such a response affirms the person's professionalism. It focuses attention where it belongs: not on the person's supposed weaknesses, but on the intensity of what they've been through.

In contrast, when colleagues respond with comments like:

> *I can see that this really got to you. But you're still quite new in the field ... / You've always been very sensitive ... / You're going through a tough time at home ...*

... the impact is very different. These remarks shift focus away from the incident and towards the person's perceived vulnerability. Instead of feeling seen and supported, the professional may feel criticised, exposed, or weak.

The principle of focusing on the incident is, in simple terms, about playing the ball—not the person. It's about recognising that powerful emotional responses are not signs of failure, but reflections of the difficult and meaningful work professionals do everyday.

Counselling and Professional Support

An important part of collegial support concerns supporting each other professionally. Knowledge sharing can occur through internal training, perhaps after a colleague has attended a course, or through conferences, meetings, or supervision. Regular professional discussions that are specially convened, before, during, or after a mentally demanding task can be incredibly valuable for colleagues who are in the middle of the task and navigate emotional chaos.

> *Even as a very experienced doctor, I need to constantly discuss complex cases with colleagues. That way I can reassure myself that I haven't missed anything. My powerlessness is also easier for me to accept when my colleagues are supportive and understanding.*

Professional support can also be given by solving tasks together. While not strictly necessary, it can be a way of exchanging tacit knowledge (Diehm, Mankowitz and King, 2019). As mentioned, tacit knowledge refers to information shared from one individual to another through practical demonstration of how a task is performed and managed. People are frequently unaware of the tacit knowledge they possess and how valuable it can be to others.

Broadly speaking, counselling and professional support are essentially about knowledge sharing.

> *I often reassure myself that I'm part of a strong team. So if I don't know something myself, someone else probably does. Luckily, the experienced people in my current team are really good at sharing their experiences.*

Practical Support

Just like any other human being, helping professionals have their highs and lows. Divorce, caring for parents with dementia, illnesses, workplace threats, or violent incidents are all integral aspects of a helping professional's life. These challenges often demand additional effort and may limit the time and energy available to maintain the usual level of commitment. It is crucial to foster a work culture where it is acceptable to speak up if your energy levels are low. This enables colleagues to better navigate challenges and support one another. Additionally, some team members may occasionally face periods of increased workload due to unexpected tasks.

Under such circumstances, practical, here-and-now assistance is often the best way to support your colleague. Such relief should come quickly and efficiently, even if it is just a temporary task reallocation. Practical help sends a clear signal to the whole group that they will look after each other.

> *I'm so tired of phrases like, 'Take care of yourself.' If you're under pressure, you just think 'Yes, thanks, but how? I've promised myself not to say it again to an employee or colleague, but instead ask: 'Is there anything I can help you with?'*

References

Ashley-Binge, S. and Cousins, C. (2020) "Individual and organisational practices addressing social workers' experiences of vicarious trauma," *Practice*, 32(3), pp. 191–207. Available at: https://doi.org/10.1080/09503153.2019.1620201.

Beck, J.S. and Beck, A.T. (2021) *Cognitive Behavior Therapy: Basics and Beyond* (3rd ed). New York; London: The Guilford Press.

Diehm, R.M., Mankowitz, N.N. and King, R.M. (2019) "Secondary traumatic stress in Australian psychologists: individual risk and protective factors," *Traumatology*, 25(3), pp. 196–202. Available at: https://doi.org/10.1037/trm0000181.

Gilbert, P. and Simos, G. (2022) *Compassion Focused Therapy: Clinical Practice and Applications* (1st ed). London: Routledge. Available at: https://doi.org/10.4324/9781003035879.

Martin, R.A. et al. (2003) "Individual differences in uses of humor and their relation to psychological well-being: development of the Humor Styles Questionnaire," *Journal of Research in Personality*, 37(1), pp. 48–75. Available at: https://doi.org/10.1016/S0092-6566(02)00534-2.

Mathieu, F. (2012) *The Compassion Fatigue Workbook: Creative Tools for Transforming Compassion Fatigue and Vicarious Traumatization* (1st ed). New York, NY: Routledge (Routledge Psychosocial Stress Series). Available at: https://doi.org/10.4324/9780203803349.

19

Individuals: Roles and Responsibilities

Again, there are two essential points that everyone in the organisation must understand to support a sustainable workplace:

- If trauma exposure is not handled professionally, it can lead to mental tilting and increase the risk of strain and psychological disorders.
- Trauma exposure can affect *everyone* in the organisation—employees, managers, and even the organisational culture—which in turn can impair the group's collective ability to think clearly and act professionally.

Fostering resilience and preventing traumatisation happens at every level of an organisation—and can be seen as a team sport, where everyone involved must contribute actively. In this chapter, you will learn about the role of the individual helping professional—that is, your role.

Here's the employee who hasn't understood their roles and responsibilities.

As discussed in Part I, many of the signs of mental tilting are invisible, making them difficult for others to detect. Ultimately, only you know what is happening inside you—though psychological blind spots can sometimes cloud that awareness. Your most important responsibility as an individual helper is to stay connected with yourself and speak up if you feel your inner balance beginning to tip. Taking care of yourself is not only a responsibility to yourself but also to those around you (Sonnentag, 2012).

The Strategic Diamond

In this chapter, you will find 12 principles—or strategies—that you can use to build resilience and prevent psychological strain. The chapter is structured around a model called *The Strategic Diamond*, inspired by the well-known cognitive model that links thoughts, emotions, physical sensations, and behaviour (Naczenski et al., 2017). It provides a simple way to organise reflections, while recognising that all aspects are inherently interconnected.

At the heart of the model is the central 'why'—a symbolic reminder of the deeper meaning that motivates professionals to stay in high-strain jobs. This sense of purpose helps sustain motivation and resilience—especially when facing emotional overload or moments of doubt.

People differ in their preferences and needs. That is why the 12 strategies described here vary in style and scope—some are reflective, others practical. For the sake of inspiration, we have chosen to briefly describe a broad range of strategies rather than exploring only a few in depth.

There are many excellent books, websites, and podcasts available for those who wish to go further. Some of the techniques in this chapter will be familiar to readers with a background in psychotherapy. But this chapter is not just for them. It is written for all professionals working in mentally high-risk roles—regardless of discipline or seniority.

Importantly, the chapter focuses on strategies that can be integrated into the workday—because that is where the strain happens, and that is where it must be addressed. This does not mean that self-care outside of work is unimportant—but leisure time is, after all, one's own.

Model 11: The Strategic Diamond

Strategies Targeting Thoughts

The Principle of Being Caring and Friendly

This first principle is one of the most important. As a helping professional in a mentally high-risk setting, you frequently encounter individuals in a state of powerlessness. This powerlessness may be expressed not only through silence or quiet tears, but also through anger, doubt, criticism, complaints, mistrust, or

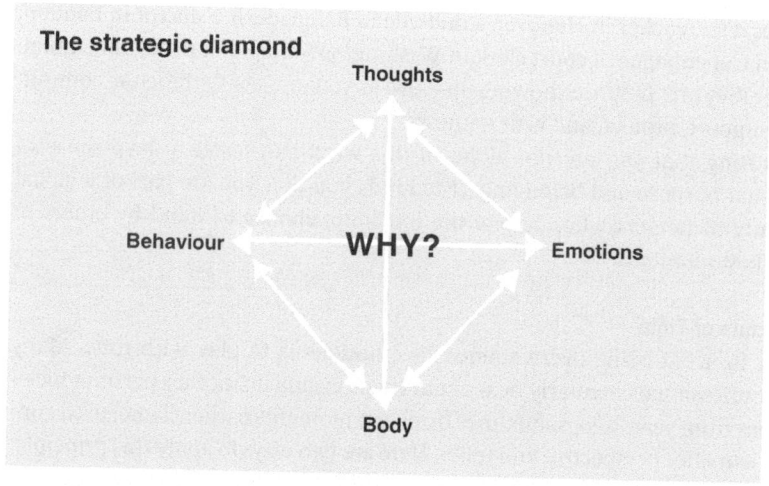

The strategic diamond

Thoughts

Behaviour — WHY? — Emotions

Body

scolding. These emotional reactions can be difficult to deal with, which is why it is essential to recognise them for what they are—and to manage your own response with care.

Be mindful and avoid reacting in ways that are defensive, dismissive, or judgemental—either towards others or yourself. Equally important is avoiding the inward path, where frustration can turn into insecurity, shame, or harsh self-criticism.

Instead of reacting, try to meet both yourself and the other person with compassion. Tell yourself: *They're in shock. They're trying to make sense of what's happening.* Or: *They're struggling to reclaim some control and dignity—and their protest isn't really about the food or the waiting. It's about the situation they've been forced into.*

Then turn that same compassion inward. Remind yourself: *I'm doing what I've trained for. I'm as prepared as I can be.* Or: *Right now, I may be the best support available—and I'm doing my best.* Say these words gently, with kindness. Repeat them if you need to. They help you stay grounded.

At its core, this principle is about maintaining compassion—for those you help, and for yourself (Sonnentag, 2012).

The Principle of 'You Are Not Alone'

This principle is about breaking the isolation that can arise when you find yourself alone in a shocking or horrific situation. In such moments, it can help to mentally connect with a broader community of professionals who are facing similar challenges. You might think to yourself: *There are others like me—right now—sitting with someone who has been raped, lost a child, is facing a terminal diagnosis, or is recounting every detail of abuse for a court case.*

Perhaps it's a teacher in Hanover, a midwife in Bangladesh, a doctor in London, a priest in Copenhagen, a court clerk in Washington, or a police officer in Dublin. Wherever they are, they are showing up—just as you are—with the same commitment to support, protect, and bear witness.

Recognising that you are not alone in this work can foster a deep sense of professional purpose and belonging. It reminds you that you are part of a global community of helpers who, despite the hardship, choose to stand by others in their darkest moments.

The Principle of Time

One way to avoid being overwhelmed by emotions is to play with time. Many helping professionals regularly hear about tragic events in another person's life—sometimes from years ago, sometimes from just moments earlier. Time, used consciously, can offer perspective and relief. Here are two ways to apply this principle:

1. **Anchor yourself in the present.** Remind yourself: *The father is safe now and is being listened to.* Or: *We are two adults lovingly caring for the inner child who was once hurt.* Or: *This person actually survived and is sitting here with me today.* Let yourself grow curious: *What did this person do to get through it?* This shift helps you see them not only as a victim of something terrible—but as a survivor.

2. **Imagine the future.** Ask yourself: *How will the patient speak about this moment in a year, five years, or ten years?* And how will you speak about it? What will you have learned? You might also imagine the person in a better future—safe, calm, and happy.

The principle of playing with time can help you stay grounded in your professional role and find a sense of calm. That calm presence allows you to hold hope on behalf of the other person—silently communicating that you believe in their capacity to recover, grow, and heal.

Strategies Targeting Emotions

The Principle of *Feeling with* (and Not *Feeling as*)

As mentioned in the section on mirror neurons, humans naturally sense what others are feeling—a trait that is often beneficial in everyday life. However, challenges arise when, as a helping professional, you are repeatedly exposed to another person's deepest pain and emotions.

In such moments, it is essential to remain mindful not to let the other person's suffering overwhelm or drain you. Your emotional energy is a vital resource for providing calm, stable, and compassionate support. It is a misconception to believe that caring means fully placing yourself in the other person's shoes. Imagining yourself as a mother who has just lost her child, for example, would only result in two deeply distraught individuals. *Feeling with* someone is not the same as *feeling as* them.

A wise colleague once put it this way: *It's about thinking: Yes, it could have been me. But it's not.* This perspective offers a compassionate recognition of shared human vulnerability, while still respecting the grieving mother's unique pain and honouring your own emotional boundaries.

If your empathic resonance becomes too intense—if you feel yourself being pulled into the other person's emotional state—it is important to take small, deliberate steps to restore psychological distance. For instance, you can:

- Avoid sitting directly opposite the other person; instead, position yourself slightly to the side.
- Get up briefly—perhaps to throw something away or to make a note on a whiteboard.
- Break eye contact for a moment and focus on a calming object in the room.
- Remind yourself that your own calm presence is already a powerful form of support, offering the other person a sense of groundedness amid emotional turbulence.
- Silently repeat: *Yes, it could have been me. But it's not.*

The principle of *feeling with, not as* is about recognising and making space for emotions without being overtaken by them. See also 'The Principle of Self-awareness' on page 167 for further discussion.

The Principle of Being Able to Recognise, Name, and Talk About Emotions

Saying yes to a mentally high-risk job means saying yes to working with emotions. Just as a gardener needs to recognise and name plants, professionals in this field must be able to identify emotions—and have a language for them. In psychological terms, this is part of what is known as *emotional literacy*.

Without it, you risk:

- missing important signals from the people you are trying to help,
- crossing your own or others' boundaries,
- absorbing emotional states without noticing, or
- being unable to give or receive support.

Most emotions have names: joy, anger, fear, grief. But emotions can also be expressed through metaphors, images, or physical sensations. I once met a man at the Danish Cancer Society who was terminally ill. When I asked how he was feeling, he said: *Hmm ... I don't really know what I feel. But it's like I'm standing in the sea with both feet cast in concrete. Just my nose above the surface. And it feels like a storm is coming.*

He taught me that emotions can be expressed in many ways. The principle of recognising and having a language for emotions is also about being able to notice and understand how others express what they feel—sometimes not through words, but through tone, metaphor, silence, or posture.

The Principle of the Emotional Weather Forecast

Being a professional in a high-strain job means regularly checking in with your emotional weather. Just like we notice shifts in the sky, it's helpful to notice when your inner atmosphere changes—perhaps from calm to tense, from light to heavy, or from focused to distracted.

Emotions work like an internal compass or barometer. They help us make sense of what's happening around us—and how it affects us. Paying attention to our emotions, naming them, and reflecting on them allow us to stay oriented, instead of drifting away from your role.

Sometimes, when emotions go unacknowledged, they can mislead us. A trauma response, for instance, can make someone feel afraid even when there is no real danger. The body and mind may still be reacting to something in the past.

Being professional means not just noticing how you feel, but being able to reflect on it and act with awareness. Your emotional state carries valuable signals—both about your own well-being and about your team's climate.

> *I once had a manager who couldn't really hide his mood—which he was aware of. But he was good at saying: 'I'm in a bad mood today, or maybe just a bit off—but it's not about you'. Honestly, that made all the difference. It helped us relax.*

Strategies Targeting the Body

The Principle of Breathing, Eating, Drinking, and Sleeping

Mental strain causes muscle tension and breathing difficulties. You should be aware of these symptoms. Deep, conscious breathing helps to calm the body and is a quick way to regain control. There are other helpful techniques—see the following box.

Breathing Exercises

Tactical breathing

- Breathe in while counting to four.
- Hold your breath while counting to four.

> • Exhale while counting to four.
> • Hold your breath while counting to four.
>
> Also draw air into the lower part of your lungs so that your stomach bulges. Keep doing this until you feel your heart rate drops. Remember to use this technique before your heart rate gets too high. If your heart rate is already high, start with straw exhalation.
>
> **Straw exhalation**
>
> Imagine exhaling through a long, thin straw. Feel free to purse your lips, but make sure they are relaxed. Continue exhaling until your lungs are completely empty of air. Now release the tension and feel your body take a deep breath all by itself.

Having a mentally high-risk job—even if it is not physically demanding—requires extra energy. For your body and brain to function optimally, especially under pressure, you need adequate food, hydration, and rest. This becomes even more important when your attention is focused on others and their needs. In such situations, it's easy to underestimate your own vulnerability and over-estimate your stamina.

> *The work of identifying bodies after the tsunami had been going on for several days when a psychologist came and told us to get some sleep and take a break for a few days. Otherwise, we would burn out too quickly. In the midst of all the chaos, we hadn't even thought about that.*

Sleep Is Essential for Mental Balance

Getting a good night's sleep is especially important during busy or stressful periods. The following are some tips that may help improve sleep quality:

> **Tips for Better Sleep**
>
> • Limit coffee and other sources of caffeine, especially in the afternoon and evening.
> • Avoid drinking or eating foods with a high liquid content during the final one to two hours before bedtime.
> • Avoid alcohol and tobacco near bedtime.
> • Avoid screens (TV, computer, phone) for a few hours before going to sleep.
> • Avoid heavy meals close to bedtime.
> • Refrain from intense physical activity within three hours of going to bed.

(Continued)

(Continued)

- Establish a consistent bedtime and wake-up routine. In the morning, get up at the same time—regardless of how much or how little you've slept.
- Avoid daytime naps.
- Keep the bedroom cool and comfortable (18–21 °C), and minimise light and noise.
- Use the bed only for sleep—and sex.
- If you can't fall asleep after 30 minutes, get out of bed and do something relaxing until you feel sleepy.
- Remind yourself that one or two nights of poor sleep may feel unpleasant, but are not harmful.

The Principle of Physical Activity

Another way to relieve muscle tension is through massage or exercise. When you actively use the body's muscles, you will experience a relaxing effect, as relaxation typically follows tension. Some workplaces have introduced exercise during working hours in their own training facilities, while others offer massage programmes. Some workplaces even cover employees' gym memberships. In any case, physical activity is beneficial (Rees, 2017), and it does not need to occur in a specific location or require special clothing to be effective.

For me, high-intensity workouts are the absolute best way to unload. Without them, I do not think I would be able to sustain life as a paramedic.

Ideas for Physical Exercises

- Run or walk up and down the stairs for 5–10 minutes. If you work in a tall office building or high-rise hospital, a single walk all the way up the stairs, followed by a walk all the way down and then back to your own floor, is probably enough.
- Keep a mat in your office and lie down to do 10 push-ups, 10 crunches, and 10 back lifts.
- Use the mat for yoga exercises.
- Buy a punching bag and hang it in a room away from patients, clients, or service users, and train your arms for five minutes.
- Keep an exercise band in your drawer and use it for a quick set of different exercises.
- Take a walk with a colleague or business partner instead of sitting at a meeting table.

Above all, the principle of physical activity is about noticing your physical strength and making your body even stronger.

The Principle of Self-awareness

Everything beneath your skin is you, and everything outside it is the rest of the world. This somewhat strange phrase underscores a profound truth: as a helping professional in a mentally high-risk job, you are vulnerable to being deeply affected by the horror and pain of traumatic events. Your skin is the largest organ of your body and draws the boundary between you and others.

Coming back to your body—to your breath, your skin, your muscles—is a way to stay present and grounded. It reminds you that the pain and horror you are witnessing belong to someone else. You are here to help, not to absorb it.

Grounding helps you stay connected to yourself and remain emotionally steady in challenging situations.

Different methods of reconnecting with yourself include:

(Re)gaining Self-awareness

- Stand up and shake your arms and legs; feel your feet on the ground.
- Move your head from side to side and back and forth, or in small circles.
- Feel the contact between your body and the ground.
- Tighten different muscles in your body, including your pelvic floor.
- Keep a good hand lotion in your office and briefly savour its scent after rubbing it on your hands.
- Stroke your arms or legs.
- Massage your forehead and perhaps your jaw.

The principle of self-awareness emphasises the importance of remaining separate—reminding you that your interaction with a person in crisis is a powerful encounter between someone who wants to help (you) and someone who needs help.

Strategies Targeting Behaviour

The Principle of Avoiding Self-induced Overdose

Be aware of when and why you ask for details of a violent or painful case. Is it truly professionally relevant to know all the details? When it comes to mental tilting, there is a classic dose–response relationship (Masten and Narayan, 2012;

Gerber et al., 2018): the greater and more intense the strain, the stronger the reaction. There are several reasons why a professional in a high-risk job may be at risk of a self-induced 'overdose'.

> *Over time, working at the call centre, I've learnt to focus on just the information I actually need about accidents and other cases. And I deliberately avoid violent photos and things like that if they're not relevant to my job. I know I have to look after myself if I'm going to keep enough space in my head to hold everything that's already there.*

A sense of duty: Sometimes, it may feel like a matter of duty—a moral obligation to bear witness to the terrible events that another human being has endured. It may feel like a way of showing respect to the victims when you ask about the details of abuse or torture, or when you choose to look through all photos from the accident or crime scene, even if you have already found one you can use for the report.

Be aware of when and why you ask for—or read—details of a violent case. Is it professionally relevant? You risk an 'overdose'.

A need to demonstrate strength: When you are regularly exposed to others' traumas, you will also regularly encounter your own vulnerability. As a counterbalance to this vulnerability, you might feel compelled to demonstrate your strength—to yourself, your colleagues, or even your manager. However, this urge can lead to seeking unnecessary details or viewing photographs and videos that are not essential to your professional responsibilities. In the event of a terrorist attack where a perpetrator kills a hostage on camera, your disdain for the act might compel you to prove that you are not intimidated by 'daring' to watch it. However, remember that by watching the video, you are doing exactly what the perpetrators intend. Such powerful images are rarely forgotten; they linger in your mind and could one day become the proverbial straw that breaks the camel's back, pushing you towards a state of mental tilting.

The principle of avoiding self-induced overdose is about keeping a cool head and a warm heart, and remembering that you are actually diminishing your ability to help the other person—or even to write a good report—if you are too overwhelmed by the horror or pain.

Is There Anything Wrong with Wanting to Hear About or Look at Photos of Traumatic Events? No, there is not. It is common and quite human to be curious about phenomena that threaten one's existence, and it can be seen as an attempt to gain power over the situation. For example, when we instinctively slow our cars down at the scene of an accident and look, it is part of a survival reaction where we give our brains the data to figure out whether to fight or flee.

The need to understand danger can probably also explain why some people are attracted to horror films. However, the appeal of such films is frequently lost on many helping professionals. Many professionals report that they no longer experience excitement from watching horror films, describing it instead as a false thrill and an unnecessary strain on their mental well-being.

The Principle of Taking Breaks

You become more efficient and can perform better when you prioritise and insist on taking breaks, both in the day-to-day routine and during peak periods. A two-minute break where you simply sit and look out of the window is better than nothing. Take breaks in green areas if possible. If working conditions allow, a power nap or a mindfulness exercise can make the break even more effective in terms of boosting your concentration and helping you stay connected afterwards.

The principle of taking breaks can also refer to slightly longer pauses from work, perhaps in the form of a leave of absence or a job swap, where you exchange roles with someone else—such as an employee or manager from your own organisation (Schrøder et al., 2022).

The Principle of Conscious Transitions

The word *transit* comes via the Italian *transito* from the Latin *transitus*, meaning 'transition' or 'passage'. Many people know the term from airports and associate it with joy, anticipation, and calmness. Your bags are checked in, the packing is done, and before departure, everything necessary has been taken care of.

The transition from home to work and back again, however, involves both a physical shift (unless you work from home) and a mental one. To avoid carrying suffering or despair home from work, it is important to be mindful of this transition. It can be helpful to create a kind of 'transit room' at work, where you pause for a few minutes each time you check in or out. This might be a literal space where you change clothes, such as a locker room for uniforms or lab coats. It could also be a symbolic space—something created through small, daily rituals. What matters most is taking a moment to tune in and out of the two worlds.

On my way to work, I've been listening to a particular song for a long time. I crank up the volume and sing so loudly it feels like the car roof might lift off. It's a happy song that always gives me a boost—lifting my energy and outlook. So when the emergency call centre handle is pulled ... I'm ready!

A transition can also involve a yoga exercise, the scent of something pleasant, gazing out of the window or at a beautiful object in the room, playing a piece of music, talking briefly to a colleague, or saying something supportive to yourself. It can also be a good time to complete your daily journal entry. All these actions help create distance between your private life and your work.

That said, just as you are the same person at home and at a holiday resort, you are also the same person in both your professional and private lives. It is unrealistic to expect complete separation. I mention this because I often meet committed and dedicated professionals who are unkind to themselves for thinking about work during time off—and who feel guilty about it.

> *We see the world with the same brain that makes us partners, siblings, and family. We can't just leave our minds soaking in salt water at the office overnight. Of course we bring work home with us. I really wish we'd stop pretending it's a choice.*

Rather than having the ambition to completely separate work and private life, it is more helpful to accept that, just as you sometimes spend time at work booking appointments with a hairdresser or dermatologist, you will also sometimes spend time at home thinking about your work.

> *Over the years, I've become better at accepting and giving space to my emotions and thoughts without getting too carried away by them. I recognise them and then focus on what I'm doing or what I want to do.*

Exercises

Working with graphic material on screen

Exposure to disturbing images—including child sexual-abuse material (CSAM), graphic violence, war footage, or natural-disaster scenes—can be profoundly distressing. Such content is encountered not only by journalists, but also by hotline analysts, content-moderation teams, law-enforcement personnel, healthcare staff, educators, and humanitarian workers.

The following checklist offers practical, field-tested steps for prevention—limiting the emotional impact of graphic images, reducing the risk of potential traumatisation and cumulative strain, and helping you regain calm after each viewing session.

- **Be intentional:** Clarify your purpose before reviewing graphic content. Know what you are looking for—and stop when that need is met. Avoid unnecessary replays or extended exposure.

- **Mark key timestamps:** If you are working with video, log the time codes of relevant sections. This minimises the need to rewatch disturbing material later.
- **Manage visual focus:** When possible, avoid lingering on victims' faces. Focus on the contextual or evidentiary aspects of the image, rather than personal suffering.
- **Adjust your screen environment:** View images in black and white or shrink the window. If possible, work in a well-lit space with natural daylight, and keep soothing visual elements in sight—such as artwork, plants, or photos that ground you.
- **Pause and reset:** Take regular breaks. Stand up, stretch, or look out the window. Even short pauses can help regulate your nervous system and reduce cumulative strain.
- **Use sound mindfully:** If you're working with audio, consider turning off the visuals while listening. Distancing one sense from another can reduce overall impact.
- **Signal and protect others:** Label distressing files clearly. Alert colleagues before sharing graphic material. Consider implementing internal labelling practices or content warnings.
- **Debrief ethical tension:** Repeated exposure to traumatic material may raise ethical dilemmas or emotional conflict—especially when there's limited room for action or response. Klas Backholm refers to this as a form of moral injury. Sharing your thoughts with peers or supervisors can prevent isolation and normalise reflection.

These guidelines draw on the *Dart Center Style Guide for Trauma-Aware Journalism* and on training materials developed by Elena Newman, Gavin Rees (Dart Center Europe), and others affiliated with the Dart Center for Journalism and Trauma. They are further informed by research from Trond Idås and Klas Backholm (Idås and Backholm, 2023), whose work shows that repeated  exposure to traumatic visuals can create ethical dilemmas and moral stress—phenomena closely related to moral injury. A fuller discussion of moral injury appears in Chapter 10 'Moral Stress and Moral Injury'.

> *For a long time, I told myself that drinking helped me deal with the pictures—that it sharpened my view and helped me stay professional. But it was a lousy excuse. Now I'm sober, and I process the pictures more clearly than ever.*

Dealing with Intrusive Thoughts, Images, and Sounds

Strong impressions from the day's experiences or stories can turn into intrusive thoughts and mental images or sounds later in the day—for example, at bedtime. It is a common experience, but it can be frustrating. The following section outlines some techniques to deal with these thoughts or mental images.

Thought-stopping

Purpose: To interrupt distressing thought loops and replace them with more constructive alternatives.

After a violent or traumatic event, it is common to be haunted by intrusive thoughts—not only about what actually happened but also about what might have happened if you had acted differently. These thoughts can become destructive, fuelling guilt, shame, or helplessness. One helpful way to counter them is through a simple form of mental reprogramming using *replacement thoughts*. A replacement thought is a constructive, reality-based reflection that acknowledges your effort or intention. For example: *'My actions helped reduce their suffering—it could have been worse without my support'.*

This kind of thought gently replaces a destructive one, such as: *'They were suffering so much, and I couldn't take away their pain'.* Over time, consistently reinforcing replacement thoughts can help ease emotional distress and support healing.

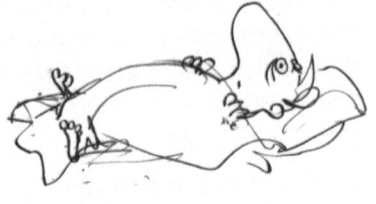

This method involves actively interrupting unwanted thoughts by saying *'STOP'*—out loud if you're alone, or silently to yourself if others are present. Immediately afterwards, bring in your replacement thought. With practice, this technique can become automatic, like fastening a button or driving a car.

In short:

- Consciously identify and verbalise the unwanted thought.
- Say or think *'STOP'.*
- Replace it immediately with your replacement thought.

The more consistently you practise, the more natural and effective the technique becomes. It works well for most people.

The Highway Exit

Purpose: To redirect mental focus using guided imagery.

Imagine your mind travelling at high speed on a multilane motorway. Now, in plenty of time, spot the exit a little ahead, slow down, and prepare to take it. Imagine turning off the motorway and driving along a picturesque country road. Perhaps you turn onto a small dirt road, past some fields or into a forest. Feel the car bumping along the uneven road and take in the vibrant colours. You can even roll down the window and listen to the crunch of gravel under the tyres and the birds singing outside.

Distraction—Shift Focus

Purpose: To gently bring your attention back to here and now when caught in a loop of distressing thoughts or images.

This method involves distracting yourself when an unwanted thought or mental image appears. The technique can be practised in different ways. A classic version is to wear an elastic band around your wrist and give it a light snap, then focus on the brief pain and on your current surroundings.

You can also try one of the activities listed in the section '(Re)gaining Self-awareness' on page 167.

Manipulation—Reframe the Image

Purpose: To regain agency over how you mentally process difficult images or sounds.

There are different techniques for manipulating your inner images—some are about imagining something pleasant, while others aim to reduce the emotional impact of something unpleasant.

Amplifying the Nice

Imagine a difficult situation—then add someone supportive to the scene. Picture someone who looks after both the patient, client, or service user and you. This person stands or sits nearby, calmly sending good energy into the room—whether it is at the site of an accident, a refugee camp, or a hospital ward. It could be someone from the other person's life or from your own: a

(Continued)

(Continued)

former mentor, colleague, manager, or even a patient or client who once left a lasting impression on you.

You might also reimagine the situation with a different, more positive outcome—giving the episode a new ending, or imagining yourself in the future where you can clearly see that your help made a difference (see *The Principle of Time* on page 162.)

Finally, some people find it calming to picture the entire scene bathed in white light—as if held by a divine or protective force. Try out these visualisations and see what works best for you.

Reducing the Uncomfortable

A useful technique to reduce discomfort is to imagine that the troubling image is playing on a screen—a smartphone, TV, or computer. The screen helps create distance between you and the image. You can also visualise a remote control or keyboard. When the image appears, you might 'turn it off', change the channel, switch it to black and white, or zoom out until the image shrinks into a small dot in the centre of the screen. If sounds accompany the image, you can lower the volume, distort the audio, or play it at an extremely fast or slow speed.

Externalising—Putting It Down for Now

Some experiences cling—not because you choose to hold onto them, but because they hold onto you. You may find yourself replaying them later or carrying them home in your body or mind. When that happens, externalising can help.

This method involves placing the emotional residue outside yourself. You might imagine putting it into a box or envelope, or sliding it into a drawer. You can also write a few words on a piece of paper as a signal to yourself: *'I'll come back to this later—in supervision, or tomorrow—but not now'.*

The goal is *not* to forget. It *is* to pause—so you can re-enter your own life with presence. Externalising allows you to mark a boundary. Not to deny what happened, but to honour your need for rest, balance, and recovery.

Closing Note

Regaining control over intrusive thoughts, images, or sounds can help restore a sense of calm after a demanding workday. The techniques described here—from mental reframing to simple distraction—are ways of reclaiming space inside yourself when your mind feels hijacked by what you have seen or heard.

Some professionals also benefit from grounding techniques—physical strategies that help you reconnect with your body and remind you where you end and the outside world begins. These are described in the section *'The Principle of Self-awareness'*.

If intrusive thoughts, images, or sounds persist beyond a few days, it may be a sign of early strain or mental overload. In such cases, don't carry it alone—reach out to a trusted colleague, supervisor, or professional support system.

References

Gerber, M.M. et al. (2018) "Influence of multiple traumatic event types on mental health outcomes: does count matter?," *Journal of Psychopathology and Behavioral Assessment*, 40(4), pp. 645–654. Available at: https://doi.org/10.1007/s10862-018-9682-6.

Idås, T. and Backholm, K. (2023) "Anniversary reactions amongst journalists covering terror: stress reactions and well-being 10 years after the terror in Norway," *European Journal of Psychotraumatology*, 14(2), p. 2220632. Available at: https://doi.org/10.1080/20008066.2023.2220632.

Masten, A.S. and Narayan, A.J. (2012) "Child development in the context of disaster, war, and terrorism: pathways of risk and resilience," *Annual Review of Psychology*, 63(1), pp. 227–257. Available at: https://doi.org/10.1146/annurev-psych-120710-100356.

Naczenski, L.M. et al. (2017) "Systematic review of the association between physical activity and burnout," *Journal of Occupational Health*, 59(6), pp. 477–494. Available at: https://doi.org/10.1539/joh.17-0050-RA.

Rees, G. (2017) "Handling traumatic imagery: developing a standard operating procedure," *Dart Center for Journalism & Trauma*. Available at: https://dartcenter.org/resources/handling-traumatic-imagery-developing-standard-operating-procedure (Accessed: 21 August 2025).

Schrøder, K. et al. (2022) "Evaluation of 'the Buddy Study', a peer support program for second victims in healthcare: a survey in two Danish hospital departments," *BMC Health Services Research*, 22(1), p. 566. Available at: https://doi.org/10.1186/s12913-022-07973-9.

Sonnentag, S. (2012) "Psychological detachment from work during leisure time: the benefits of mentally disengaging from work," *Current Directions in Psychological Science*, 21(2), pp. 114–118. Available at: https://doi.org/10.1177/0963721411434979.

20

Additional Preventive Measures

In Chapters 17, 18, and 19, I described many preventive strategies. While I've placed them where they fit best in terms of role and responsibility, the ideas can of course be used by anyone in the organisation. In this chapter, I will discuss other methods that can be used in everyday life to build resilience and prevent mental tilting.

Supervision—Group or Individual

We have previously discussed how supervision serves as a protective factor by providing a dedicated space for reflection. It allows professionals to adjust their expectations in light of what's realistically possible—based on both their own abilities and the demands of the job (Hensel et al., 2015; O'Connor, Muller Neff and Pitman, 2018).

To benefit from supervision, it is crucial that the atmosphere feels safe—free from the risk of destructive criticism. As mentioned earlier, a key aspect of supervision is the counsellor's relationship with the client(s). For example, do you feel well-connected and balanced in your role, or have you developed a tendency towards either over-involvement or under-involvement (Peled-Avram, 2017)?

In mentally high-risk jobs, it is essential that the supervisor recognises the strain experienced by their supervisee and actively works to normalise their emotional reactions. Research suggests that relationship-oriented supervision contributes to a lower risk of secondary traumatisation. This type of supervision is characterised by a positive, appreciative approach, where the supervisor partly steps out of the traditional expert role and instead adopts a more open and vulnerable position.

Buddy Systems

A buddy system involves pairing two (or three) colleagues who commit to supporting each other in the day-to-day work. This increases the likelihood that team members will talk to each other if one begins to feel overwhelmed or has been exposed to a violent or particularly emotionally taxing situation. Many people find it difficult to ask for help after a stressful event, so a buddy system creates a framework where such conversations feel natural and are genuinely welcomed.

Some workplaces make buddy systems mandatory, while others offer them on a voluntary basis. If participation is required, it is important that employees are allowed to choose their own buddy to ensure there is good chemistry and mutual trust.

Buddy systems are especially useful in large workplaces or in environments with rotating shifts, where employees may not see each other regularly. They help ensure that no one is left alone with the emotional residue of difficult experiences (Kinchin, 2007).

Mentoring Programmes

Mentoring is another effective tool in high-risk professions. To promote learning and development, organisations can establish mentorship pairings between experienced professionals and newer colleagues. The mentor's role is to guide and support the mentee, helping them navigate the complexities of the job.

This kind of mentoring speeds up learning for the newcomer but also reinforces the idea that mentally high-risk work is, at its core, a collective endeavour.

> *I always encourage other managers to mentor their new hires—especially recent graduates. When you're young, you often need a lot of help to get off to a strong start in mental high-risk work.*

Leadership Mentoring and Coaching

In a complex and high-pressure work environment, where leaders are short on time and face constant demands, regular sparring with a fellow leader, consultant, or coach can offer much-needed clarity and perspective.

As a manager, it is important to have a space for reflection—separate from day-to-day operations—where you can examine your leadership style, gather inspiration, and stay attuned not only to your organisation and staff but also to yourself and your own reactions.

Trauma Therapy

During a specific task, a professional may uncover—or unintentionally aggravate—a vulnerability linked to past trauma. If left unprocessed, earlier traumatic experiences can lead to re-traumatisation or increase the risk of secondary traumatisation (Hensel et al., 2015; La Mott and Martin, 2019). Both outcomes may impair the individual's quality of work and, in severe cases, endanger patient or client safety.

If trauma is suspected or clearly present, the person affected should be offered trauma therapy either individually or in a group setting.

When strain shows up in the body—through pain, tension, or other physical symptoms—body-centred therapy can be a powerful way to support recovery.

References

Hensel, J.M. et al. (2015) "Meta-analysis of risk factors for secondary traumatic stress in therapeutic work with trauma victims," *Journal of Traumatic Stress, 28*(2), pp. 83–91. Available at: https://doi.org/10.1002/jts.21998.

Kinchin, D. (2007) *A Guide to Psychological Debriefing: Managing Emotional Decompression and Post-Traumatic Stress Disorder*. London; Philadelphia: Jessica Kingsley Publishers.

La Mott, J. and Martin, L.A. (2019) "Adverse childhood experiences, self-care, and compassion outcomes in mental health providers working with trauma," *Journal of Clinical Psychology, 75*(6), pp. 1066–1083. Available at: https://doi.org/10.1002/jclp.22752.

O'Connor, K., Muller Neff, D. and Pitman, S. (2018) "Burnout in mental health professionals: a systematic review and meta-analysis of prevalence and determinants," *European Psychiatry, 53*, pp. 74–99. Available at: https://doi.org/10.1016/j.eurpsy.2018.06.003.

Peled-Avram, M. (2017) "The role of relational-oriented supervision and personal and work-related factors in the development of vicarious traumatization," *Clinical Social Work Journal, 45*(1), pp. 22–32. Available at: https://doi.org/10.1007/s10615-015-0573-y.

21

In Times of Crisis: A Tiered Approach

No matter how well an organisation prepares for the everyday challenges of working life, acute events will occur. A serious accident. A violent threat. A sudden loss. These situations may affect a single employee, a team, or the entire organisation. While risks can be reduced, they can never be fully eliminated. That is why workplaces need well-prepared and regularly practised contingency plans—not just to manage the event itself, but to protect both mental health and the team's sense of connection.

In the public sector especially, when a service user, client, or patient experiences a critical event, the first line of response is often a professional —a nurse, teacher, social worker, paramedic, or other front-line worker. These professionals are not only expected to support the person affected but often find themselves impacted by the situation as well. In such moments, it helps to remember that we are all part of a wider support system: We support others—and we support each other. That simple principle strengthens both professional integrity and human connection.

In this chapter, we introduce two interrelated models:

The *Workplace Support Pyramid*, which outlines how psychosocial support can be organised internally.

And the *Community Support Pyramid*, which shows how the broader societal support system can be mobilised in times of crisis.

Both are tiered models—grounded in international best practice—that help organisations and communities tailor their support efforts in proportion to the situation. Together, they provide a framework for understanding how help can be activated, adapted, and escalated when people are exposed to serious strain or trauma.

The Workplace Support Pyramid and the Community Support Pyramid were originally introduced in the Danish handbook as mentioned elsewhere, the English version is in preparation to be published by Wiley.

This chapter draws on that work and has been adapted and translated for an international readership.

From Everyday Prevention to Targeted Crisis Response

The Workplace Support Pyramid offers a practical framework for evaluating how much support needs to be activated in response to psychological strain. At its foundation are universal, everyday practices such as self-care, peer support, and a culture of psychological safety. These form the baseline for all employees and are relevant regardless of the situation.

As strain increases—whether through prolonged stress or acute incidents—support must be intensified accordingly. Structured interventions such as psychological first aid, leadership check-ins, or group-based follow-up conversations (such as defusing) may be required. In more complex cases, further steps are necessary: professional debriefing or individual trauma-focused assistance.

Importantly, the pyramid does not replace broader preventive models like the IGLO-E framework, which clarifies who holds responsibility at different organisational levels. Instead, it answers a different question: When should support be activated—and how much is needed?

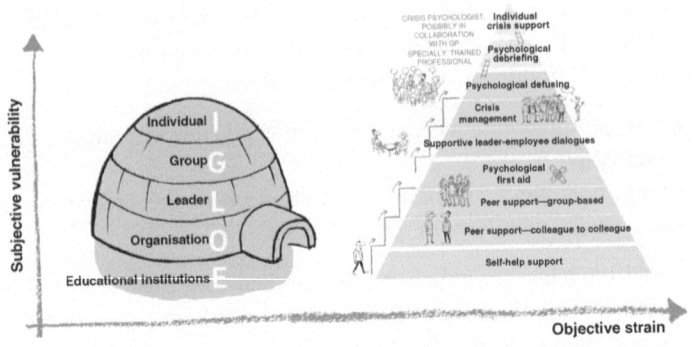

Use the IGLO-E for prevention in everyday work life and—the Workplace Support Pyramid in situations of accumulated or acute strain.

In this sense, the shift from prevention to crisis response is not a change in values, but a change in intensity and coordination. A strong culture of prevention makes this adjustment possible. Rather than allowing psychological strain to build unnoticed or erupt unmanaged, the workplace can respond with care, clarity, and shared responsibility.

The model aligns with internationally recognised tiered-response frameworks, which indicate that most people recover well with early, proportionate, and trusted support—especially from within their immediate environment. Only a historically marginalised require specialist intervention. The stronger the inner foundation, the less need for external escalation. This perspective echoes evidence that recovery is shaped less by the event itself and more by how it is met—through leadership, workplace culture, and supportive others (Zalta et al., 2021).

A Note on Global Alignment

The tiered approach used in the Workplace and Community Support Pyramids reflects internationally recognised best practice. Similar multi-layered models have been endorsed by the World Health Organization (WHO) and the Inter-Agency Standing Committee (IASC) in their Guidelines on Mental Health and Psychosocial Support in Emergency Settings (2007). These frameworks emphasise scalable support—starting with informal and everyday resources, and escalating only when needed to specialist care. The aim is to match support to need, while avoiding over-medicalisation and promoting community-based resilience.

The Workplace Support Pyramid—A Tiered Overview

The Workplace Support Pyramid outlines a progressive approach to psycho-social support—beginning with individual coping strategies and escalating to professional assistance when needed. Each level represents a distinct form of help, activated according to the intensity and scope of the strain.

Model 12: The Workplace Support Pyramid

- Self-help
  The first response to strain often comes from the person themselves. Short breaks, adjusting personal expectations, talking to someone trustworthy, or regaining a sense of control through familiar activities can help stabilise the situation. Basic awareness of one's own stress reactions is key.

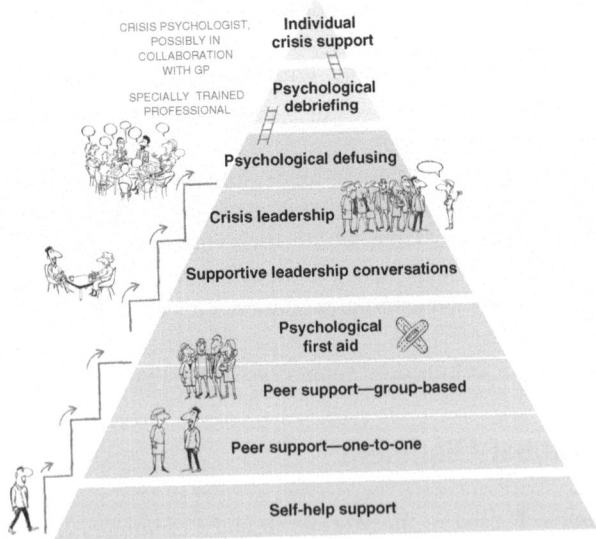

- Peer Support
  Colleagues play a vital role in early support. Whether through simple presence, active listening, or shared experience, being available to one another creates a safety net at the heart of the workplace community.
- Psychological First Aid
  Trained peer supporters provide structured assistance in the initial phase after a difficult experience. The goal is to calm, connect, and support the affected person in regaining overview—without clinical intervention.
- Supportive Leadership Conversations
  Managers—whether direct supervisors or trusted figures in leadership—can create psychological safety by initiating check-ins, showing concern, and helping frame the experience. A proactive and sincere leader presence reduces isolation and strengthens trust.
- Crisis Leadership
  When a wider team or entire organisation is affected, coordinated leadership becomes essential. Clear communication, collective briefings, and visible care help stabilise the situation and guide the group through uncertainty.
- Psychological Defusing
  This is a brief, structured conversation held shortly after a critical incident. It offers space to share initial reactions, reduce confusion, and identify support needs. Led by an experienced colleague or designated crisis contact.
- Psychological Debriefing
  Some events require deeper collective processing. A professionally facilitated debrief enables those involved to reflect on what happened, how it

affected them, and what support may still be needed. Timing and consent are essential.

- Individual Crisis Support

  In a few cases, an employee may need specialised help—such as trauma therapy or individual counselling. This level of support complements, rather than replaces, the shared efforts at workplace level.

A Closer Look at Two Key Layers

While all levels of the Workplace Support Pyramid matter, two stand out for their practical relevance in the early phase of a crisis: psychological first aid and crisis leadership. These interventions often unfold within the first hours or days after a critical incident—and can make a decisive difference for how individuals and teams recover.

The following sections provide a closer look at these two layers: not as comprehensive manuals, but as hands-on guidance for those expected to act swiftly, supportively, and with care.

---

10 Steps of Psychological First Aid in Acute Situations

A practical guide for immediate support following a critical incident

Step 1: Stop the incident and call for medical help if needed

Make sure everyone is safe. If necessary, call emergency services. In chaotic situations, ask others to help create calm and shield those involved from further exposure.

Step 2: Get an overview

Who needs help? Who can help? Prioritise. Divide responsibilities. If possible, work in pairs—one focuses on the affected person, the other on practical matters.

Step 3: Move to a quiet and private space

Stay nearby and offer comfort—a warm drink, a blanket, or simply your presence. If you need to leave, make sure someone else steps in and maintains contact.

Step 4: Stay calm

Breathe slowly and speak clearly. Your calmness will help others remain calm. Eye contact, a gentle tone, or a light touch can be reassuring—but always respect the other person's boundaries. Do not hug or touch others unless you are sure it is welcome.

(Continued)

(Continued)

Step 5: Help the person connect with loved ones

People in crisis often need to reach someone they trust. Offer support in contacting family or friends—to share what happened, to arrange transport, or simply to avoid being alone. Even small practical acts help restore normalcy.

Step 6: Listen

Ask simple, concrete questions to help the person piece together what happened:

- 'When did you realise ...?'
- 'What happened then?'
- 'Who else was there?'

Avoid 'why' questions. They often trigger pressure to explain or justify, which the person may not be able to do.

Do **not** criticise, minimise, offer clichés, share your own stories, or steer the conversation away from their experience.

If the person repeats themselves, let them. It's often a way of processing and finding order.

If they don't want to talk about what happened, respect that—and talk about something they bring up instead.

Important: Many people feel guilt or shame in the immediate aftermath of a crisis. Don't dismiss those feelings. Accept and acknowledge them gently. You might say: 'It's very common to feel guilt after something like this. You might see things differently in a few days'.

Feeling heard—without judgement—can ease internal pressure and prevent isolation.

Step 7: Keep it simple—and repeat

When a person is in shock, it's hard to concentrate or retain information. Stick to the basics, and repeat key points gently. Speak as you would to someone overwhelmed—the brain needs clarity, not complexity.

Step 8: Normalise reactions

The body and mind may react in unfamiliar or frightening ways during crisis. Reassure the person that strong feelings—confusion, physical tension, fear, or shame—are normal reactions to abnormal situations.

This is especially important if the person has never experienced a crisis before.

Step 9: Clarify the immediate next hours

Ask what they need right now. Help make a short plan for the rest of the day or evening. If appropriate, agree to check in the next day—even just briefly.

Step 10: Hand over the responsibility

Make sure the person's immediate supervisor or another relevant party is informed about what happened and what support has been provided so far. From there, the leadership takes over responsibility for continued follow-up and care.

Crisis Leadership: 10 Supportive Actions for Leaders in the Immediate Aftermath

1. **Make Safety the First Priority**

   Your most urgent task is to prevent further harm. Stay calm and act quickly to secure the area. Ensure that anyone who is injured or at risk receives the necessary care—and don't hesitate to call emergency services. If others are nearby, ask them to help create calm and clarity.

2. **Bring People Together and Clarify Roles**

   In chaotic moments, people look to leadership for orientation. Invite key staff together—including care coordinators, psychological first aiders or health and safety reps—and gently clarify who does what. Make sure those affected are moved to a quiet and private space, away from unnecessary attention.

3. **Keep a Shared Record of What Happens**

When emotions run high, it's easy to lose track. Ask someone to document key steps and decisions. This simple log can support later evaluation, help people understand what was done and why—and, if needed, provide accountability.

4. **Host a Brief, Honest All-staff Meeting**

Bring the team together—on-site or online—and share a short, factual briefing. Acknowledge what has happened, clarify what's being done, and reassure staff that support is available. Use the psychological ABC as a guide:

- A: Reactions are normal when something unusual happens.
- B: Let's take care of each other—and ourselves—in the days ahead.
- C: If you need anything, speak to your manager or a trusted colleague.

End with clarity: when and how will more information be shared?

5. **Consider a Short Pause in Operations**

Sometimes, it's helpful to slow down briefly—especially after a serious event. A short pause shows that people's well-being is more important than productivity. But aim to resume work as soon as it feels manageable: normal routines can bring grounding and calm.

6. **Reach Out Compassionately to Next of Kin**

If someone is seriously injured or has passed away, make contact with their family with care and respect. Listen more than you speak. Ask what kind of support they need—now or later—and respect their wishes regarding communication and remembrance.

7. **Check In Personally in the Days After**

Shock may fade quickly, but emotional reactions often surface later. Make time to ask how people are doing—not only those directly affected but also their close colleagues. Let them know that it's okay to struggle, and offer flexibility and follow-up if needed.

8. **Mark the Event in a Caring Way**

If someone has died, consider how to acknowledge the loss. A simple moment of silence, a condolence message, or attending a memorial can be deeply meaningful. Even small acts show that people—and their lives—matter.

9. **Accept That Recovery Takes Time**

People process things differently. Some bounce back quickly; others need more space. Communicate clearly that all reactions are valid, and let people know that adjustments and support will be made where needed.

10. **Keep the Dialogue Open**

Follow up regularly, even if there is little new to say. A brief update or check-in can reduce uncertainty. What matters is not having all the answers—but showing that you care, and that the workplace stands together when things get tough.

Sick Leave and Reintegration

Being exposed to a critical incident—and reacting strongly to it—should not automatically lead to time off work. For many, returning to familiar routines and being part of the work community can offer a sense of structure, belonging, and meaning. What matters is that the individual is only assigned tasks that align with their current capacity and that pressure is avoided.

In some cases, a short period of full or partial sick leave may be helpful—not as avoidance, but as a needed pause to regain stability. Whatever the approach, it is the leader's responsibility to stay in close contact and to ensure a safe and thoughtful return. After sick leave, gradual reintegration and careful task adjustment help ensure that expectations match real time capacity—and that recovery is supported in practice, not just in words (Clayton, 2018).

While the workplace plays a critical role in immediate recovery, it is rarely the only source of support. The next section explores how the broader community can contribute to sustainable care and continuity.

Beyond the Workplace: Community Support Pyramid

Every organisation is embedded in a broader social context—including communities, welfare systems, and healthcare structures. This wider reality is captured in the Community Support Pyramid, which complements the workplace-level efforts described above.

This relationship has several key implications:

- **Shared responsibility and limits**: While workplaces play a vital role in early response and prevention, some events will exceed what internal support systems can carry. In those cases, external resources—such as specialised trauma therapy, psychiatric services, social support, or legal protection—must be activated.
- **Better coordination, smoother transitions**: When organisations take responsibility for their part of the pyramid, they create stronger bridges to public services. A coherent handover—from internal support to community-based care—helps prevent long-term harm and unnecessary escalation.
- **Multi-level prevention**: Community systems also shape what workplaces are able to do. Laws, collective agreements, healthcare access, and public health campaigns all set the conditions for psychological safety at work. When these broader structures support the workplace's preventive efforts, more people receive timely and proportionate help.

Both pyramids follow the same basic logic: Support is most effective when it begins within the natural relationships and routines of daily life—and adapts upward only as needed. The stronger the foundation, the less pressure is placed on top-tier services.

Together, these two pyramids reflect a shared responsibility across individual, organisational, and societal levels—ensuring that no one is left without support, whether as an employee or as a user.

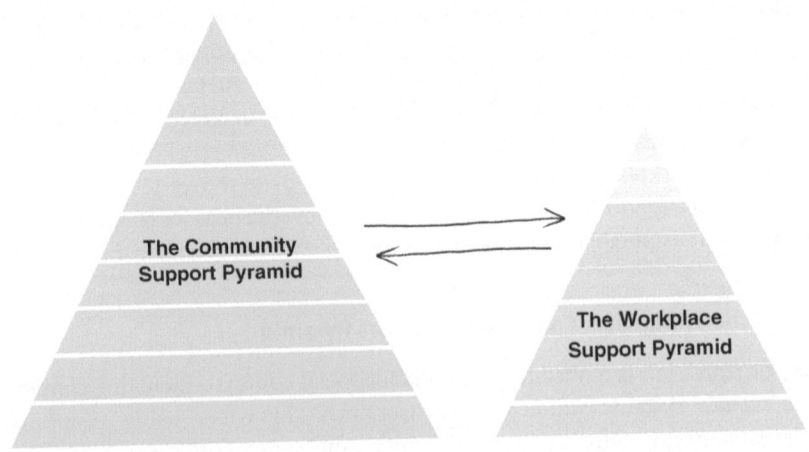

The Community Support Pyramid and the Workplace Support Pyramid complement each other, forming a coherent and integrated support system before, during, and after critical incidents.

The Community Support Pyramid

The Community Support Pyramid illustrates how assistance following a distressing event can be provided across multiple levels—from individual self-care and informal support networks to specialised professional services. For most people, the most accessible and effective support is found in the lower tiers of the pyramid, where close relationships and local communities play a key role.

Model 13: The Community Support Pyramid

Self-help

The first level of support begins with the individual. Simple actions like stepping outside, taking a deep breath, journaling, or engaging in a familiar routine can offer relief and help restore emotional balance.

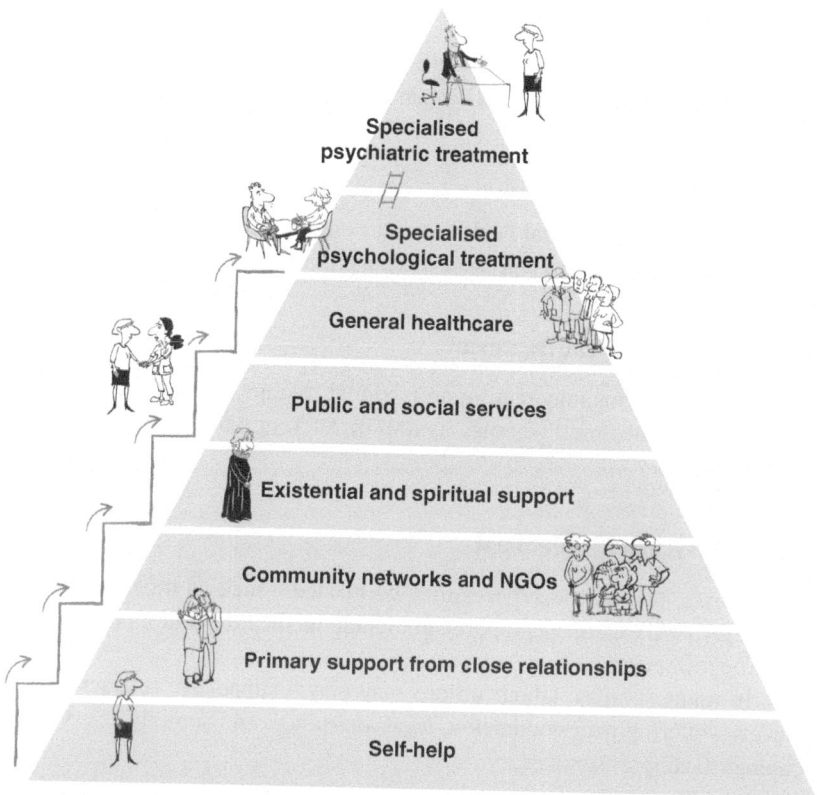

Close Relationships

Family, friends, colleagues, and fellow students can offer essential emotional and practical support. A walk, a message, or just being present can reduce isolation and provide comfort in a time of strain.

Community Networks and NGOs

In addition to close personal ties, people may also find support in local associations, faith communities, sports clubs, or NGOs. Shared experience and voluntary engagement often foster a sense of belonging and mutual understanding.

Existential and Spiritual Support

For some, faith or existential reflection can provide meaning in the face of crisis. Conversations with spiritual leaders or participation in rituals may offer clarity, peace, or connection.

Public and Social Services

Government and municipal services can assist with practical needs—housing, finances, legal advice, or access to crisis centres.

General Health Care

General practitioners and local health services often represent the first step into the professional system. They can assess needs, provide guidance, or refer further.

Specialised Psychological Treatment

More complex reactions may require professional therapy. Trained psychologists offer trauma-informed methods such as EMDR, CBT, or narrative approaches to support recovery.

Specialised Psychiatric Treatment

In severe cases, psychiatric services may be needed—such as inpatient care or treatment for PTSD. Clinical support can include medication and more intensive therapeutic frameworks.

Note: In many settings, labour unions may play a supportive role across several levels—offering peer connection, legal assistance, and sometimes access to psychological support services.

Facilitating Support Pathways

Personal relationships often serve not only as a source of care, but also as a bridge to further help. Family members, friends, or colleagues may be the ones who help a person take the next step—whether by identifying support options, making initial contact, or simply being present during the process.

Clear and caring transitions between levels of support are vital—they help people feel safe and stay connected. Needs can shift over time, and the ability to adjust support accordingly is key to effective recovery. The earlier help is offered—and the more closely it is integrated into everyday life—the greater the chance of preventing serious strain.

This is why professional services must be complemented by an active and compassionate support culture amongst individuals, communities, and workplaces.

Structural Foundations of Support

Whether support is offered in the workplace or within the broader community, access to help is shaped by the systems and structures that surround us. No support model operates in isolation—each is influenced by national legislation, public policy, and social frameworks that determine how care is organised and delivered.

These structural factors may either expand or limit what is possible. They set the conditions for how workplaces handle crises, how individuals are referred to professional care, and how fairness and compensation are addressed in high-strain situations.

Relevant frameworks may include mental health strategies, occupational safety regulations, workers' compensation systems, access to legal advice, or public health coverage. All of these shape both the Workplace and Community Support Pyramids—and ultimately influence how people are met, supported, and helped to recover.

Strong public systems form the foundation of an inclusive support culture—one that ensures no one is left behind, whether as employees or citizens.

References

Clayton, S. (2018) "Mental health risk and resilience among climate scientists," *Nature Climate Change*, 8(4), pp. 260–261. Available at: https://doi.org/10.1038/s41558-018-0123-z.

Zalta, A.K. et al. (2021) "Examining moderators of the relationship between social support and self-reported PTSD symptoms: a meta-analysis," *Psychological Bulletin*, 147(1), pp. 33–54. Available at: https://doi.org/10.1037/bul0000316.

22

Proactive Psychosocial Prevention

Good prevention is like a washing machine: no single cycle fits all loads—and no single strategy fits all strain. Some situations call for quick action, others for gentle care. Some require clear routines and structure; others require pause, support, or space to breathe.

The key is to have a wide selection of responses to match the variety of challenges professionals face. Prevention needs to be flexible, responsive, and well-practised—just like knowing when to run a delicate cycle or when to spin at full speed.

A balanced strain strategy requires as many settings as a modern washing machine. From fast cycles to gentle care, every program has its place.

Prevention efforts can be grouped into three interconnected levels:

- Primary prevention: to avoid strain-related injuries
- Secondary prevention: to detect early signs and respond quickly
- Tertiary prevention: to reduce the impact of existing injury and prevent relapse

Each of these approaches falls into one of four categories: proactive or reactive, and individual or collective. A proactive and collective measure—such as embedding psychological safety into everyday culture—is quite different from a reactive and individual one, like treating burnout after sick leave. All categories matter, but a healthy prevention culture relies especially on those that are both proactive and collective.

This chapter outlines the three prevention levels and their practical implementation in strain-related work.

Primary Prevention

Primary prevention focuses on reducing risk factors before strain-related issues arise. It includes contingency plans, knowledge building, clear work procedures, and continuous analysis and evaluation of potential risks.

Key Components of Primary Prevention

Contingency Plans
Well-crafted contingency plans are essential. They should be grounded in knowledge of strain psychology (see Parts I and II of this book), and describe how the organisation prepares for and responds to psychologically demanding situations—from violence and threats to overload, helplessness or moral conflict.

Knowledge of Strain Psychology
Employees need basic knowledge about how psychosocial strain arises, how to recognise early signs, and how to respond constructively. Strain reactions are part of being human—and of being deeply engaged in one's work. Recognising them early supports timely dialogue, ethical responsibility, and a culture of care.

Documentation, Analysis, and Evaluation
Organisations should document work situations that contribute to strain—such as violence, threats, lack of mandate, understaffing, or unmanageable complexity. They should also document what works: which tasks, teams or workflows help prevent overload. This allows for continuous evaluation and allows organisations to learn and adapt preventive efforts over time.

Examples of Primary Prevention

- Clear work procedures
- Contingency planning
- Physical safety measures
- Mentoring systems
- Access to supervision
- Psychological first aid and defusing routines
- Strategic competence development
- Regular training and drills
- Clear division of tasks and responsibilities

Secondary Prevention

Secondary prevention involves early detection of strain and rapid action to reduce its impact. This requires timely support at multiple levels: individual, group, managerial, and organisational.

Individual Level

At the individual level, secondary prevention includes:

- Physical tools to regulate the nervous system
- Conscious transitions at the start and end of the workday
- Awareness of personal coping strategies to maintain healthy boundaries

Group Level

At the group level, it includes:

- Extra collegial sparring or knowledge sharing
- Emotional support
- Additional practical assistance

Managerial Level

At the managerial level, prevention may involve:

- Clear prioritisation of tasks
- Adjustments that allow time for recovery
- Strategic distribution of responsibilities
- Explicit recognition of employees' efforts

Organisational Level

At the organisational level, secondary prevention includes:

- Flexible personnel policies (e.g., flexible hours or remote work options)
- Interventions that strengthen psychological safety
- Social support for managers and teams during high-strain periods

Tertiary Prevention

Tertiary prevention aims to prevent an existing strain-related condition from worsening and to support sustainable recovery.

This includes access to treatment (psychotherapeutic, medical, or both), meaningful contact during sick leave, and carefully managed return-to-work processes. These efforts are most effective when combined with continued documentation, analysis, and adaptation of preventive strategies.

Examples of Tertiary Prevention

- Help navigating access to professional treatment
- Extra managerial and collegial support during part-time sick leave
- Ongoing adjustments to tasks and pace based on energy and capacity
- Regular contact with colleagues or manager during full-time sick leave (if desired)
- Reduced demands on teams affected by sick leave
- Reallocation of organisational resources to reduce pressure
- Support for leaders managing affected teams

Better Safe Than Sorry—Especially in High-strain Work

Organisations working in high-strain sectors should adopt the mindset that it is always better to prevent than to repair. Proactive, dynamic, and collective prevention improves not only employee well-being and resilience but also the safety and quality of service delivery—for the benefit of both professionals and those they support.

As summarised in the model below, effective prevention works best when actions are matched to the nature and level of strain.

PROACTIVE AND REACTIVE PSYCHOSOCIAL PREVENTION

Proactive

Reactive

Individual prevention

Collective prevention

Primary prevention

To avoid
strain-related injuries

⇩

Primary prevention concerns:
- Contingency plans
- Knowledge of strain psychology
- Documentation and analysis
- Clear work procedures

⇩

Examples of prevention efforts:
- Clear work procedures
- Contingency planning
- Physical safety measures
- Mentoring systems
- Access to supervision
- Psychological first aid and defusing routines
- Strategic competence development
- Regular training and drills
- Clear division of tasks and responsibilities

Secondary prevention

To detect early signs and
respond quickly

⇩

Secondary prevention concerns:
- Early identification
- Timely support
- Adjustments to tasks and schedules
- Tools and methods to reduce strain

⇩

Examples of prevention efforts:
Individual level
- Physical tools; conscious transitions; coping strategies
Group level
- Collegial sparring; emotional support; practical assistance
Managerial level
- Prioritisation; adjustments for recovery; task distribution; recognition
Organisational level
- Flexible personnel policies; strengthening psychological safety; social support during high strain

Tertiary prevention

To reduce the impact of existing
injury and prevent relapse

⇩

Tertiary prevention concerns:
- Access to treatment
- Support during sick leave
- Return-to-work practices
- Ongoing documentation and evaluation
- Coordinated support across all levels of the Support Pyramid

⇩

Examples of prevention efforts:
- Help accessing treatment
- Extra support during part-time sick leave
- Adjustments to tasks and pace
- Contact during full-time sick leave (if desired)
- Reduced demands on affected teams
- Reallocation of resources
- Support for leaders managing affected teams
- Coordinated support across all levels of the Support Pyramid

Epilogue

Being Human

I would like to end this book by acknowledging some of the remarkable professionals I've had the privilege to learn from over the years. Let me mention just a few of them here.

The first who comes to mind is the late Danish psychiatrist and professor Preben Hertoft. He often used to say:

"Now, let's remember we can't walk on water".

Perhaps it sounds banal—but it's a truth worth holding on to when your work takes place in the landscape of tragedy. I often repeat this phrase to myself.

Another person I want to mention is a former colleague I met during a training course at Falck, a Danish emergency response organisation known for its ambulance and rescue services. Unfortunately, I no longer remember his name. He told me about an accident in which a pair of siblings were standing by a road they were about to cross. Suddenly, the younger child ran into the street and was hit by a car, dying instantly. When the paramedic was later asked what went through his mind upon arriving at the scene, he said:

I thought: it's good for the parents that the other child didn't run after the first one.

A brutal thought—but deeply human.

Back in 1998, I wrote my thesis on primary and secondary traumatisation at the University of Copenhagen and had since developed both solid knowledge and broad practical experience. Still, when I came across *Trauma Stewardship* by Laura van Dernoot Lipsky in 2009, something clicked. Lipsky gave a clear and accessible language to something complex—and conveyed it with warmth, precision, and humour. She showed how trauma exposure, if not addressed professionally, can lead to psychological strain in both staff and leaders—and shape the entire organisational culture in ways that make it harder to think clearly and act professionally.

I also carry with me the teachings of my former supervisor, the late British psychotherapist and pastor Peter Lang. He was a master at helping people recognise that, even in trauma, they are not just passive victims, but active agents.

One story in particular has stayed with me. An African family had taken refuge in a church during a civil war. Enemy soldiers found them and dragged the father outside, preparing to execute him in front of his wife and children. Afterwards, the mother was tormented by guilt for not having done anything. The following conversation between Peter and the woman took place:

Peter: Tell me what happened.

Woman: They had pulled my husband out into the square, and I just stood there watching.

Peter: Where were the children?

Woman: They stood on either side of me. I placed a hand on each of their shoulders.

Peter: Why did you do that?

Woman: They needed to feel me—and I had to stop them from running towards their father. That could have made things worse. It also stopped me from running forward. But it was hard.

Peter: So there you were, in the worst moment of your life, and you managed to comfort your children. You assessed the situation and took action to prevent it from escalating—protecting everyone from even greater danger. What do you think your husband was thinking at the time?

(Long silence)

Woman: I think he knew that was why I stood still. He knew I would do anything to protect our children.

Peter: What else did you do?

Woman: I kept eye contact with him so he wouldn't feel alone in the horror around him.

Peter: So even in the worst situation imaginable, you continued to show your husband your love. Is that right?

The woman broke down in tears. She said her husband had known how deeply she loved him—and that she would always be a good mother to their children.

During my time in the Danish Armed Forces, I met hostage negotiator Jens Serup—someone whose grounded approach to extreme situations has stayed with me. His work involves resolving complex conflicts around the world—often in highly dangerous situations—and he has successfully negotiated the release of many hostages. When I asked him how he maintains his mental resilience, he said:

> *The key to surviving a dangerous—and in many ways extreme—job is to carry a solid dose of normalcy and stability with you. I think practically: I always have a long to-do list of chores I'm behind on at home. And then it's about having something more important than your own ego, money, recognition, or status—and remembering that. At least that's what works for me.*

Finally, I want to share a piece of advice from one of my great professional heroes, the American psychiatrist and author Irvin D. Yalom. In one of his books, he writes:

> *There is nothing you have told me that is not human.*

That sentence has stayed with me ever since. As a crisis psychologist, you often meet clients burdened by shame or guilt connected to violent or traumatic events. I remember a soldier who felt devastated and ashamed because, during a mortar attack, his only thought was for his own safety—not the safety of the entire group. In that moment, Yalom's sentence lifted the conversation to a judgement-free space—allowing a shared understanding of the human element in what had happened.

And that, at its core, is what strain psychology is all about:

Reminding us of the deeply human reactions to extreme stress—and reminding us to take good care of one another.

Thank you for reading,
Rikke Høgsted

Appendix 1

Guide to the Well-Being Index: WHO-5

The WHO-5 is a measure of well-being. It consists of five questions about how an individual has felt in the past two weeks. It captures the degree of positive experiences and serves as an indicator of a person's overall well-being.

The WHO-5 has been tested across diverse populations in multiple countries. It is simple to administer and supported by robust evidence confirming its reliability as a well-being measure. Developed by Professor Per Bech for the World Health Organization, the WHO-5 is freely available for use in assessing psychological well-being.

However, it is important to note:

- The WHO-5 does not directly measure daily functioning, though there is believed to be a correlation between functional ability and well-being.
- The WHO-5 is not a diagnostic tool but rather a measure of well-being. A low score suggests that an individual requires support or treatment, which would need to be further assessed by a medical professional.

Well-Being Index WHO-5

For each of the five statements, tick the box that comes closest to how you have been feeling in the past two weeks. Note that a higher number represents better well-being.

Example: If you've felt cheerful and in good spirits a little more than half of the time in the last two weeks, tick the box with the number 3 in the first question.

The World Health Organization-Five Well-Being Index (WHO-5).

		All of the time	Most of the time	More than half of the time	Less than half of the time	Some of the time	At no time
1	I have felt cheerful and in good spirits	5	4	3	2	1	0
2	I have felt calm and relaxed	5	4	3	2	1	0
3	I have felt active and vigorous	5	4	3	2	1	0
4	I woke up feeling fresh and rested	5	4	3	2	1	0
5	My daily life has been filled with things that interest me	5	4	3	2	1	0

Source: The WHO-5 Well-Being Index is copyright ©1998 World Health Organization.

How to Calculate the Result

The score is calculated by adding the numbers in the ticked boxes and then multiplying the sum by four. This gives a number between 0 and 100. The more points, the higher the well-being. If the number is below 50, the test person may be at risk of depression or may be exposed to long-term stress.

Interpretation of Results

Standard: The average for the population is a score of 68; however, a score above 50 means that the test person is not at an immediate risk of depression or long-term stress.

Scores between 0 and 35: You may be at high risk of depression or stress. You score significantly lower than the average for the rest of the population. This score suggests that you are not at your best and there may be a serious risk of suffering from depression or long-term stress. You should consider seeking help from your doctor.

Scores between 36 and 50: You may be at risk of depression or stress. Your score is lower than the average. This score suggests you may not be feeling well. Pay attention to whether you feel better or worse and seek medical attention if needed.

Score above 50: There is no immediate risk of depression or stress. You are within the average (68), with a lower limit around 50.

Age: The WHO-5 has been tested on people aged from 16 years old. Individuals aged 16–20 years typically score slightly lower than 20–80 year olds (people over 80 typically score the lowest).

Gender: Women typically score slightly lower than men (67 vs 69 points on average, respectively).

Appendix 2

Professional Quality of Life Scale – The ProQOL

The "Professional Quality of Life Scale" is a measurement tool originally developed by Charles Figley. This section provides a refined version of the "Professional Quality of Life Scale" by B. Hudnall Stamm.

Professional Quality of Life Assessment

Helping people involves forming direct connections with their lives. Caring for others can affect you in both positive and negative ways. Below you will find some questions about your experiences, both positive and negative, as a carer. Consider each of the following questions about you and your current work situation. Choose the answer that most closely reflects your experiences in the past 30 days. Professional Quality of Life Scale (ProQOL).

Your Results in ProQOL

Professional Quality of Life Screenings
Now place the results from your scoring below. If there is anything you are unsure or worried about, discuss your results with a relevant professional.

Compassion Satisfaction
Carer satisfaction refers to the joy you get from being able to do your job well. For example, you may feel happy that your work allows you to help others, or you may take pride in your relationships with colleagues, your contributions in the workplace, or the positive impact you have on society. Higher scores on this scale reflect greater satisfaction with your ability to be an effective carer.

| 1 = Never | 2 = Rarely | 3 = Sometimes | 4 = Often | 5 = Very Often |

_____ 1. I am happy.

_____ 2. I am preoccupied with more than one person I *[help]*.

_____ 3. I get satisfaction from being able to *[help]* people.

_____ 4. I feel connected to others.

_____ 5. I jump or am startled by unexpected sounds.

_____ 6. I feel invigorated after working with those I *[help]*.

_____ 7. I find it difficult to separate my personal life from my life as a *[helper]*.

_____ 8. I am not as productive at work because I am losing sleep over traumatic experiences of a person I *[help]*.

_____ 9. I think that I might have been affected by the traumatic stress of those I *[help]*.

_____ 10. I feel trapped by my job as a *[helper]*.

_____ 11. Because of my *[helping]*, I have felt "on edge" about various things.

_____ 12. I like my work as a *[helper]*.

_____ 13. I feel depressed because of the traumatic experiences of the people I *[help]*.

_____ 14. I feel as though I am experiencing the trauma of someone I have *[helped]*.

_____ 15. I have beliefs that sustain me.

_____ 16. I am pleased with how I am able to keep up with *[helping]* techniques and protocols.

_____ 17. I am the person I always wanted to be.

_____ 18. My work makes me feel satisfied.

_____ 19. I feel worn out because of my work as a *[helper]*.

_____ 20. I have happy thoughts and feelings about those I *[help]* and how I could help them.

_____ 21. I feel overwhelmed because my case [work] load seems endless.

_____ 22. I believe I can make a difference through my work.

_____ 23. I avoid certain activities or situations because they remind me of frightening experiences of the people I *[help]*.

_____ 24. I am proud of what I can do to *[help]*.

_____ 25. As a result of my *[helping]*, I have intrusive, frightening thoughts.

_____ 26. I feel "bogged down" by the system.

_____ 27. I have thoughts that I am a "success" as a *[helper]*.

_____ 28. I can't recall important parts of my work with trauma victims.

_____ 29. I am a very caring person.

_____ 30. I am happy that I chose to do this work.

Source: Stamm, 2009/Center for Victims of Torture.

WHAT IS MY SCORE AND WHAT DOES IT MEAN?

In this section, you will score your test so you understand the interpretation for you. To find your score on **each section**, total the questions listed on the left and then find your score in the table on the right of the section.

Compassion Satisfaction Scale

Copy your rating on each of these questions on to this table and add them up. When you have added then up you can find your score on the table to the right.

3. ____
6. ____
12. ____
16. ____
18. ____
20. ____
22. ____
24. ____
27. ____
30. ____

Total: _____

The sum of my Compassion Satisfaction questions is	And my Compassion Satisfaction level is
22 or less	Low
Between 23 and 41	Moderate
42 or more	High

Burnout Scale

On the burnout scale you will need to take an extra step. Starred items are "reverse scored." If you scored the item 1, write a 5 beside it. The reason we ask you to reverse the scores is because scientifically the measure works better when these questions are asked in a positive way though they can tell us more about their negative form. For example, question 1. "I am happy" tells us more about the effects of helping when you are *not* happy so you reverse the score

*1. ____ = ____
*4. ____ = ____
8. ____
10. ____
*15. ____ = ____
*17. ____ = ____
19. ____
21. ____
26. ____
*29. ____ = ____

Total: _____

The sum of my Burnout Questions is	And my Burnout level is
22 or less	Low
Between 23 and 41	Moderate
42 or more	High

You Wrote	Change to
1	5
2	4
3	3
4	2
5	1

Secondary Traumatic Stress Scale

Just like you did on Compassion Satisfaction, copy your rating on each of these questions on to this table and add them up. When you have added then up you can find your score on the table to the right.

2. _____

5. _____

7. _____

9. _____

11. _____

13. _____

14. _____

23. _____

25. _____

28. _____

Total: _____

The sum of my Secondary Trauma question is	And my Secondary Traumatic Stress level is
22 or less	Low
Between 23 and 41	Moderate
42 or more	High

Source: Stamm, 2009/Center for Victims of Torture.

The average score on Carer Satisfaction scale is 50 (SD 10; reliability 0.88). About 25% score above 57, and about 25% score below 43. A higher score suggests you are likely experiencing a strong sense of professional fulfilment. A score below 40 might indicate challenges in your work or suggest that your satisfaction is primarily derived from activities outside of work.

Burnout

Most people have an intuitive understanding of what burnout is. In research, burnout is considered one component of compassion fatigue. It is characterised by the feelings of hopelessness and difficulty in effectively carrying out one's work. These feelings typically develop gradually and may stem from a sense that one's efforts are unproductive or lack meaningful impact. Alternatively, burnout can result from ongoing excessive work demands or a lack of support in the work environment.

A higher score on this scale indicates a greater risk of burnout.

The average score is 50 (SD 10; reliability 0.75). About 25% of respondents score above 57, while another 25% score below 43.

If your score is below 43, it may reflect a generally positive outlook on your professional capabilities. If your score is above 57, it could be a sign to reflect on what aspects of your work may be making you feel less effective. Your score might simply reflect a difficult day or the need for rest. However, if the high score persists or reflects deeper concerns, it is worth paying attention to and discussing with a supervisor or professional.

Secondary Traumatic Stress

The third component of caregiver fatigue is secondary traumatic stress (STS), which refers to work-related exposure to extreme or traumatic events. Although it is relatively uncommon to develop issues purely from exposure to others' trauma, helping professionals may experience STS following repeated exposure to distressing or traumatic stories.

For example, you may frequently listen to accounts of traumatic events experienced by others—this is known as vicarious traumatisation. If your job involves direct personal danger, such as in war zones or front-line police work, this is referred to as *primary* exposure. In contrast, *secondary* exposure applies when you are affected by others' trauma in the course of your work as a therapist, emergency responder, or similar role.

The symptoms of STS often arise quickly and are typically linked to a specific event. These symptoms may include fear, disturbed sleep, vivid mental images, or intrusive thoughts. You may find yourself avoiding situations, people, or places that remind you of the event.

The average STS score is 50 (SD 10; reliability 0.8). About 25% of individuals score below 43, and 25% score above 57.

If your score is above 57, it may be helpful to reflect on what aspects of your work—or possibly your personal life—could be contributing to this. A high score does not necessarily indicate a problem, but it does suggest that you might benefit from considering your current work situation and emotional state. It may be useful to speak with a supervisor, colleague, or mental health professional.

Further Reading

Literature on Work Strain and Crisis Management

Birkmose, D. (2016) *Når gode mennesker handler ondt. Tabuet om forråelse [When Good People Act Evil: The Taboo of Brutalisation]*. University Press of Southern Denmark.

Covey, S.R. (2020) *The 7 Habits of Highly Effective People*. Simon & Schuster Ltd.

David, J.T. (2011) *Police Psychology: A New Specialty and New Challenges for Men and Women in Blue*. Praeger.

Fraher, A.L. (2010) *Thinking Through Crisis: Improving Teamwork and Leadership in High-Risk Fields*. Cambridge University Press.

Hodgkinson, P.E. and Stewart, M. (1998) *Coping with Catastrophe: A Handbook of Disaster Management*. Routledge.

Isdal, P. (2018) *Medfølelsens pris [The Price of Compassion]*. Akademisk Forlag.

Leick, N. (1994) "The disaster: an encounter with death, meaninglessness, loneliness – and with freedom," in Hodgkinson, P.E. and Stewart, M. (eds.) *Coping with Catastrophe: A Handbook of Disaster Management*. Routledge.

Lind, M., Hagelquist, J.Ø. and Rasmussen, H. (2022) "Mentalization-based principles within the organization: elevated empowerment and lower depressive symptoms," *Current Psychology*, 41(6), pp. 2319–2326. Available at: https://doi.org/10.1007/s12144-020-00749-6.

Southwick, S.M. and Charney, D.S. (2018) *Resilience: The Science of Mastering Life's Greatest Challenges*. Cambridge University Press.

van Dernoot Lipsky, L. (2018) *The Age of Overwhelm: Strategies for the Long Haul*. Berrett-Koehler Publishers.

van Dernoot Lipsky, L. and Burk, C. (2009) *Trauma Stewardship: An Everyday Guide to Caring for Self While Caring for Others.* Berrett-Koehler Publishers.

Wedell-Wedellsborg, M. (2015) *Battle Mind: How to Navigate in Chaos and Perform Under Pressure.* Akademisk Forlag.

Literature on Trauma

Briere, J. and Scott, C. (2014) *Principles and Practice of Trauma Therapy: Using DSM-5 and ICD-10.* SAGE Publications.

Elklit, A. and Kurdahl, S. (2013) "The psychological reactions after witnessing a killing in public in a Danish high school," *European Journal of Psychotraumatology,* 4, p. 19826. Available at: https://doi.org/10.3402/ejpt. v4i0.19826.

Figley, C.R. (1988) "Posttraumatic family therapy," in Ochberg, F.M. (ed.) *Post-Traumatic Therapy and Victims of Violence.* Brunner/Mazel, pp. 83–109.

Figley, C.R. (1989) *Treating Stress in Families.* Brunner/Mazel.

Janoff-Bulman, R. (1985) "The aftermath of victimisation: rebuilding shattered assumptions," in Figley, C.R. (ed.) *Trauma and Its Wake.* Brunner/Mazel, pp. 15–35.

Kardiner, A. and Spiegel, H. (1947) *War Stress and Neurotic Illness.* Paul B. Hoeber, Inc.

Lifton, R.J. (1993) "From Hiroshima to the Nazi doctors: the evolution of psychoformative approaches to understanding traumatic stress syndromes," in Wilson, J.P. and Raphael, B. (eds.) *Handbook of Traumatic Stress Syndromes.* Plenum Press, pp. 11–24.

Mansour, M. et al. (2023) "Post-traumatic stress disorder: a narrative review of pharmacological and psychotherapeutic interventions," *Cureus,* 15(9), p. e44905. Available at: https://doi.org/10.7759/cureus.44905.

Mitchell, J.T. and Dyregrov, A. (1993) "Traumatic stress in disaster workers and emergency personnel," in Wilson, J.P. and Raphael, B. (eds.) *Handbook of Traumatic Stress Syndromes.* Plenum Press, pp. 905–914.

Rothschild, B. (2000) *The Body Remembers: The Psychophysiology of Trauma and Trauma Treatment.* W. W. Norton & Company.

van der Kolk, B.A. (2015) *The Body Keeps the Score: Brain, Mind, and Body in the Healing of Trauma.* Penguin.

Weisæth, L. and Eitinger, L. (1993) "Posttraumatic stress phenomena," in Wilson, J.P. and Raphael, B. (eds.) *Handbook of Traumatic Stress Syndromes.* Plenum Press, pp. 69–78.

Wilson, J.P. and Raphael, B. (eds.) (1993) *International Handbook of Traumatic Stress Syndromes.* Plenum Press.

Literature on Grief and Bereavement

Dyregrov, A. and Dyregrov, K. (2008) *Effective Grief and Bereavement Support: The Role of Family, Friends, Colleagues, Schools, and Support Professionals*. Jessica Kingsley Publishers.

Guldin, M. and Leget, C. (2024) *Loss Grief and Existential Awareness: An Integrative Approach*. Routledge.

Literature on Psychotherapeutic Approaches

Eagleman, D. (2015) *The Brain: The Story of You*. Canongate Books.

Gilbert, P. and Simons, G. (eds.) (2022) *Compassion Focused Therapy: Clinical Practice and Applications*. Routledge.

Harris, R. (2021) *Trauma-Focused ACT: A Practitioner's Guide to Working with Mind, Body, and Emotion Using Acceptance and Commitment Therapy*. Context Press/New Harbinger Publications.

Jacobsen, B. (2008) *Invitation to Existential Psychology: A Psychology for the Unique Human Being and Its Applications in Therapy*. John Wiley & Sons.

van Deurzen, E. (2002) *Existential Counselling & Psychotherapy in Practice*. Sage Publications.

van Deurzen-Smith, E. (1996) "The survival of the self," *Journal of the Society for Existential Analysis*, 7(1), pp. 56–66.

Yalom, I.D. (1980) *Existential Psychotherapy*. Basic Books.

Yalom, I.D. (2002) *The Gift of Therapy: An Open Letter to a New Generation of Therapists and Their Patients*. Harper.

Index